LAW, PERSONALITIES, AND POLITICS

OF THE MIDDLE EAST

Essays in Honor of Majid Khadduri

LAW, PERSONALITIES,

AND POLITICS

OF THE MIDDLE EAST

Essays in Honor
of Majid Khadduri

EDITED BY JAMES PISCATORI

AND GEORGE S. HARRIS

WESTVIEW PRESS

THE MIDDLE EAST INSTITUTE

Designed by Maria Josephy Schoolman

Copyright © 1987 by The Middle East Institute, Washington, D.C.

Published in 1987 in the United States of America by Westview Press, Inc., Frederick A. Praeger, Publisher, 5500 Central Avenue, Boulder, Colorado 80301; and by The Middle East Institute, 1761 N Street N.W., Washington, D.C. 20036

Library of Congress Catalog Card Number: 87-61445
ISBN 0-916808-32-7

Composition for this book was provided by the editors.
This book was produced without formal editing by Westview Press.

Printed and bound in the United States of America

∞   The paper used in this publication meets the requirements of the American National Standard for Permanence of Paper for Printed Library Materials Z39.48-1984.

6   5   4   3   2   1

CONTENTS

V

PREFACE

This book is a tribute to Majid Khadduri, written by his friends
and former students. It is testimony to the intellectual inspiration which he has been to two generations of students and
scholars in Washington and elsewhere, and is divided into sections corresponding to the three principal fields of his own work:
  (1) Islamic and international law;
  (2) ideas and personalities in the Arab world;
  (3) politics and diplomacy in the Middle East.

ISLAMIC AND INTERNATIONAL LAW

Judge Gamal M. Badr's "Islamic Law and the Challenge of
Modern Times" is a commentary on the need for Islamic law to
adapt to current conditions. He emphasizes the need for *ijtihad* or
independent judgment and questions the relevance of *qiyas* or
analogy as a means today of evolution of legal doctrine. This
recalls Professor Khadduri's demonstration that jurists in the
early Abbasid period questioned the equity of *qiyas* and that
al-Shafi'i, while limiting *ijtihad* to *qiyas* only, attempted to restrict
its usage to details and to prescribe rules for its employment.

Badr also endorses *maslaha* or the public interest when it is
consistent with general directives of the *shari'a*, in the process
criticizing the Hanbali Najm al-Din al-Tawfi as advocating too
loose an interpretation of *maslaha*. He specifically cites Khadduri's discussion of al-Tawfi, and although he takes a somewhat
critical view of this jurist, he follows Khadduri's general approval
of *maslaha* as "positive in character, intended to promote general
welfare and reduce social vices" (*The Islamic Conception of
Justice*, p. 182). Although there are important differences in their
arguments, Badr and Khadduri also share a relatively liberal view
of *riba*, interest in economic dealings, and both register their
specific approval of the Egyptian Civil Code, which was written
by 'Abd al-Razzaq al-Sanhuri, whom Professor Khadduri knew
and greatly admired.

Henry Cattan writes on the "Legal Status of Jerusalem." Like Khadduri, he relates international law to situations of conflict. While never a dominant theme in Khadduri's work, the Arab-Israeli dispute appears throughout a book he edited, *Major Middle Eastern Problems in International Law*, and in *Political Trends in the Arab World*.

James Piscatori's article on "Saudi Arabia, Culture Change, and the International Legal Order" is an extension of Khadduri's work on classical international law. It argues, first, that there is a mixture of traditional and modern political and legal perspectives in Saudi Arabia, just as Khadduri, in *Political Trends in the Arab World*, argues of the contemporary Middle East in general; and, second, that this mixture affects the elite's attitudes toward international law. The basic conclusion—that Saudi Arabia is willingly part of the international legal system—is consistent with Khadduri's conclusion that Muslim states are reconciled to the norms of modern international law.

IDEAS AND PERSONALITIES IN THE ARAB WORLD

Ambassador Hermann Eilts, with his customary attention to detail, presents what we believe will be the definitive account of Ameen Rihani's attempt to mediate the conflict between 'Abd al-'Aziz Ibn Sa'ud and Sharif Husayn in the Hijaz in the period 1919–1925. This complements and fills in the story of Saudi Arabia that Khadduri tells in his portraits of King Faysal and Kings Khalid and Fahd. Eilts shows Rihani to be pre-eminently dedicated to Arab nationalism, naturally a subject of some fascination for Khadduri.

John Peterson writes on "Arab Nationalism and the Idealist Politician: The Career of Sulayman al-Baruni," an early Libyan nationalist and political thinker. In calling al-Baruni an idealist and an intellectual politician, Peterson follows the categorization used by Khadduri in *Arab Contemporaries: The Role of Personalities in Politics*. Peterson helps to shed light on al-Baruni by comparing him to a figure of interest to Khadduri as well, 'Aziz 'Ali al-Misri.

Mudhafar Amin and Edmund Ghareeb explain the origins and political philosophy of the Ahali group, Iraqi social reformers and political activists who first made their mark in the 1930s. It is a topic to which Khadduri devoted considerable attention in *Independent Iraq*. In addition to this, Amin and Ghareeb rely on Khadduri's treatment of Kamil al-Chadirchi, who, while not a founder, quickly became one of the intellectual guides of the group. Khadduri's scholarly interest is not surprising: Ahali members were of his generation. He was in secondary school when anti-British nationalist sentiments seized many of his contemporaries, and, like some of them, he went on to the ideologically tolerant campus of the American University of Beirut where, however, their paths were to diverge.

POLITICS AND DIPLOMACY IN THE MIDDLE EAST

Tareq Ismael writes on "The Communist Movements in the Arab World." It is a subject to which Professor Khadduri has turned time and again, particularly in his studies of Iraq. Ismael refers several times in the course of his exposition to Khalid Bakdash, head of the Syrian Communist Party, on whom Khadduri has offered a full assessment.

George Harris presents a case study of a little understood episode in Iranian history in which a communist movement briefly held power in the province of Gilan. This study, in a specific way, develops themes on the interplay of ideology and power, communism and nationalism, that are discussed by both Khadduri and Ismael.

Stephen Grummon writes on "The 1820 Expedition to the Gulf and the Decline of British Commercial Shipping," challenging the conventional view of motives and results of British policies in the Gulf. This covers an earlier period than is usually associated with Khadduri, but his interest in the British role in the region is seen, of course, throughout *Independent Iraq*.

It is only fitting that the contributors to this volume have ties of intellectual and personal friendship to Professor Khadduri.

ix

Gamal Badr and Khadduri have read and admired each other's work on Islamic law for years, and there has been a long association between Khadduri and Henry Cattan. Cattan contributed a chapter to Khadduri's joint enterprise with Herbert Liebesny, *Law in the Middle East*, still a standard on the subject. James Piscatori benefited from Professor Khadduri's advice on his doctoral research and now teaches the courses formerly taught by him at the Johns Hopkins School of Advanced International Studies (SAIS).

Hermann Eilts is a graduate of SAIS although just prior to Khadduri's time. Later, however, he arranged to study Islamic law under Khadduri. The two have maintained regular professional and personal contact for many years, not least through the Shaybani Society of International Law, of which Professor Khadduri has been President since 1969. John Peterson's graduate work was supervised by Khadduri, and although Mudhafar Amin was never formally Khadduri's student, his work on the Ahali group puts him in Khadduri's tradition as well. Edmund Ghareeb, happily, is linked to Khadduri both by the scholarly ties of research on Iraq and by family ties.

Tareq Ismael came to know Professor Khadduri as a visiting student at Johns Hopkins and since then has collaborated with him on various professional projects in the United States and Canada. George Harris has been Khadduri's friend for a number of years and taught with him at the School of Advanced International Studies for more than a decade. The two have served on the Washington lecture circuit and Middle East Institute committees together and share a scholarly interest in Ottoman diplomacy. Stephen Grummon was Dr. Khadduri's student at Johns Hopkins and wrote his doctoral dissertation under his guidance.

Majid Khadduri's association with the Middle East Institute, the publisher of this volume, has been similarly close. In fact, it is not an exaggeration to say that almost in tandem the two established themselves as institutions of Middle Eastern scholarship in Washington and the nation. Professor Khadduri became the Institute's Director of Research in 1950, only four years after it came into existence, and, for the next decade, shaped its program. He regularly advised the Institute's founder, George Camp Keiser, and, in 1960, he was asked to join the Board of

Governors. As one would expect of an academic of his stature, Dr. Khadduri has been principally interested in the publishing side of the Institute and was chairman of its Publications Committee for many years. The Institute published two of his own books—*Socialist Iraq: A Study in Iraqi Politics Since the Revolution of 1968* and *Arab Personalities in Politics*—and he encouraged the publication of works by other distinguished writers. In 1980, he became emeritus member of the Board of Governors, but no less a vigorous supporter of the Institute's activities.

We and the Institute are pleased to acknowledge, finally, that several people have been involved in putting this volume together. Particular thanks should go to Kathleen H.B. Manalo for her work in collating and editing the various contributions, to Maria Schoolman for designing the book, to Patricia Dockham for copyediting the manuscript, and to Richard B. Parker for his assistance and guidance from beginning to end.

—George S. Harris and James Piscatori

CONTRIBUTORS

MUDHAFAR AMIN, New York-based specialist on modern Iraq, formerly taught at The University of Mosul, author of *al-'Iraq fi'l-Tarikh*

GAMAL MOURSI BADR, Legal Adviser to the Permanent Mission of Qatar to the United Nations and Professor of Islamic Law at New York University, former judge of the Algerian Supreme Court, author of *al-Niyaba fi'l-Tasarufat al-Qanuniyya*

HENRY CATTAN, Paris-based international lawyer, member of the Bars of Jerusalem and Damascus, author of *Palestine and International Law; The Legal Aspects of the Arab-Israeli Conflict*

HERMANN FREDERICK EILTS, Distinguished University Professor of International Relations at Boston University, former U.S. Ambassador to Saudi Arabia and Egypt, author of "Ahmad bin Na'aman's Mission to the United States in 1840: The Voyage of al-Sultanah to New York City"

EDMUND GHAREEB, Adjunct Professor of International Studies, the American University, author of *The Kurdish Question in Iraq*

STEPHEN R. GRUMMON, Analyst in the Office of Counterterrorism in the Office of the Secretary, U.S. Department of State, author of *The Iran-Iraq War*

GEORGE S. HARRIS, Director of the Office of Analysis for Near East and South Asia, Bureau of Intelligence and Research, U.S. Department of State, former Professorial Lecturer, the School of Advanced International Studies, The Johns Hopkins University, author of *Turkey: Coping With Crisis*

TAREQ Y. ISMAEL, Professor of Political Science at the University of Calgary, author of *The Arab Left*

J. E. PETERSON, Washington-based writer, formerly taught at The College of William and Mary, author of *Oman in the Twentieth Century*

JAMES PISCATORI, Associate Professor of Middle Eastern Studies at the School of Advanced International Studies, The Johns Hopkins University, author of *Islam in a World of Nation-States*

PART I

Introduction

Majid Khadduri

CHAPTER ONE

The Life and Work of Majid Khadduri

JAMES PISCATORI

In a career spanning half a century, Majid Khadduri has made manifest contributions to the study of the Middle East. His writings on the Islamic law of nations, Arab ideas and personalities, and his native Iraq have assured places in the modern scholarship of the region. Although obviously the research and writing took place at different times and places, there is a natural unity to the *corpus*, a sense that all along he perceived certain themes to be enduring and inter-connected: Islamic law elaborates a sophisticated theory of the state and of state-to-state relations; ideas such as these, but so too others based on far different premises, have shaped Arab history; extraordinary individuals, whether by setting goals for a people to achieve, or nudging these to the side, or even sacrificing them, have turned the intellectual history of the Arabs into political history. While scarcely unique, this balancing of religious and legal imperatives and secular trends, and of ideas and statesmen, makes a favorable contrast with both the stern juristic commentaries and the breathless chronicling of great men and deeds found in much of the contemporary as well as earlier writing of the Middle East.

* * * * *

Majid Khadduri is himself a balance of Eastern and Western outlooks, having found in the West the tools to make sense of his

3

own civilization. Like so many of his generation and class, he gravitated to the American University of Beirut and, no doubt, found confirmation there of the view that Arabs would be at the threshold of development if only they acquired the modern skills which the West could offer. His own interests were not technical or scientific. But influenced by the nationalist agitation growing throughout the area—as every university student to some degree would have been—and specifically by the drive to terminate Britain's mandate over Iraq, he recognized that his interests lay in the larger questions of law, institutions, and political society. He sought to deepen his understanding of these subjects by doing graduate work in America, and he was especially fortunate to have arrived at the University of Chicago when, in the 1930s, it was the center of American political science. He studied with distinguished scholars of that discipline—Western political thought with Charles Merriam, international organization with Pitman Potter, diplomatic history with Bernadotte Schmitt—and benefited from the emphasis on rigorous research and precise writing.

It was Quincy Wright, however, who influenced him the most. Wright was to make his enduring mark with the publication of the monumental *A Study of War* in 1942,[1] but his concern with the causes and regulation of conflict as well as with the problems of the Middle East were already apparent when Khadduri arrived in Chicago. Researching his book, *Mandates Under the League of Nations*,[2] Wright traveled widely in the Middle East and was particularly affected by the French bombardment of Damascus in October 1925. The conclusion in this case was to become characteristic of his approach: international law had been violated and those on the wrong side of the law—this time, the French—should be held responsible before the international community.[3] In the dispute between Turkey and Great Britain over Mosul, he recognized the possibilities of arbitration, and he came to regard this as a valuable complement to the formal

1. Chicago: University of Chicago Press, 1942. 2 volumes.
2. Chicago: University of Chicago Press, 1930.
3. "The Bombardment of Damascus," *The American Journal of International Law*, 20, No. 2 (April 1926), pp. 263–280.

4

mechanisms of international law.[4]

With these as signposts, Khadduri acquired his knowledge of the connection between international law and politics and their roles in situations of conflict, and did his doctoral research on the Islamic law of war and peace. Unlike many students returning home from education in the West, he went back to Iraq appreciative of how much the experience in Chicago had taught him of law and politics, but also conscious of how much more he needed to learn of Islamic law. While teaching such modern subjects as the Constitutional Law of Iraq and Treaties in the Law College and Political Science and Modern History at the Teachers' College (later, the College of Arts and Sciences of Baghdad University), he determined to read in the classical texts of Islamic jurisprudence. This he did alone, or, as when he read al-Shafi'i's *Kitab al-Risala fi Usul al-Fiqh* [*Epistle on the Sources of Jurisprudence*], under the guidance of Taha al-Rawi, Secretary to the Council of Ministers and a distinguished jurist.

It was also during this period that Khadduri came into contact with a figure of some consequence for the development of law in the modern Middle East, 'Abd al-Razzaq al-Sanhuri (1895–1971), dean of the Law School in Cairo. They met in 1936 when unhappy circumstances brought al-Sanhuri to Iraq: as a member of the "Sa'dist" faction of the Wafd Party opposed to Nahhas Pasha, he was obliged to accept, and fortunate to have been offered, the deanship of the Law College in Baghdad when Nahhas came to power in Cairo. Khadduri, as local secretary of the PEN Club, the international writers' club, invited him to speak, and from then on they were intermittently to meet. Al-Sanhuri, having gone back to Cairo when the political climate improved, returned to Baghdad once Nahhas, in 1943, became Prime Minister again. It was then that he completed the work begun in 1936 and drafted the Iraqi Civil Code, which, like the Syrian and Egyptian codes of 1949, was a blend of the Majalla (the Ottoman codification of Hanafi law) and of European civil law. While believing that al-Sanhuri never built a solid theoretical

4. "The Mosul Dispute," *The American Journal of International Law*, 20, No. 3 (July 1926), pp. 453–464.

bridge between Islamic and Western law,[5] Khadduri regrets nonetheless having missed the opportunity to work with him on the formulation of this draft, which finally became Iraqi law in 1951.

But Khadduri was not to lack for practical experience. In the period when Rashid 'Ali al-Gaylani dominated the government (1940–1941), he assisted the Foreign Ministry with the preparation of a "white book." This set out Iraq's position in the dispute over the disposition of its internal affairs with Britain that culminated in the Anglo-Iraqi war of May 1941. Later Khadduri was a delegate to one of the great international convocations of our age, the San Francisco Conference of 1945, which drew up the Charter of the United Nations. Second to Fadil al-Jamali, then Director-General of the Foreign Ministry and later Prime Minister (1954), Khadduri helped to represent Iraq in the committees concerned with the questions of trusteeship and regional arrangements. He was, in addition, sole Iraqi representative to the important committee dealing with what became Chapter VI, the Charter's provisions on the peaceful settlement of disputes. He could well have made a success of a diplomatic career and, indeed, was invited to set out on this path by Tawfiq al-Suwaydi, Foreign Minister in 1940 and later Prime Minister (1946).

Khadduri was committed, however, to the scholarly life, and it was the opportunities which American universities afforded in this regard that, once and for all, attracted him away from government and from Iraq. Visiting professor at the University of Indiana in 1947–1948 and at the University of Chicago in 1948–1949, he moved to Washington in 1950 and joined the School of Advanced International Studies of The Johns Hopkins University. There, for slightly over the next quarter-century, he taught hundreds of students, many of whom became diplomats and academics of note both in the United States and in the Middle East.[6]

---

5. *The Islamic Conception of Justice* (Baltimore: The Johns Hopkins Press, 1984), pp. 207-209, especially note 16, p. 209. Also see *Political Trends in the Arab World: The Role of Ideas and Ideals in Politics* (Baltimore: The Johns Hopkins University Press, 1970), pp. 239–241.

6. He dedicated the book he edited, *Major Middle Eastern Problems in International Law* (Washington, D.C.: American Enterprise Institute

* * * * *

Majid Khadduri has been as productive a writer as a teacher, and, in many ways, his works on the Islamic law of nations have been the most compelling of his writings. From the earliest book, *The Law of War and Peace in Islam*,[7] to the most recent, *The Islamic Conception of Justice*, Khadduri has substantially advanced our knowledge of Islamic legal and political theory in the domain of international relations. Others, of course, before him had studied it and presented it to a Western audience; Najib Armanazi, for example, described the basic principles,[8] and al-Sanhuri advocated transforming the institution of the caliphate into a kind of League of Nations system.[9] One can also certainly say that Khadduri's work in this area deals with more general aspects of Islamic law and philosophy; this is particularly true of *The Islamic Conception of Justice*. Yet the fact remains that his work on Islamic international law has become the standard scholarly formulation and, because written in English, the means by which a wide audience has gained an appreciation of the subject.

The erudition of these writings is based on a broad reading of the classical and medieval texts, and also on Khadduri's ability to compare and contrast the ideas gleaned from them with Western categories of thought. He shows, for instance, how the *jihad* is similar to the European Christian concept of *bellum iustum* because there are clear guidelines as to how and when fighting in a just cause may legally occur. Yet it is also unique because, following Islam's imperative of universalism, it is a permanent state of warfare with the ideological enemies of Islam, particularly the polytheists.[10] Taking it one step further, he shows how

for Public Policy Research, 1972), to these students.

7. London: Luzac and Company, 1941. This was revised and expanded, published as *War and Peace in the Law of Islam* (Baltimore: The Johns Hopkins Press, 1955).

8. *Les Principes Islamiques et les rapports internationaux en temps de paix et guerre* (Paris: Picart, 1929).

9. *Le Califat: son évolution vers une Société des Nations Orientales* (Paris: Paul Geuthner, 1926).

10. *War and Peace in the Law of Islam*, chapter 5; *The Islamic*

it would be wrong simply to conclude that *jihad* is synonymous with offensive war, for that would overlook that the doctrine changed as political conditions changed. As the Islamic empire came to face more powerful enemies abroad and disorder at home, *jihad* became a defensive concept. By the fourteenth century, in Ibn Taymiyya's formulation, any other kind of *jihad* than self-defense against the aggression of the infidels was thought to be tantamount to what the Qur'an specifically prohibits—religious compulsion.[11] When dealing with another area, treaties, Khadduri shows how the idea of *pacta sunt servanda* (compacts must be honored) is intrinsic—and central—to the Islamic law of nations, just as it is to Western contract law.[12]

The reader may feel that not all such comparisons are as helpful. Given that *jihad* is a permanent state of warfare between Islam and polytheism, for instance, one might wonder if it can also be thought of as "litigation" between them.[13] Moreover, it may be felt that he does not rely on all the schools of law equally.[14] But these are minor objections when set against the comprehensive learning of his analysis as a whole.

All would surely agree that he is correct to focus as much attention as he does on the contributions of Muhammad ibn al-Hasan al-Shaybani (750–804). By translating and explaining his *siyar*, Khadduri demonstrates that the Islamic law of nations is really found in jurisprudential writings such as these, and not simply in the Qur'an or traditions of the Prophet. Noting how al-Shaybani was the first Muslim jurist to deal with the subject in a precise and deliberate manner and that he did so over eight centuries earlier than the major European exposition of the subject, he concludes, not unreasonably, that it does al-Shaybani

---

Conception of Justice, pp. 164–167.

11. *The Islamic Conception of Justice*, pp. 168–170.

12. *War and Peace in the Law of Islam*, p. 204.

13. *Ibid.*, p. 59.

14. This is the criticism of the Saudi intellectual Abdul-Hamid Abu Sulayman in his doctoral dissertation, "The Islamic Theory of International Relations: Its Relevance, Past and Present" (University of Pennsylvania, 1973), for example pp. 36–42.

less than justice to refer to him as the Grotius of Islam.[15]

Khadduri's concise and structured presentation of Muslim thinking on the law of nations over the centuries is a major contribution to the literature of Islam, but there are implications for the study of international law as well. Many international lawyers since the end of the Second World War have preoccupied themselves with looking for the basis of a truly world-wide law, and it is in the hope that comparative studies will advance this cause that Khadduri set out on his work: "To draw on experiences of an increasing number of other nations is as logical as it is pragmatic, for diversity of experience serves the common interests of an expanding community of nations."[16]

If indeed it was ever welcome, this message, particularly since the Iranian hostage crisis when Islam was made to seem antithetical to the general legal order, has scarcely been taken to heart. Yet it would seem from what Khadduri has to say that Islam, when viewed from the longer perspective, has much to offer: its encounters with Christianity, sometimes violent and sometimes amicable, suggest the possibility of divergent ideological orders coexisting; unlike the traditional law but rather like the emerging law of human rights, it puts the individual at the center of things; and as a moral code—as opposed to a religious or ideological code—it encourages tolerance and humanitarianism, especially at times of conflict.[17] This would not be everyone's view of Islam, but he does draw his conclusions from his empirical evidence and in the end, like all good scholars, makes us appreciate the complexity of his subject.

In a second major area of contribution, Khadduri has written extensively on important ideas and personalities in the Arab world. If not exactly like al-Muzani who claimed to have read

15. *The Islamic Law of Nations: Shaybani's Siyar* (Baltimore: The Johns Hopkins Press, 1966), p. 57.

16. *Ibid.*, p. xii.

17. *Ibid.*, pp. 68–69. Also see "The Islamic System: Its Competition and Co-existence with Western Systems," *Proceedings of the American Society of International Law* (1959), p. 52. For similar conclusions about the role of justice, see *The Islamic Conception of Justice*, pp. 231–232.

al-Shafi'i's *Risala* 500 times with profit,[18] Khadduri has returned again and again to this book which he read first as a young lecturer in Baghdad. He sees it as the most comprehensive treatment of *usul al-fiqh*, the study of the sources of jurisprudence. In introducing his English translation of it, he points out that the preoccupation with the Prophet's *sunna* or traditions led al-Shafi'i(767–820) to restrict independent reasoning (*ijtihad*) to reasoning by formal analogy only (*qiyas*). However well-intentioned this may have been, Khadduri says, the effect was to idealize the law as "a perfect legal order" and thus to give vent to *taqlid* or imitation of precedent,[19] over the centuries creating not perfection but legal rigidity and stagnation.

Just as ideas affect the development of history, historical conditions sometimes affect the development of ideas. In *The Islamic Conception of Justice*, Khadduri shows this to be the case of the development of the various meanings of justice. The early debate between voluntarism (*qadar*) or free will and involuntarism (*jabr*) or predestination, and on whether man was responsible or not for his unjust acts, was greatly influenced by the political circumstances of the age. The ruling Umayyads (661–750) saw in *jabr*—i.e., the question of human responsibility for one's acts does not arise because everything, including "the drama of history," is the product of God's will—validation of the *status quo* and of their own right to rule. By way of contrast, the Kharijites and Shi'a, political opponents of the Umayyads, argued for *qadar*: because men are free to choose, those who choose injustice have no right to rule over others.[20]

Khadduri is right to see the debate over social justice as the most important in our own time. In *Political Trends in the Arab World*, he argues that both a "revivalist" and a "collectivist" response to the problems of modernization have emerged among the Arabs. In the late nineteenth century and early twentieth century, people such as Jamal al-Din al-Afghani (1839–1897) and Muhammad 'Abduh (1849–1905) set revivalism into motion by

18. *Islamic Jurisprudence: Shafi'i's Risala* (Baltimore: The Johns Hopkins Press, 1961), p. 42.

19. *Ibid.*, pp. 42–43; also see pp. 288, 304–306.

20. *The Islamic Conception of Justice*, pp. 23–27, quotation at p. 25.

creatively looking for ways to reconcile Islam and reason, religion and science, but groups such as the Muslim Brotherhood derailed the process, advocating instead "the re-establishment of principles and practices no longer compatible with modern conditions of life." In reaction to this, leftist, mainly secular, ideologies of collectivism developed.[21] This was a natural conclusion for Khadduri to draw given that, when writing the book in the late 1960s, Nasirism and, to a lesser extent, Ba'thism appeared predominant and the Brotherhood's politics had taken a violent turn.

But from the perspective of a decade later and with the example of Ayatullah Khumayni now in mind, Khadduri's interpretation in *The Islamic Conception of Justice* is more subtle and theoretically suggestive. In this book, revivalists can be "Rationalists," such as al-Afghani or 'Abduh, or "Revelationists," such as the Brotherhood or Khumayni. Yet the line is not so clearly drawn between them: the Brotherhood, for example, is seen as an intellectual, though a somewhat wayward, descendant of al-Afghani and 'Abduh and as attempting in its ideology to keep "a balance between freedom and equality."[22] More importantly, all must now contend with Islamic versions of collectivism. Although a satisfactory synthesis, such as "Islamic equilibrium" (*al-takaful al-ijtima'i*) might one day be, has yet to come into existence, collectivist criticisms of free enterprise and private property and notions of distributive justice have found a place in the contemporary dialogue of Muslims. Khadduri stands on fertile ground when he concludes that rather than it being a betrayal or deviation, this is part of "the process of accommodation and the assimilation of foreign elements." Seen in the larger perspective, then, ostensibly conflicting ideas such as revivalism and collectivism, or rationalism and revelationism, are not antithetical but, rather, complementary.[23]

One must add to this sophisticated view of the role of ideas in history his analysis of the relationship between ideas and

21. *Political Trends in the Arab World*, chapters 4 and 5, quotation at p. 87.

22. *The Islamic Conception of Justice*, pp. 196–227, quotation at p. 221.

23. *Ibid.*, pp. 227–229, quotation at p. 228.

individual thinkers and doers. He explores this relationship in two books, *Arab Contemporaries: The Role of Personalities in Politics*[24] and *Arab Personalities in Politics*.[25] He personally knew many of the individuals he writes about,[26] but is able to remain the discerning analyst. He employs different schemes in each book, but neither is used as a blunt instrument to bludgeon the data into some artificial order. He seems, in fact, somewhat uncomfortable with his own typologies[27] and wisely lets the individuals themselves emerge.

In the end, it matters less that a particular man is an "idealist," "ideologue" or "realist,"[28] or, indeed, a "monarchical," "military" or "centralizing" leader[29] than that Khadduri firmly ties him both to his ideas and to the circumstances which formulated his thinking and defined his place in the world. This is exactly what he does in *Political Trends in the Arab World*, but here the approach is explicitly identified. Calling it "empirical idealism,"[30] he means that ideas cannot be dissociated from action any more than the man can be dissociated from his circumstances; they are connected of course.

This sense of "the man-in-the-circumstances"[31] is consistently found in Khadduri's writings on politics and diplomacy—

24. Baltimore: The Johns Hopkins University Press, 1973.

25. Washington, D.C.: The Middle East Institute, 1981.

26. For example, of the seven individuals studied in *Arab Personalities in Politics*, Khadduri personally interviewed five, and he knew a significant number of intellectuals discussed in *Political Trends in the Arab World*.

27. He says with hindsight, for example, that the structure of *Arab Contemporaries* "needs to be recast": *Arab Personalities in Politics*, p. 8.

28. *Arab Contemporaries: The Role of Personalities in Politics*, pp. 3–4.

29. *Arab Personalities in Politics*, p. 12.

30. *Arab Contemporaries: The Role of Personalities in Politics*, p. 3; *Arab Personalities in Politics*, p. 13. Khadduri says here (p. 13) that although he may not have used the term "empirical idealism" before *Arab Contemporaries*, "I have always tried to apply it in earlier studies on the contemporary Arab World."

31. *Arab Contemporaries: The Role of Personalities in Politics*, p. 228.

the third area of his contributions. His *Modern Libya: A Study in Political Development*[32] demonstrates the absolutely crucial role that Sayyid Idris al-Sanusi (r. 1951–1969) played, first, in gaining independence for Cyrenaica from the Italians and, then, in winning the support of the Tripolitanians for a united Libya. Religion, in particular the Sanusi revivalist movement, helped to create nationalist sentiment, and much as Mu'ammar al-Qadhdhafi might regret it, a "nationalist" hero such as 'Umar al-Mukhtar (1862–1931) fought in the Sanusi cause.[33] Khadduri also highlights the diplomatic history of Sayyid Idris and other Libyan leaders who, by pitting one great power against another, won complete independence for Libya and avoided the intermediate stage of a trusteeship under the new United Nations system.[34]

Khadduri's major contribution in this area of politics and diplomacy are his studies of modern Iraq. His origins and his employment both in the university and occasionally in government gave him the vantage point from which to mount these studies, and his formal training in the West gave him the discipline of dispassionate observation which he needed to carry them out. He benefited too from the immense learning and intellectual friendship of 'Abbas al-'Azzawi, the distinguished historian and author of an important book on Iraq, *Tarikh al-'Iraq Bayna Ihtilalayn* [*The History of Iraq Between Two Occupations*].[35] Khadduri's *Independent Iraq: A Study in Iraqi Politics Since 1932*[36] and *Republican Iraq: A Study in Iraqi Politics Since the Revolution of 1958*[37] are models of meticulous research, together giving a picture of Iraq from the 1920s to the 1960s and filling in an emormous void in the literature of Middle Eastern history and politics. *Socialist Iraq: A Study in Iraqi*

32. Baltimore: The Johns Hopkins Press, 1963.

33. *Ibid.*, pp. 23–25.

34. *Ibid.*, chapter 5.

35. Baghdad: Matba'at Baghdad, 1353–1376 A.H./1935–1956. 3 volumes.

36. London: Oxford University Press, 1951. This was revised and expanded, published as *Independent Iraq: A Study in Iraqi Politics from 1932 to 1958* (London: Oxford University Press, 1960).

37. London: Oxford University Press, 1969.

Politics Since the Revolution of 1968,[38] which is based on many direct interviews of Iraqi officials, takes the story through the 1970s.

These largely tell the history of military involvement in politics. In the period from independence in 1932 to the revolution in 1958, the military's overriding commitment was to the unity of the nation-state; ideology played a secondary role.[39] But, as Khadduri shows, after 1958 and even though the military had seized power, factionalism developed in tandem with factionalism among civilians. Iraqi politics became polarized, the actors all in principle Arab nationalists but in reality divided into bitterly opposed camps over union with Egypt and Syria and cooperation with the Ba'thists and communists. After the Ba'thists, in 1968, decisively came to power, they resolved to subject the military to civilian rule and were able to do so, in part, because of the prestige that Ahmad Hasan al-Bakr (r. 1968–1979) had in military circles. But Khadduri's studies remind us that older military men do not really dominate: younger, nationalist military officers in Iraq used Brigadier Bakr Sidqi (r. 1936–1937) to assert their own power in the *coup d'état* of 1936,[40] much as the Free Officers in Egypt used Major-General Muhammad Najib (r. 1952–1954) to make the revolution of 1952.

* * * * *

Majid Khadduri's work, in the end, stands or falls on the basis of its empirical exactitude and analytical rigor. Both have been impressively high. But, in addition to these, a personal voice is sometimes heard that makes one see the author as the Liberal man of letters. Balancing East and West in his own life, time after time he proposes tolerance and reconciliation as the way out of ideological and political impasses. Thus, as we have seen, he thinks that Islam as a code of morality, but not as religious

38. Washington, D.C.: The Middle East Institute, 1978.

39. "The Role of the Military in Iraqi Society," in Sydney Nettleton Fisher (ed.), *The Military in the Middle East* (Columbus: Ohio State University Press, 1963), p. 47.

40. *Independent Iraq*, pp. 78–82; *Socialist Iraq*, pp. 21–24, 69–71, 75.

dogma, can contribute to the development of a moderate international system. Of the central Arab-Israeli problem, he believes that only when the national ideologies of both sides are renounced, and replaced by the "the principles of accommodation and consent" within a bi-national Palestine, can there be peace.[41] With regard to a new penal code for Egypt, he argues, if only it could combine "the best elements from Islamic and Western standards," it would be an example to the whole Muslim world,[42] and if social justice in general is to prevail, the principle of egalitarianism must be balanced by that of individual freedom.[43] Finally, he feels that although the military might carry out necessary reforms, there is the grave risk of its perpetuating itself in power and destroying the possibility of democratic government. Democracy is "the safest way towards ultimate stability and progress," and to ensure this, the Middle Eastern peoples must be educated into accepting the idea of constitutional limitations on arbitrary rule.[44]

Ironically, Khadduri's eagerness to see balance and harmony prevail sometimes leads him to minimize the force of his own conclusions. For example, he says that Islam in the twentieth century has "completely reconciled" itself to the Western secular order,[45] yet he shows how basic differences, such as on the concept of human rights and generally on the role of the individual, remain.[46] He fastens on to accommodation and reconcilia-

---

41. *Political Trends in the Arab World*, pp. 281–288, quotation at p. 287.

42. *The Islamic Conception of Justice*, p. 216.

43. *Ibid.*, pp. 223–224.

44. "The Role of the Military in Middle East Politics," *The American Political Science Review*, 47, No. 2 (June 1953), p. 524.

45. "The Islamic System: Its Competition and Co-existence with Western Systems," p. 51. Cf. *The Islamic Law of Nations: Shaybani's Siyar*, p. 67; and *War and Peace in the Law of Islam*, pp. 293–296.

46. Even in his most recent book, *The Islamic Conception of Justice*, where he explicitly deals with Khumayni (pp. 224–227) and Muslim views on the evolving law of human rights (Appendix), he concludes: "Islamic as well as other states have accepted the principle that religious doctrines should be separated from the standard of justice in international relations." (p. 229)

tion where others see differences and conflict, but whether or not the broader currents of Islamic history are with him, there is no doubt that a steady vision such as his has the salutary effect of forcing us to re-examine basic assumptions. Certainly, as Khadduri says of the distinguished Egyptian liberal Ahmad Lutfi al-Sayyid (1872–1963), one may say of Khadduri: he has insisted on applying reason and intellect to everything he has done, and what holds him in high regard is "the consistency throughout his life of his moral and intellectual attitudes."[47]

47. *Arab Contemporaries: The Role of Personalities in Politics*, p. 192.

16

CHAPTER TWO

Curriculum Vitae

MAJID KHADDURI

Place and Date of Birth
Mosul, Iraq, September 27, 1908
American citizen, 1954

Education
High School, Mosul, 1928
American University of Beirut, B.A., 1932
University of Chicago, Ph.D., 1938

University Posts in Iraq
Law and Higher Teachers Colleges, 1939–1947 (Professor)

Visiting Professor
University of Indiana, 1947–1948
University of Chicago, 1948–1949
Columbia University, 1955, 1962, 1968 (weekly seminars)
University of Vermont, 1963 (bi-weekly seminars)
University of Virginia, 1964, 1965, 1974
Oxford University, Spring, 1970
Harvard University, Summers, 1950, 1970
American University of Cairo, December–January 1973
University of Baghdad, December–January 1976
University of Basra, March 1978

Professor of Middle East Studies
The Johns Hopkins University School of Advanced International Studies, 1949–1970
Director of the Center for Middle East Studies, 1960–1980

University Distinguished Research Professor
The Johns Hopkins University School of Advanced International Studies, 1970–1980
Distinguished Research Professor Emeritus, 1980–

Other Academic Activities
Director of Research at the Middle East Institute, 1950–1960
Member of the Board of Governors, Middle East Institute, 1960–1980
Member of the Board of Governors, Middle East Institute, Emeritus, 1980–
Member of the Near and Middle East Committee, Social Science Research Council, New York, 1950–1960

Membership in Academic and Intellectual Societies
P.E.N. Club (World Association of Writers), 1934–
American Society of International Law, 1938–
American Political Science Association, 1947–
The Middle East Institute, 1947–
American Historical Association, 1960–1974
The Shaybani Society of International Law (President), 1969–
International Association of the Philosophy of Law and Social Philosophy, 1975–
Corresponding Member of the Academy of the Arabic Language (Egypt), 1983–
Corresponding Member of the Iraqi Academy, 1986–
International Association of Middle East Studies (President), 1986–

Research Fellowships and Grants
Ford Foundation Fellow, 1955
Rockefeller Foundation Grants, 1958, 1963, 1966
Philosophical Society Grant, 1959
American Council of Learned Societies Travel Grant, 1960

Social Science Research Council Travel Grants, 1966, 1968, 1974

Fulbright-Hays Travel Grant, 1970

Other research grants from the School of Advanced International Studies, the Johns Hopkins University

International Conferences Attended

P.E.N. Congress, Buenos Aires, 1936

Congress of Orientalists, Moscow, 1960

World Congress on Philosophy of Law and Social Philosophy, St. Louis, 1975

World Congress on Philosophy of Law and Social Philosophy, Basel, 1979

International Congress on Islam, Seville, 1980

Public Service

Iraq Foreign Office, 1945

Member of the Delegation of Iraq to the United Nations Conference at San Francisco, 1945

Member of several educational committees, Iraq Ministry of Education, 1939–1947

Participated in the establishment of the University of Libya and served as Dean of the University, 1957

Served as adviser on various occasions to the U.S. State Department

Honors

Order of the Rafidain, Government of Iraq, 1953

Order of Merit (First Class), Government of Egypt, 1978

L.H.D. (honorary), the Johns Hopkins University, 1985

Publications

BOOKS

The Law of War and Peace in Islam: London: Luzac Company, 1941.

The Government of Iraq. Baghdad: The New Publishers, 1944. Revised and enlarged Arabic edition, 1946.

Independent Iraq: A Study in Iraqi Politics Since 1932. First edition. London: Oxford University Press, 1951. Revised and enlarged under the title *Independent Iraq: A Study in Iraqi Politics from 1932 to 1958.* London: Oxford University Press, 1960.

War and Peace in the Law of Islam. Baltimore: The Johns Hopkins Press, 1955. (Reprinted in 1960, 1962, 1969, and 1979). Translated into Arabic, Persian, Urdu, and Indonesian.

Law in the Middle East, Vol. 1: *Origin and Development Of Islamic Law.* Washington, D.C.: The Middle East Institute, 1955. Edited with Herbert J. Liebesny.

Islamic Jurisprudence: Shafi'i's Risala. Baltimore: The Johns Hopkins Press, 1961

Modern Libya: A Study in Political Development. Baltimore: The Johns Hopkins Press, 1963 (Reprinted 1968). Translated into Arabic, 1966.

The Islamic Law of Nations: Shaybani's Siyar. Baltimore: The Johns Hopkins Press, 1966. Translated into Arabic, 1975.

Republican Iraq: A Study in Iraqi Politics Since the Revolution of 1958. London: Oxford University Press, 1969. Translated into Arabic, 1974.

Political Trends in the Arab World. Baltimore: The Johns Hopkins Press, 1970. Paperback edition, 1972. Translated into Arabic, 1972.

Major Middle Eastern Problems in International Law (Editor and contributor). Washington, D.C.: American Enterprise Institute, 1972.

Arab Contemporaries: The Role of Personalities in Politics. The Johns Hopkins University Press, 1973. Translated into Arabic, 1973.

Socialist Iraq: A Study in Iraqi Politics Since the Revolution of 1968. Washington, D.C.: The Middle East Institute, 1978. (Reprinted 1979).

Arab Personalities in Politics. Washington, D.C.: The Middle East Institute, 1981.

The Islamic Conception of Justice. Baltimore: The Johns Hopkins University Press, 1984.

The Gulf War (in preparation for Oxford University Press)

ARTICLES
"The Franco-Lebanese Dispute and the Crisis of November

1943," *The American Journal of International Law*, 30 (October 1944), pp. 601–620.

"The Alexandretta Dispute," *The American Journal of International Law*, 30 (July 1945), pp. 406–425.

"Human Rights in Islam," *The Annals of the American Academy of Political and Social Science*, 243 (January 1946), pp. 77–81.

"Towards an Arab Union: The League of Arab States," *The American Political Science Review*, 40 (October 1946), pp. 90–100.

"The Arab League as a Regional Arrangement," *The American Journal of International Law*, 40 (October 1946), pp. 756–777.

"Nature of the Islamic State," *Islamic Culture*, 21 (October 1947), pp. 327–331.

"The Background of Arab Nationalism," *Foreign Notes* (Chicago Council on Foreign Relations), 25 (June 18, 1948), pp. 3–4.

"The Coup d'Etat of 1936: A Study of Iraqi Politics," *The Middle East Journal*, 2 (July 1948), pp. 270–292.

"Constitutional Development in Syria with Emphasis on the Constitution of 1950," *The Middle East Journal*, 5 (Spring 1951), pp. 137–160.

"The United States and Political Stability in the Near East," *World Affairs*, 114 (Spring 1951), pp. 41–42.

"The Juridical Theory of the Islamic State," *Muslim World*, 41 (July 1951), pp. 181–185.

"Iran's Claim to the Sovereignty of Bahrayn," *The American Journal of International Law*, 45 (October 1951), pp. 631–647.

"The Anglo-Egyptian Controversy," *Proceedings of the Academy of Political Science*, 24 (January 1952), pp. 82–99.

"Coup and Counter-Coup in the Yaman, 1948," *International Affairs*, 28 (January 1952), pp. 59–68.

"Governments of the Arab East," *Journal of International Affairs*, 6 (Winter 1952), pp. 37–50.

"The Role of the Military in Middle East Politics," *The American Political Science Review*, 47 (June 1953), pp. 511–524.

"Nature and Sources of Islamic Law," *The George Washington Law Review*, 22 (October 1953), pp. 3–28.

"Islam and the Modern Law of Nations," *The American Journal of International Law*, 50 (April 1956), pp. 358–372.

"The Problem of Regional Security in the Middle East: An

21

Appraisal," *The Middle East Journal,* 11 (Winter 1957), pp. 12–22.

"The Islamic System: Its Competition and Co-existence with Western Systems," *Proceedings of the American Society of International Law* (1959), pp. 49–52.

"American Foreign Policy in the Middle East, 1948–1960: An Appraisal," *SAIS Review,* 5 (Spring 1961), pp. 18–22.

"General Nuri's Flirtations with the Axis Powers," *The Middle East Journal,* 16 (Summer 1962), pp. 328–336.

"Political Trends in Iraq and Kuwait," *Current History,* 52 (February 1967), pp. 84–89, 115.

"The Greater War," *ARAMCO World Magazine,* 19 (July-August 1968), pp. 24–27.

"Closure of the Suez Canal to Israeli Shipping," *Law and Contemporary Problems,* 33 (Winter 1968), pp. 147–157.

"Marriage in Islamic Law: The Modernist Viewpoints," *The American Journal of Comparative Law,* 26 (Spring 1978), pp. 213–218.

"Who Are the Palestinians?," *The Sunday Sun,* Baltimore (February 5, 1978).

"The Resurgence of Islam," *The Sunday Sun,* Baltimore (February 25, 1979).

"Maslaha (Public Interest) and 'Illa (Cause) in Islamic Law," *Journal of International Law and Politics,* 12 (Fall 1979), pp. 213–217.

ESSAYS IN BOOKS AND ENCYCLOPAEDIAS

"The Scheme of Fertile Crescent Unity: A Study in Inter-Arab Relations," in R. N. Frye (ed.), *The Near East and the Great Powers* (Cambridge: Harvard University Press, 1951), pp. 137–177.

"The Army Officer: His Role in Middle Eastern Politics," in S. N. Fisher (ed), *Social Forces in the Middle East* (Ithaca: Cornell University Press, 1955), pp. 162–183. Reprinted with slight revision from *The American Political Science Review,* 47 (June 1953), pp. 511–524.

"From Religious to National Law," in R. N. Anshen (ed.), *Mid-East: World Center* (New York: Harper and Brothers, 1956), pp. 220–234.

"Baghdad Pact," *Encyclopaedia Britannica* (Chicago and London: William Benton, 1961), vol. 2, p. 921.

"Pan-Islamism," *Encyclopaedia Britannica* (1961), vol. 17, pp. 184–185.

"Dustur—Egypt, Iraq, Syria, and Lebanon, Jordan, Libya," *Encyclopaedia of Islam*, New ed. (Leiden: E. J. Brill, 1963), vol. 2, pp. 647–649, 659–662, 667–668.

"The Role of the Military in Iraqi Society," in S. N. Fisher (ed.), *The Military in the Middle East* (Columbus: Ohio State University Press, 1963), pp. 41–51.

"An Introduction to the Islamic Law of Nations," in Joel Larus (ed.), *Comparative World Politics* (Belmont, California: Wadsworth Publishing, 1964), pp. 230–238. Reprinted from *Law in the Middle East*, vol. 1, pp. 349–372.

"The Islamic Philosophy of War," in Joel Larus (ed.), *Comparative World Politics* (Belmont, California: Wadsworth Publishing, 1964), pp. 166–174. Reprinted from *War and Peace in the Law of Islam*, pp. 51–66.

"Aziz Ali al-Misri and the Arab Nationalist Movement," in Albert Hourani (ed.), *St. Antony's Papers: Middle Eastern Affairs*, No. 4 (London: Oxford University Press, 1965), pp. 140–163.

"Islamic Law," in Arthur Larson and C. W. Jenks (eds.), *Sovereignty Within the Law* (Dobbs Ferry, New York: Oceana Publications, 1965), pp. 165–183.

"The Islamic Theory of International Relations and its Contemporary Relevance," in J. Harris Proctor (ed.), *Islam and International Relations* (New York: Frederick A. Praeger, 1965), pp. 24–39.

"Dustur—Egypt, Iraq, Syria and Lebanon, Jordan, Libya," in *Dustur: A Survey of the Constitutions of the Arab and Muslim States* (Leiden: Brill, 1966), pp. 24–32, 59–61, 65–71, 85–87. Reprinted with additional material from the *Encyclopaedia of Islam*, vol. 2, pp. 647–649, 659–662, 667–668.

"From Religious to National Law," in J. H. Thompson and R. D. Reischauer (eds.), *Modernization of the Arab World* (Princeton: Van Nostrand, 1966), pp. 37–51. Reprinted with slight revision from R. N. Anshen (ed.), *Mid-East: World Center* (New York: Harper and Brothers, 1966), pp. 220–234.

"Harb—Legal Aspect," *Encyclopaedia of Islam* (1966), vol. 3, pp. 180–181.

"Hudna," *Encyclopaedia of Islam* (1967), vol. 3, pp. 546–547.

"Iraq, 1958 and 1963," in W. G. Andrews and Uri Ra'anan

23

(eds.), *The Politics of the Coup d'Etat* (New York: Van Nostrand Reinhold Co., 1967), pp. 65–88.

"Some Legal Aspects of the Arab-Israeli Conflict of 1967," in Albert Lepawski, E. H. Buehrig and H. D. Lasswell (eds.), *The Search for World Order* (New York: Appleton-Century-Croft, 1971), pp. 238–264.

"Baghdad Pact," *Encyclopaedia Britannica* (1973), vol. 2, p. 1026.

"Jihad," *Encyclopaedia Britannica* (1973), vol. 12, p. 1084.

"Property: Its Relations to Equality and Freedom in Accordance with Islamic Law," in Carl Wellman (ed.), *Equality and Freedom: Past, Present and Future* (Wiesbaden: Franz Steiner, 1977), pp. 177–188.

"Diplomacy, Islamic," *Dictionary of the Middle Ages* (New York: Charles Scribners Sons, 1983), vol. 4, pp. 197–201.

"International law, Islamic," *Encyclopedia of Public International Law* (Amsterdam: North-Holland, 1983), vol. 6, pp. 227–233.

"The Emergence of Modern Iraq," in Z. Michael Szaz (ed.), *Sources of Domestic and Foreign Policy in Iraq* (Washington, D.C.: American Foreign Policy Institute, 1986), pp. 3–7.

"Foreword" to Daniel Silverfarb, *Britain's Informal Empire in the Middle East; A Case Study of Iraq, 1929–1941* (New York: Oxford University Press, 1986), pp. v–vii.

"al-Mawsil (Mosul)," *Dictionary of the Middle Ages* (1987), vol. 8, pp. 500–501.

"Maslaha," *Encyclopaedia of Islam* (in press).

"al Shafi'i," *Encyclopaedia of Religion* (in press).

"Tenure of Land, Islamic," *Dictionary of the Middle Ages* (in press).

PART II

Islamic and International Law

CHAPTER THREE

Islamic Law and the Challenge of Modern Times*

GAMAL MOURSI BADR

ISLAMIC LAW IN CRISIS

Of late, Islamic law has been facing a crisis both in countries where it has been, uninterruptedly and exclusively, the law of the land for fourteen centuries, and in countries where since the mid-nineteenth century it has had to give way to Western-type codifications in many areas of the law. Awareness of the crisis is enhanced in the latter countries by a recent popular demand for a return to the application of Islamic law in all areas. Yet even in those countries where Islamic law has remained in exclusive application, the need to regulate new types of transactions and economic situations not specifically provided for in classical Islamic law poses critical problems.

The roots of the crisis go back to the fourth century of the Islamic era (the tenth century AD) when a consensus emerged among Sunni jurists that all the rules of Islamic law had been fully and definitively expounded. These jurists agreed that there

*This paper is a revised version of the author's address at the annual meeting of the Shaybani Society of International Law, held on September 28, 1985, in Washington, D.C.

27

was no further need for exercising independent reasoning *(ijtihad)* to formulate new rules of law. This is what came to be known in Sunni Islam as the "closing of the door of *ijtihad.*" Although exceptional talent and innovative spirits existed in subsequent generations of jurists, they remained an uninfluential minority. By and large, the Sunni scholars of Islamic law stagnated and were unable to meet changing social conditions. The output of juristic scholarship assumed a non-original and commentatorial character. That was especially important because of the absence of a separate lawmaking process. In classical Sunni conception, formulation of the rules of law is the responsibility of the jurists alone. No legislative power is vested in the state and the judges merely apply the law; no legal norms are created through judicial precedent.

As the Muslim world was confronted with the challenges of modernization in the last century, the ossified and static condition of its law was one reason why some Muslim countries opted for the easy way out of the problem by adopting codes on the European model in certain areas of the law. In those countries, the crisis was compounded by a duality of legal education and practice. Separate law schools, separate courts, and a separate legal profession were created to deal with the teaching and application of the new Western-type legislation. Islamic law became only one of several subjects taught at the new law schools and, for both scholars and practitioners, it lost importance except in the area of family and inheritance law, where it continued to apply.

RESPONSES TO THE CRISIS

Response to the crisis was neither immediate nor forceful. Over fifty years from the time European codes were introduced in the nineteenth century, a new interest in the study of Islamic law, in the areas where it had been displaced by modern legislation, began to assert itself slowly and gradually among the faculty and students of the new law schools. They began to take a fresh look at those areas of Islamic law and no longer cared much about the traditional rigid separation of the various schools *(madhahib)* of law. Islamic law was now considered an integrated whole and there was no compulsion to restrict oneself to any one particular

28

school.[1] This electicism and inter-school fertilization was evident in the amendments to family law that were introduced in Egypt in the 1920s. The revival of Islamic legal studies also benefited from a comparative approach, where the principles and rules of Islamic law were compared to corresponding principles and rules of other legal systems, thus shedding more light on the former and proving their lasting merit and relevancy under present-day conditions.

A milestone in the slow process of reasserting the *shari'a* (Islamic law) in those areas of the law where its application had been discontinued is the Egyptian Civil Code of 1949 and its progeny of civil codes in other Arab countries. The code contains a definitive *shari'a* input and, more importantly, designates the *shari'a* as a supplemental source of legal norms. This does not only mean that gaps in the code are to be filled by rules of Islamic law. It also means that interpretation of the provisions of the code is to be carried out in the light of the principles and rules of Islamic law. This tendency is reinforced by the fact that the judge and the interpreter are cautioned against the use of foreign sources in understanding and interpreting the provisions of the code.[2]

More recently, new constitutions or constitutional amendments in several Muslim countries have proclaimed the *shari'a* the principal source of legislation. Concurrently with the adoption of those provisions or closely following upon it, there has been an increasingly vocal demand, mostly by lay citizens, that the existing laws, perceived as being of foreign origin, be abrogated in favor of an immediate return to the application of the classical *shari'a*. This popular demand focuses on the restoration of the corporal punishments *(hudud)* in criminal cases and on a

---

1. 'Abd al-Razzaq al-Sanhuri, *al-Wasit fi Sharh al-Qanun al-Mandani*, (Cairo: Dar al-Nahda al-'Arabiyya, 1981), vol. 1, p. 70; Gamal M. Badr, *al-Niyaba fi'l-Tasarufat al-Qanuniyya* (Cairo: Al-Hay'ah al-Misriyya al-'Amma li'l-Kitab, 1980), p. 22; Muhammad Mustafa Shalabi, *al-Madkhal fi'l Fiqh al-Islami* (Beirut: Al-Dar al-Jami'yya, 1985), p. 156.

2. *Travaux préparatoires* of the Egyptian Civil Code, vol. 1, p. 133; al-Sanhuri, *Al-Wasit*, pp. 73–79.

strict ban on *riba* (interest) in civil and commercial transactions.[3] It represents one of two distinguishable responses to the crisis of the *shari'a*. The first response is characterized by atavistic emotionalism and champions the *shari'a* simply because it reflects the ways of the forefathers; it does not admit that the *shari'a* needs to evolve with the times. Most of the proponents of this trend know very little of the *shari'a* as a legal system and even less of the existing laws that they are opposed to maintaining. Theirs is an emotional, non-rational approach to the problem.

The second response to the challenges confronting Islamic law in our times may, by contrast, be described as enlightened rationalism. The proponents of this trend hold that the *shari'a's* claim to excellence as a legal system is based on objective grounds and believe it to have the intrinsic potential to undergo necessary changes without loss of its Islamic character. Their indispensable premise is that the process of independent and innovative formulation of new rules of law which are derived from the original sources *(ijtihad)* must be resumed, and that nothing precludes such an exercise by present-day jurists. In fact, opposition to the so-called closing of the door of *ijtihad* and a firm position in favor of resuming the process have come to be generally endorsed at the level of individual scholarship.[4] They

---

3. Criminal law is outside the scope of this paper and deserves a separate treatment. The question of *riba* will be briefly addressed below.

4. The closing of the door of *ijtihad* was never a position unanimously accepted by Muslim jurists. The reason for this is quite simple: a law that ceases to evolve would be incapable of meeting the social and economic needs of society. The *shari'a* being, according to the well-known maxim, "appropriate to all times and in all places," it owes it to itself to evolve constantly in order to adapt to the changing circumstances of Islamic society. Thus, both in the past and in the modern era, the most illustrious of Muslim jurists have vehemently refuted the assertion that the door of *ijtihad* has been closed. Ibrahim ibn Musa al-Shatibi (d. 790 A.H./1388), in his authoritative work, *al-Muwafaqat fi Usul al-Shari'a* (Cairo: al-Maktaba al-Tijariyya al-Kubra, 1975), expresses the idea of the necessary continuity of *ijtihad* in this concise formula: "*Ijtihad* cannot cease except at the end of the world when man's subjection to the Law will cease" (vol. 4, p. 89). Al-Suyuti (d. 911 A.H./1505) devoted a monograph to the question. Its title clearly indicates the contents: *Kitab*

have also become the stated policy[5] and the view held by collective academic bodies.[6]

THE NEED TO WORK WITH EXISTING LAWS

Present-day Islamic jurists of this second persuasion put emphasis on the need for the serious study of *fiqh* (the science of Islamic law) and of *usul al-fiqh* (Islamic jurisprudence), on the

---

al-Radd 'ala man Akhlada ila'l-Ard wa Jahila anna'l-Ijtihad fi Kull 'Asr Fard [Reply to One Who Prefers the Least Effort and Ignores the Fact that Ijtihad is Imperatively Necessary at All Times] (Beirut: Dar al-Kutub al-'Ilmiyya, 1983). Muhammad ibn 'Ali al-Shawkani (d. 1255 A.H./1839) in his book *Kitab Irshad al-Fuhul ila Tahqiq al-Haqq min 'Ilm al-Usul* (Cairo: Muhammad Amin al-Khanji, 1909), refuted the false proposition according to which contemporary jurists can no longer acquire the high qualifications that allowed the jurists of the classical era to exercise *ijtihad*. He explains that *ijtihad* has become infinitely easier than in the past because of the progress made in the Qur'anic sciences and in the science of *hadith*, and because of the publication of the compilations of juridical science (cited in Zakariyya al-Birri, *Usul al-Fiqh al-Islami* (Cairo: Dar al-Nahda al-'Arabiyya, 1979), p. 320, note 1). In our own time, the rejection of the purported closing of the door of *ijtihad* has become so common everywhere that it is difficult to cite all the jurists who defend the continuity of *ijtihad*. Some examples are:

—Muhammad Rashid Rida (d. 1935), cited in Hamid Enayat, *Modern Islamic Political Thought* (Austin: University of Texas Press, 1982), p. 70. Rida considered *ijtihad* "an imperative attribute of all legal thinking" (p. 81).

—Muhammad Mustafa al-Maraghi (Shaykh of al-Azhar in the 1930s, d. 1945), *Buhuth fi'l-Tashri' al-Islami* (Cairo, 1927), pp. 10–11 (cited in al-Birri, *Usul al-Fiqh*, p. 326).

—Mawlana Muhammad 'Ali (famous Muslim jurist of India, d. 1931), *The Religion of Islam* (Cairo: The Arab Writers, Publishers and Printers, n.d.), pp. 112–114, under the title "The Gate of Ijtihad is Still Open."

—Muhammad Muhammad al-Madani, in a 1942 article reproduced in *al-Dawha* (monthly review published in Qatar), January 1986, pp. 101–103.

—Al-Birri, *Usul al-Fiqh*, pp. 326–330.

—Shalabi, *al-Madkhal*, pp. 156–157 and note 1.

31

advisability of reviewing the existing laws in order to relate their provisions to the principles and rules of the *shari'a*, and on interpreting the existing laws in the light of the principles of the *shari'a* so as to bring them even closer to it. They do not concur in the demand that existing codes be summarily abrogated in favor of what is perceived as an immediate return to the application of the *shari'a*.

In fact, several considerations militate against an immediate wholesale discarding of the current codes. First, there is the need for a prior sustained exercise in *ijtihad* to fill the gaps between classical Islamic law and the current requirements of social and economic life in the Muslim world. These gaps resulted, obviously, from the early discontinuation of the process of *ijtihad*, by

—Khalid Muhammad Khalid, in *al-Wafd* (Cairo weekly), May 23, 1985, p. 7.
—Al-Sadiq al-Mahdi (well-known Sudanese legal scholar and currently Prime Minister of Sudan), in *al-Mustaqbal* (Arabic weekly published in Paris), June 1, 1985, p. 53, and in *al-'Arab* (daily published in Qatar), June 8, 1985.
—Yusuf al-Qaradawi, in *al-Dawha*, January 1985, pp. 8–11, and February 1985, pp. 6–11.
—Al-Habib Belkhoja (well-known Tunisian legal writer and Mufti of the Tunisian Republic), in *al-Umma* (monthly review published in Qatar), November 1985, pp. 66 and 69b.
—'Abd al-Munaym al-Nimr (former Minister of Awqaf in Egypt), *al-Ijtihad* (Cairo: Dar al-Shuruq, 1986).
—Jad al-Haq 'Ali Jad al-Haq (currently Shaykh of al-Azhar and former Mufti of Egypt) is writing a book on *"ijtihad* and contemporary developments."* See *al-Ahram*, February 7, 1986.

In summing up ancient and contemporary Islamic legal thinking, Enayat writes in his above cited book that *ijtihad* "had never in practice been totally abandoned among Muslims of any description" (p. 160).

5. In June 1983 Kin Fahd of Saudi Arabia publicly called for an international conference of Islamic jurists to update the *shari'a* through rigorous *ijtihad*.

6. The first conference (1964) of the Academy of Islamic Studies, cited in al-Birri, *Usul al-Fiqh*, pp. 328–329; the Fiqh Academy of the Muslim World League in Mecca announced in February 1985 that *ijtihad* should be set in motion to tackle new issues and problems unheard of in the old days.

which alone Islamic law can progressively develop. Second, the level of scholarship among the majority of present-day Islamic jurists, who were trained exclusively in the old-type educational institutions, is unacceptably low. Most of them are hardly aware of the needs of the economic life of society or of the workings of new types of business transactions not regulated by classical law. The legal framework that they propose for these new situations is glaringly inadequate. An example of this inadequacy is the poor quality of recent draft codes drawn up by committees created in Egypt when the popular demand for a return to the *shari'a* was at its highest.

Third, the majority of lawyers in the Arab world attach great value to the current Egyptian Civil Code. When enacted in 1949 this code was heralded as the harbinger of a Uniform Arab Civil Code, and has in fact been adopted by six other Arab countries. In the view of many lawyers, it contains nothing un-Islamic. As such, it has come to be considered a precious part of the Arab legal landscape and a potential factor for unity, which is dear to all pan-Arabists. The prospect of this code and the others modeled after it being abandoned in the cavalier fashion proposed by the adherents of the atavistic emotional approach is viewed with decided aversion. Because Islamic law is not a monolithic system and considerable diversity of opinion on details exists, new codifications of the *shari'a* by individual countries are likely to result in eliminating the measure of unity represented by the Egyptian Civil Code and its progeny. Only a joint multi-national exercise in codification could lead to the adoption of uniform rules of Islamic law among the countries concerned.

Two recent events appear to indicate that the atavistic emotional approach to the revival of Islamic law is losing steam. The controversial results of Sudan's experiment point to the pitfalls of a precipitate and ill-conceived return to the application of the *shari'a* without adequate preparation.[7] Moreover, in Egypt Parliament in effect

---

7. Faraj 'Ali Fuda, *Qabl al-Suqut* (Cairo: Published by the author at P.O. Box 5677, Heliopolis, 1985), pp. 126–141; al-Mahdi, *al-Mustaqbal.* See generally Carey N. Gordon, "The Islamic Legal Revolution: The Case of Sudan," *The International Lawyer,* 19, No. 3 (Summer 1985), pp. 793–815.

shelved the drafts referred to above, which purported to codify the *shari'a* and were intended to replace existing codes. In May 1985 Parliament resolved that the codification of Islamic law should proceed "in a gradual and scientific fashion." Emphasis was put on removing from existing laws those provisions, if any, which are contrary to the principles and mandatory rules of Islamic law, rather than on abrogating wholesale the current codes and statutes.

REVIEWING EXISTING LAWS

If the enlightened rational approach to the revival of the *shari'a* finally prevails, legal scholarship throughout the Muslim world will be called upon to undertake a renewed in-depth study of Islamic law and to conduct, with the benefit of the lessons of such a study, a review of the existing codes to determine whether they contain non-Islamic elements. A gradual disappearance of the dichotomy of legal education, noted above as a factor in the current crisis of the *shari'a*, could make this task easier to perform. In fact, interest in the comparative study of Islamic law is on the increase in the modern-type law schools and the recent publications of their faculty, on non-*shari'a* subjects, contain more Islamic inputs than ever before. In Egypt, to mention only one Muslim country, modern legislation and comparative law have become part of the curricula of the law schools of al-Azhar and its affiliated institutions. There is thus a narrowing of the gap between lawyers trained in Islamic law institutions and those trained in modern-type law schools. Shared knowledge of both systems is bound to reduce, and ultimately eliminate, that natural antipathy toward the unknown with which each group used to view the system in which it was not trained.

Such a renewed study of the *shari'a* and a concurrent review of the existing codes in the light of its teachings would bring these codes even closer to the *shari'a*. They would also produce results that are likely to surprise the vociferous champions of an immediate replacement of the existing codes, which they view as un-Islamic, by others ostensibly based on the *shari'a*.

One example of the closer identification of the existing codes with the *shari'a* that would stem from a better knowledge of the latter is the rule of the undisclosed principal in the area of agency law. Under a number of codes (e.g., Article 106 of the Egyptian

Civil Code), the effects of a contract concluded by someone who does not declare that he is an agent and identify his principal do not devolve on the "undisclosed principal," despite the existence of agency. From this general rule the codes provide for an exception "where it is immaterial for the third party to deal with the agent or the [undisclosed] principal." On the face of it, this last provision lends itself to a subjective interpretation whereby it must be ascertained in each individual case whether it mattered or did not matter to the third party to deal with one or the other. Looked at in the light of the Islamic regulation of agency, this provision merits an interpretation which is objective and not subjective; this, indeed, would greatly extend the scope of the rule of the undisclosed principal. In fact, Islamic law knows such a rule, which is as extensive as that of the Common Law.[8] Under this interpretation, the direct effects of agency would be realized, despite lack of disclosure of its existence or of the principal's identity, in a whole category of contracts objectively defined. The provision of the existing code would thus be brought closer to the rules of Islamic law.

Another example of a more perfect alignment between the codes and Islamic law through interpretation relates to the effect of supervening unexpected events on contractual obligations. When such events represent an obstacle to performance by one of the parties, they might excuse his non-performance. But the conditions required for such an outcome differ according to the interpretation given the provisions of the codes. If understanding those provisions is influenced, as it should not be, by the foreign sources of some of the wording or terminology used in them, the result would be very stringent conditions for excusing performance, such as the extraneous character of the event and the absolute impossibility of performance. Islamic law, by contrast, is content with much less strict conditions and may consider as valid excuses events personal to the obligator, or may be satisfied with a supervening hardship in performance rather than actual

---

8. Badr, *al-Niyaba*, pp. 309–332; Badr, "La tendence objective en matière de représentation dans la common law and en droit islamique," *La Revue internationale de droit comparé*, 17, No. 1 (January–March 1965), pp. 379–394.

impossibility to perform.[9] Deriving guidelines from the *shari'a* in this area would further bring the existing codes closer to it.

THE ISLAMIC ROOTS OF MODERN CONCEPTS

On the other hand, a serious renewed study of the *shari'a* and a review of the existing codes in its light would demonstrate that even those provisions of the codes ostensibly derived from foreign codifications can be traced back to Islamic law. Identifying such Islamic roots of the provisions of the codes and relating those provisions directly to Islamic sources is a much more worthy endeavor than preparing half-baked draft codes claiming to be the embodiment of Islamic law. Such an exercise would prove to one and all what the adherents of the enlightened rational approach knew all along: that the existing codes contain nothing which violates mandatory rules of Islamic law. Even matters that conventional wisdom tends to concede are contrary to the rules of Islamic law will be proven, upon scrutiny, not to be so. The two major, and possibly only, examples of this kind are interest on capital and the contract of insurance.

Interest

The equation of interest, as practiced in today's economy, with the *riba* prohibited in the Qur'an is the result of an uncritical approach to the problem based on an imprecise notion of what constitutes *riba*. The Qur'anic verses on *riba* were among the last to be revealed. There is precious little in the *sunna*, or traditions of the Prophet, that serve as legal precedent, to clarify the applicability of the prohibition in conditions other than those which prevailed at the time or its applicability to practices other than those pre-Islamic ones which were being discontinued as immoral and exploitative. 'Umar, the third Caliph, is even reported to have said that he regretted the fact that the Messenger of God departed this world before elucidating for the believers all the aspects of *riba*.[10] The famous *hadith* of the Prophet mentions

9. N. J. Coulson, *Commercial Law in the Gulf States: The Islamic Legal Tradition* (London: Graham & Trotman, 1984), pp. 83–87.
10. Ibn Kathir, *Tafsir*, as cited in Shalabi, *al-Madkhal*, pp. 516–517.

only gold and silver (in addition to four edible items with which we are not concerned). Like all prohibitive rules, this one should be construed restrictively and should not be extended to other items through interpretation. This is why, when coinage of base metals later appeared in the Muslim world, jurists of all schools were unanimous in ruling that the prohibition of *riba* did not apply to transactions in such coinage. The lender of one thousand copper coins could lawfully stipulate that he would receive back 1200 pieces or more of the same coinage when the debt was due. Jurists of the classical period distinguished, in fact, between:

a) money *ex natura sua*, which consists only of gold and silver currencies and to which alone the prohibition of *riba* applied, and

b) *fiat* money, which comprises currencies made out of any other materials.

The same reasoning is behind the opinion expressed by some present-day Muslim jurists that paper money, being *fiat* money *par excellence*, lies squarely outside the scope of *riba*. Consequently, there can be no ceiling to the rate of interest on paper-money loans and deposits other than what maximum might be prescribed by the existing laws or fixed by banking authorities under their established practice.[11]

Shalabi states (pp. 517–518) that prohibition of *riba* is definitively established with regard to the six items mentioned in the *hadith* and that concerning other items (paper money?) the matter is subject to *ijtihad*. He further states (p. 518) that prohibitive rules, being contrary to the original and universal permissiveness, should not be expanded by analogy. But he stops short of drawing the inevitable conclusion with regard to interest in today's paper money economy. He later (pp. 519–520) indulges in some vague rhetoric against Western-type banking. This is a striking example of how most contemporary Islamic jurists feel constrained by popular attitudes to legal issues. Their timorous reaction to misguided public opinion is in sharp contrast to the moral courage and leadership of their predecessors in the golden age of Islam.

11. See the well-reasoned article by Nasr Farid Wasil, then professor at the Shari'a school of al-Azhar on secondment to the University of

A less radical contemporary opinion, to which the present writer subscribes, is based on the definition of *riba* and the rationale of its prohibition. The definition of *riba* in Islamic jurisprudence is "surplus value without counterpart" *(fadlu malin la yuqabiluhu 'iwad)*. The key word "value" must be understood to mean *real*, as opposed to formal or merely numerical, value. In the classical period of Islamic law, new coinage of gold or silver having a lesser content of the precious metal, or older units worn out so that some of the weight was lost, had to be weighed and not merely counted at the time of repayment. A loan of 1000 gold dinars could thus be paid back as 1050 dinars of equal aggregate weight. No jurists ever considered the additional 50 dinars in the example as *riba*. Because the rationale of the prohibitive rule is to ensure equivalency in real value, the surplus in numerical value was immaterial. The present writer obtained, some years ago, a formal opinion *(fatwa)* from the Mufti of Egypt to the effect that this ancient practice was perfectly lawful and did not violate the prohibition of *riba*.[12]

Now, if through religiously inspired though excessive caution we treated paper money, which has no gold cover and no intrinsic value, as money *ex natura sua* and not as the *fiat* money it really is, an interest rate lower than the current rate of inflation would not be *riba* because it only makes up for a lesser real value. In this way, the interest rate would give effect to the rule of equivalency of real values. For years, the rate of inflation in all Muslim countries has been higher than the modest maximum interest rates prescribed by the existing civil and commercial codes. Thus, there is no ground whatsoever for the claim that in today's paper-money economy interest is *riba* and that the existing provisions on interest are un-Islamic.[13]

San'a, in the first issue (1978) of the journal of the School of Shari'a and Law of the University of San'a, *Majallat al-Shari'a wa'l-Qanun*.

12. *Fatwa* No. 181/1979 dated May 19, 1979, signed by the current Rector of al-Azhar, Shaykh Jad al-Haq. The inevitable conclusion regarding interest on paper money with a constantly diminishing real value was not raised with the Mufti because of the constraints of public opinion referred to in note 10 above.

13. Gamal M. Badr, in *al-Ahram al-Iqtisadi* (Cairo), July 1, 1979, pp.

Insurance

With regard to insurance, those present-day Islamic jurists who declare it inconsistent with the *shari'a* base their position on two arguments:

1) that insurance companies invest their funds in ways involving *riba*, which taints any monies received by the insured or the beneficiaries; and

2) that insurance involves uncertainty *(gharar)* since the insurer may have to pay after receiving only one or a few relatively small premiums, and since the insured may not get anything in return for his premiums if the risk does not become an actuality.

The first point has been addressed in the preceding discussion of interest and we need not dwell on it again here. The second argument is based, from the insurer's point of view, on considering a single insurance contract in isolation. The assumption is that the insurer concludes only one contract and may thus be exposed to the uncertainty, and subsequent inequity, of paying a huge sum in return for a relatively insignificant premium. This, of course, is not the case with insurance companies, which issue thousands upon thousands of policies and whose actuarial calculations protect them against any such uncertainty. From the point of view of the insured, this argument disregards the protective coverage which he obtains and which constitutes a valid counterpart for premiums paid.

Opponents of the validity of insurance under the *shari'a* attempt sometimes to classify this new type of transaction in one of the pigeonholes provided by the nominate contracts known to classical jurists. When it does not fit into any of them, they declare it un-Islamic.[14] Some contrive a distinction between insurance bought from a mutual company, which they consider valid under Islamic law, and insurance bought from a commercial profit-making company, which they do not consider to be valid. Such a distinction is of dubious merit. Islam attaches no opprobrium to profit-making as much. The very same activity cannot

19–21 and *ibid.*, August 18, 1980, pp. 32–34; Badr, in *International Lawyers' Newsletter*, 6, No. 5 (1984), p. 5.

14. Yusuf al-Qaradawi, *al-Halal wa'l-Haram fi'l-Islam* (Cairo: Dar al-'Itisam, 1977), pp. 223–224.

be at times valid and at other times invalid according to the absence or presence of a profit motive. Others resort to a fiction which they believe validates casualty insurance, but not life insurance, by assimilating it to the recognized nominate contract of "gift with stipulated counterpart." In this view, the gift is the premiums paid and the counterpart consists of the amount of the insurance.[15] In fact, no such legal fictions are needed to validate insurance under Islamic law.

Insurance is "a social device whereby a large group of individuals, through a system of equitable contributions, may reduce or eliminate certain measurable risks of economic loss common to all members of the group. Its primary function is to substitute certainty for uncertainty as regards the economic cost resulting from the accidental occurrence of disastrous events."[16] This description of insurance by an expert on the subject contains elements which sound distinctly Islamic. Solidarity and cooperation among Muslims is in fact a cornerstone of the Islamic society which the *shari'a* regulates, and certainty in contractual relations and the elimination of loss *(darar)* are two major concerns of Islamic jurisprudence.

Furthermore, among the recognized goals *(maqasid)* of the *shari'a* are protection and promotion of the individual's interests in property *(mal)* and his interest in the well-being of his progeny *(nasl)*. Casualty insurance is perfectly consonant with the first goal and life insurance generally with the second. New types of transactions that promote the goals of the *shari'a*, that are not tainted with *riba*, and that involve no uncertainty affecting their validity are perfectly consistent with Islamic law and should not be called un-Islamic merely because they were not known in classical times or because they originated in the non-Muslim West.

THE NEED FOR SUSTAINED IJTIHAD

In a sense, the provisions of the existing codes which regulate new types of transactions and of which the immediate formal sources are foreign codifications can be said to fill the gaps in

15. *Ibid.*, p. 225.
16. J. Edward Hedges, "Insurance," *Encyclopaedia Britannica* (Chicago and London: William Benton, 1973), vol. 12, p. 337b.

40

traditional Islamic law resulting from the arrest of its progressive development through abandonment of *ijtihad*. Where such provisions do not violate any principles or mandatory rules and can be fitted into the scheme of the *shari'a*, they should be considered part and parcel of an updated Islamic law.

A thorough knowledge of the *shari'a*, not limited to the details and technicalities of the old textbooks of *fiqh*, and an objective review of the existing legislation in the light of such knowledge could thus help achieve two ends:

a) to put to rest the exaggerated claims of a basic incompatibility of the current codes and statutes with the principles and peremptory rules of Islamic law; and

b) to bring further together the two groups of jurists in the Muslim world: those trained exclusively or mainly in the *shari'a* and those who are the products of the law schools of modern universities. By undertaking this mighty exercise jointly they could herald a definitive end to the deceptive dichotomy of the law into Islamic and "modern," and pave the way for a true revival of the *shari'a* that would be responsive to the changing needs of the present and the future. Only thus could the truth of the saying, "The *shari'a* is suitable for all times and all places," be given concrete expression.

A continued development of the *shari'a* in response to the dynamics of evolving social and economic conditions requires a sustained process of *ijtihad*. But *ijtihad* can no longer be the final step in the process of lawmaking or, rather, law formulating. In the Islamic conception, it will be recalled, only God is the lawmaker, the jurists being mere expositors of the law. Theirs is a role of discovery based on the original primary sources, rather than one of creation *ex nihilo* of legal norms. This process, which we call *ijtihad*, naturally leads to a diversity of opinions, as witnessed by the historical development of Islamic law. Modern conditions, including the complexity of present-day social and economic relationships and the transnational nature of many transactions, call for certainty of legal norms and require easy access to them. The results of new *ijtihad*, whether individual or collective, should therefore be ultimately couched in texts enacted by individual parliaments. This would not be an exercise by the parliaments of a veritable legislative power, but merely a necessary act of compilation and dissemination of uniform rules selected from the results of prior *ijtihad* in order to ensure the certainty of legal norms and their ready accessibility to all concerned. This pre-enactment *ijtihad* would invest the jurists with a positive role in formulating the law, in the best historical traditions of the *shari'a*, rather than giving them merely a negative veto power on parliamentary legislation, as in the case of Iran's Council of Guardians (Articles 91–95 of the Iranian Constitution of 1980).

Of the three tools of *ijtihad*, namely analogy *(qiyas)*, consensus *(ijma')* and the consideration of the public interest or common good *(maslaha)*, the last mentioned appears to be the most promising in the context of a renewed and continuous process of *ijtihad*. This is so because the new areas of activity and the novel transactions in need of legal regulation may not lend themselves to strict *qiyas*, which is after all an analogical deduction of a new rule from an existing one by virtue of an identity of rationale between the new situation and the one covered by the existing rule. In a sense, *qiyas* may be said to have been largely exhausted by previous generations of jurists as a source of new rules of law. As to *ijma'*, it is the consensus of those who exercise *ijtihad*. Before reaching that consensus each *mujtahid* must arrive at this own conclusion by one of the other tools of *ijtihad; ijma'* does not stand by itself. This leaves *maslaha* as an open-ended possibility for formulating new rules of law.

The use by *mujtahids* of *maslaha* as a source of new rules of law must be accompanied by the two following safeguards:

1) ascertaining that the public interest invoked is one recognized by the *shari'a* in the light of its overall objectives *(maqasid)*. This would preclude deviation from the *shari'a* in the guise of rules based on an ill-conceived "public interest";

2) ascertaining further that the rules to be so adopted do not contravene or conflict with any mandatory rules of law derived directly from the Qur'an or the established *sunna*,[17] the two basic

---

17. The various schools of Islamic law, and individual jurists within each school, often invoked weak and unauthenticated *hadiths* in order to buttress their divergent opinions by relating them ostensibly to the *sunna*. Others of their contemporaries and successors rejected those *hadiths* and upheld different positions than those based on them.

original sources which provide relatively few, but mostly peremptory and always immutable, rules of law.

The use of *maslaha* as advocated here contrasts with the more radical doctrine of the seventh century, A.H. (fourteenth, A.D.) Hanbali jurist Najm al-Din al-Tawfi, who elevated *maslaha* to an autonomous source of the rules of law capable of overriding even the Qur'an and the *sunna*. His argument was that public interest is itself a basic principle of the Qur'an and the *sunna* and the ultimate purpose of the *shari'a*.[18] The trouble with this view is that a public interest defined without reference, or even contrary, to the guidelines of the Qur'an and the authenticated *sunna* would soon transcend the Islamic framework within which all *ijtihad* must be exercised. A legal system whose rules are formulated through such an unrestrained consideration of a public interest subjectively perceived outside the outer perimeters of the primary sources of Islamic law risks the loss of its Islamic character.

Provided that the renewed process of *ijtihad* through *maslaha* meets the above two requirements—i.e., the compatibility of the particular public interest in question with the overall scheme of the *shari'a* and the absence of any conflict with a mandatory rule prescribed by the Qur'an and the established *sunna*—everything is possible by way of stating new rules of law or amending existing ones. This is so because of the principle of "original permissiveness." The law which evolves along these lines would always remain, thanks to the above two safeguards, authentically Islamic. It would reflect Islamic modernization, as opposed to the indiscriminate Westernization in the legal field carried out by some Muslim countries in the second half of the nineteenth century.

Present-day Islamic jurists should consider themselves bound only by established and authenticated *sunna*. They should feel no compulsion to follow this or that opinion of the earlier jurists when based on *hadiths* not generally recognized as genuine.

For an informative study in English of the question of the authenticity of *hadith*, see G. H. A. Juynboll, *Muslim Tradition* (Cambridge: Cambridge University Press, 1983).

18. Majid Khadduri, *The Islamic Conception of Justice* (Baltimore and London: The Johns Hopkins University Press, 1984), pp. 181–182.

This process of sustained *ijtihad* requires think tanks of Islamic jurists who would, preferably at a transnational level, devote themselves, as the need arises, to the task of formulating new rules of law that would be both truly Islamic and effectively modern. This is the challenge which the *shari'a* must meet if it is to put behind it all the lingering effects of its recent crisis. The *shari'a* contains within itself all the resources necessary to achieve that end. One can only hope that current and future generations of Islamic jurists will be both open to and capable of using those resources in the enlightened way required for the successful discharge of this formidable task. It is also hoped that Islamic jurists will resume their leadership role so that they will guide lay public opinion in the right path of the *shari'a*, rather than subserviently follow that public opinion in its misguided whims and impulses.

CHAPTER FOUR

The Legal Status
of Jerusalem

HENRY CATTAN

HISTORICAL PERSPECTIVE

In order to understand the present legal status of Jerusalem, it is necessary to examine first the status of the city when Palestine was part of the Ottoman Empire. Only then is it possible to evaluate the impact of events on Palestine and on Jerusalem in particular after the disintegration of the empire at the end of the First World War.

Despite its religious and historic importance, Jerusalem did not possess its own separate legal status in Turkish times until after the Crimean War, which broke out following an incident at the Church of the Nativity in Bethlehem. The district of Jerusalem subsequently attained "autonomous" administrative status in accordance with the Administrative Regulations of 1877–1888. This status, however, did not involve autonomy in the legal sense, but only meant that the district of Jerusalem was linked directly to Constantinople, instead of being under the jurisdiction of the governor of the province.[1]

---

1. A. Heidborn, *Manuel de droit public et administratif de l'Empire Ottoman* (Vienna: C. W. Stern, 1908), vol. 1, p. 7.

Although Jerusalem was part of the Ottoman Empire, its character and population were predominantly Palestinian Arab during almost eighteen centuries following the deportation of the Jews from Jerusalem by the Romans in 132–135 after their second revolt. The Palestinian Arabs, who claim descent from the Canaanites and the Philistines, coexisted with the Jews before their deportation. The Palestinian Arab character of Jerusalem was not affected by Byzantine, Crusader, or Muslim Arab conquest. Nor did this character change with the Turkish capture of the city in 1517, because colonization of Jerusalem or of any other part of Palestine was never substantial.

The Arabs in Palestine and other Arab provinces of the Ottoman Empire enjoyed equal civil and political rights with Turks as citizens of an independent and sovereign state. In accordance with the Ottoman Constitution of December 23, 1876, they had the right to elect, and be elected as, deputies to the Chamber of Deputies in Istanbul. Jerusalem elected two deputies from the city's Arab inhabitants.

John Westlake has observed that the duties and rights of states are only the duties and rights of the men who compose them.[2] Hence, although Jerusalem was then under Ottoman sovereignty, this should be understood to mean the joint sovereignty of the Turks and the Arabs, which they shared in all the provinces of the Ottoman Empire, regardless of whether they were Turkish or Arab in character and population. However, the legal status of Jerusalem as an Ottoman city was altered at the end of the First World War as a result of the detachment of Palestine from the empire and the consequent change from Ottoman to Palestinian sovereignty.

PALESTINIAN SOVEREIGNTY

On December 9, 1917, Jerusalem was occupied by British forces under General Allenby. Subsequently it was administered, like the rest of Palestine, as occupied territory. The occupation of Palestine did not involve its annexation. The objective of the

2. *Collected Papers*, ed. by L. Oppenheim (Cambridge: Cambridge University Press, 1914), p. 78.

46

Allied powers, inspired by President Wilson's Fourteen Points and the Anglo-French pledges made to the Arabs for their independence,[3] was to liberate, rather than appropriate, the Arab territories. This objective corresponded to the aspirations of the Arab peoples who, for some time and despite their political equality with the Turks, had been agitating for independence.

The objective of the Allies was made concrete in the peace settlement which terminated the First World War. It was decided by the Treaty of Versailles and Article 22 of the Covenant of the League of Nations, which was incorporated in the Treaty, that the Arab peoples who inhabited the occupied territories would be detached from the Ottoman Empire and their existence as independent nations would be provisionally recognized, subject to the rendering of administrative advice and assistance by a mandatory power until such time as they were able to stand alone.

As a result, five new states came into existence—Iraq, Lebanon, Syria, Palestine, and the Amirate of Transjordan (which subsequently assumed the name of the Hashimite Kingdom of Jordan). These new states were placed under mandates entrusted by the Council of the League: Iraq, Palestine, and Transjordan under British mandate; Lebanon and Syria under French mandate. Turkey formally renounced its sovereignty over the detached Arab territories in accordance with the Treaty of Lausanne of July 24, 1923.

Under international law, the legal effect of the detachment of Palestine from Turkey and the recognition by Article 22 of the League Covenant of its inhabitants as "an independent nation" was to make of Palestine a sovereign state.[4] Jerusalem, which until then was the principal city of Palestine, thus became the capital of an independent and sovereign state placed temporarily under a mandate.

---

3. George Antonius, *The Arab Awakening* (Beirut: Khayat, 1938).

4. Regarding the concept of national independence and sovereignty contained in Article 22 of the Covenant of the League of Nations, see R. Erlich, "La Naissance et la reconnaissance des Etats," *Hague Recueil*, 13 (1926), p. 450; H. Duncan Hall, *Mandates, Dependencies and Trusteeships* (Washington, DC: Carnegie Endowment for International Peace, 1948), p. 80.

The fact that Palestine was placed under a British mandate did not affect its statehood or its international personality. In fact, the very existence of the mandate, which by definition was of a temporary nature, presupposed and implied the existence of Palestinian statehood. The legal status of Palestine had close similarity to that of a protected state.[5] Its international personality was distinct from the personality of Great Britain as the mandatory power. The government of Palestine established by the Palestine Order-in-Council of 1922,[6] although administered by a British High Commissioner, was legally the representative of the people and of the state of Palestine. It concluded agreements with the mandatory power and treaties with third states through the instrumentality of Great Britain. This arrangement was required by reason of the provision contained in Article 12 of the mandate which stated: "The Mandatory shall be entrusted with the foreign relations of Palestine . . ."

Moreover, the mandate did not confer sovereignty over Palestine on Great Britain as the mandatory, nor divest the state of Palestine or its people of their sovereignty. Professor P. Pic was one of the first writers to proclaim the principle that sovereignty lies in the inhabitants of the mandated territory. He said:

Les rédacteurs du Traité de Versailles, s'inspirant avant tout d'un droit pour les peuples de disposer s'eux-mêmes, ont formellement proclamé qu'il n'y aurait aucune annexion des territoires sous mandat par une puissance quelconque ... Ces territoires appartiennent virtuellment aux populations ou communautés autochtones, dont la Société des Nations s'est constituée le défenseur, et au regard desquelles elle joue un peu le rôle d'un conseil de famille. Or, en droit interne, un conseil de famille n'a pas plus que le tuteur qu'il désigne, et dont il contrôle les actes, de droit privatif sur les biens du pupille.[7]

5. Earl of Birkenhead, *International Law*, 6th ed. (London: J.H. Dent & Sons, 1927), p. 99.

6. *Legislation of Palestine, 1918–1925*, compiled by Norman Bentwich (Alexandria: Government of Palestine, 1926), vol. 1, p. 1.

7. "Le Régime du mandat d'après le Traité de Versailles," *Revue Générale de Droit International Public*, 30 (1923), p. 334.

As pointed out by J. Stoyanovsky, the people of a mandated territory are not deprived of the right of sovereignty, but are temporarily deprived of its *exercise*.[8] There was a fairly general consensus that sovereignty lay in the people of a mandated territory.[9]

There is, therefore, no doubt that sovereignty over Jerusalem as an integral part of Palestine was at all times vested in the people of Palestine, both during Ottoman times when the Palestinians shared sovereignty with the Turks as citizens of an independent and sovereign country, and also specifically after the detachment of Palestine from the Ottoman Empire by its recognition as an independent nation in the mandatory period.

The preceding discussion concerning the sovereignty of the Palestinians over Jerusalem is not simply one of historical or academic interest. The question is of relevance at the present time even though events which occurred in Palestine on the termination of the mandate have prevented its people from exercising their sovereignty. There remains still to examine the effect of the status of Jerusalem of its internationalization by the General Assembly of the United Nations in 1947 and its occupation and annexation by Israel.

INTERNATIONALIZATION

As we have seen, it was never the purpose of the mandate to keep the people of Palestine forever under mandatory tutelage. Indeed, the British government announced in a White Paper in 1939[10] that Palestine would be granted its independence within ten years. At the same time, British authorities recognized that the continuation of Jewish immigration into Palestine, which they had allowed against the wishes of the Palestinians, had caused serious prejudice to the "rights and position" of the Arab

---

8. "La Théorie général des mandats internationaux" (Sorbonne thesis), p. 83.

9. See various authorities cited in Henry Cattan, *Palestine and International Law*, 2nd ed. (London: Longman, 1976), pp. 116–120.

10. Great Britain, *Statement of Policy on Palestine, May 17, 1939*, Cmd. 6019.

Palestinians whom they were obligated to safeguard. As a consequence, the British government decided to limit Jewish immigration and, after five years, to allow it only with Arab consent. This decision prompted a Jewish campaign of violence and terrorism against the British government in order to force it to alter its policy. Subjected to untenable pressures on all sides, the British decided in 1947 to refer the question of the future government of Palestine to the new United Nations.

After an enquiry by a Special Committee, the General Assembly of the United Nations adopted on November 29, 1947, Resolution 181, which recommended the termination of the mandate, the creation of Arab and Jewish states in Palestine, and the establishment of Jerusalem as a *corpus separatum* under a special international regime to be administered by the Trusteeship Council on behalf of the United Nations. The area of the *corpus separatum* was defined to include the then existing municipality, which comprised the Old City and the New City of Jerusalem and their environs, including Bethlehem, Bethany, and Ein Karem (birthplace of St. John the Baptist). The Resolution envisaged the appointment by the Trusteeship Council of a Governor to administer the City and to conduct its external affairs. The Governor would be assisted by an administrative staff chosen whenever practical from the residents of the City and the rest of Palestine. Local autonomous units in the territory of the City, such as municipalities, would enjoy wide powers of local government and administration. The City would be demilitarized and its neutrality declared and preserved. A Legislative Council elected by the residents of the City would have powers of legislation and taxation.

The resolution declared that its provisions relating to Holy Places and to religious, minority and property rights "shall be under the guarantee of the United Nations, and no modifications shall be made in them without the consent of the General Assembly of the United Nations" (Chapter 4 of Part I).

The resolution further provided that the Trusteeship Council was to elaborate and approve a detailed Statute of the City which would contain, *inter alia*, the substance of the provisions set forth in the resolution. However, influenced by developments on the ground, the Statute, which was prepared by the Trusteeship

Council, deviated from Resolution 181. It was accordingly ignored by the General Assembly. In fact, the Assembly restated its intention in Resolution 303 of December 9, 1949, that Jerusalem should be placed under a permanent international regime, and it asked the Trusteeship Council to prepare a Statute of Jerusalem on the lines of Resolution 181. On April 4, 1950, the Trusteeship Council approved a Statute which followed substantially that embodied in Resolution 181, except in one respect: it substituted a system of communal election to the Legislative Council by Christians, Muslims, and Jews for election by universal suffrage and proportional representation. The Trusteeship Council, unable to implement the Statute because of opposition by Israel and Jordan to internationalization, simply transmitted it to the General Assembly. Attempts were made to modify the scope and nature of internationalization during a General Assembly meeting in December 1950, but no proposal made at that time was approved. As a result, Resolution 181 as well as the Statute approved by the Trusteeship Council remained unchanged.

The question which must now be considered is whether Resolution 181, by its internationalization of Jerusalem, conferred sovereignty on the United Nations, specifically on the Trusteeship Council, or affected the sovereignty of the people of Palestine over Jerusalem. The answer is that Resolution 181 had neither effect.

The resolution did not confer sovereignty over Jerusalem to the United Nations or the Trusteeship Council. The fact that it attributed to the Trusteeship Council the power to administer Jerusalem on behalf of the United Nations did not have the effect of vesting sovereignty over the City in the Trusteeship Council or in the United Nations. The power of administration of a territory and the right of sovereignty over such territory are two different things. Just as the British government did not acquire sovereignty over Palestine during the mandate, though vested by the League of Nations with full powers of legislation and administration, so too the grant to the Trusteeship Council of powers limited to administration only, to the exclusion of powers of legislation and taxation, did not confer on it sovereignty over the City of Jerusalem.

By the same token, the resolution did not divest the Palestinians of their sovereignty over Jerusalem. This is clear from the fact that the powers of legislation and taxation as well as of the judiciary, all attributes of sovereignty, were reserved for the inhabitants. Moreover, the resolution recognized the right of the residents of Jerusalem, after a period of ten years, to express by referendum their wishes as to modifications of the regime of the City (Part III, D). Further, not only did Resolution 181 not divest the Palestinians of their sovereignty, it could not have done so, even if it had intended such a result, for the United Nations did not—and does not—possess legal competence to extinguish the sovereignty that resides in the Palestinian people.

The foregoing conclusion might raise a query as to the compatability of the internationalization of Jerusalem with the survival of Palestinian sovereignty. But in accordance with international practice, sovereignty may coexist with internationalization in the same territory. Charles Rousseau points out that internationalization does not require the effective exercise of sovereignty by the international community:

> C'est ainsi qu'il n'apparaît pas, comme certains auteurs l'ont pensé . . . que les regimes d'internationalisation constituent une catégorie juridique impliquent l'exercice effectif de la souveraineté . . . par la communauté internationale.[11]

An example of the coexistence of sovereignty with internationalization was the city of Tangiers, which, despite its internationalization, remained under the sovereignty of Morocco. It follows therefore, that, without affecting Palestinian sovereignty, the effect of Resolution 181 was to clothe Jerusalem with an international legal status compatible with its historic character and its religious significance to the world.

Lastly, it is important to observe that Resolution 181 was not abrogated by reason of its non-application. It remains operative and binding despite the fact that its implementation was thwarted by military operations. Its non-implementation, or its violation, do not entail its lapse—just as the various resolutions of the United Nations which have called for the repatriation of the Palestinian refugees, or the rescission of the measures taken

---

11. *Droit International Public* (Paris: Sirey, 1974), vol. 2, p. 413.

by Israel contrary to the status of Jerusalem, have not lapsed or been abrogated by Israel's refusal to respect and implement them. There exists no principle in legal theory which would support the view that a resolution of the United Nations lapses or is abrogated by its non-implementation or its violation. Moreover, as we shall see, the legal status given to Jerusalem by Resolution 181 has repeatedly been invoked by the United Nations since 1967, and Resolution 181 was specifically reaffirmed by Resolution 35/169A adopted by the General Assembly on December 15, 1980.

ISRAELI ANNEXATION

The General Assembly had recommended in Resolution 181 that the mandate for Palestine should terminate not later than August 1, 1948, and the administration be turned over progressively by the mandatory to a commission elected by the General Assembly. However, the commission which was chosen to take over the temporary administration of Palestine was unable to assume its functions. The British government withdrew its forces and terminated the mandate on May 15, 1948, leaving the country in complete chaos without any orderly transfer of authority to a successor. On the eve of the termination of the mandate the Jews proclaimed the State of Israel, and on May 15 war broke out between the new state and the neighboring Arab states.

However, the battle for Jerusalem had erupted prior to the termination of the mandate, when Jewish forces seized several Arab residential quarters of the City before the British withdrawal. The Jews even completed the occupation of most of the area of the New City of Jerusalem before the Arab states entered the war.

After the Jews overran the New City of Jerusalem, they attacked the Old City. But its Palestinian inhabitants resisted the various assaults until the arrival on May 18 of Jordan's Arab Legion, which occupied the Old City and prevented its seizure by Jewish forces. Thus within three days of the termination of the mandate, the whole of Jerusalem was militarily occupied, partly by Israel, which controlled its modern section, and partly by Jordan, which held the Old City. This situation was frozen by a cease-fire and eventually by the Israeli-Jordanian Armistice Agreement concluded on April 3, 1949. It was to last until June 1967.

The military occupation of Jerusalem prevented the application of the international regime which was envisaged by the United Nations for a *corpus separatum*. The efforts of the Palestine Conciliation Commission to secure its implementation were defeated by the opposition of Israel and Jordan to internationalization. Israel not only rejected internationalization, but it proceeded to take steps for the annexation of the section of the City under its control. In 1949, it moved certain ministries from Tel Aviv to Jerusalem, while denying that its action possessed any political or juridical significance, or that it affected the legal status of the City. The statements made in this regard by Israel's representative to the United Nations were explicit.[12] However, despite these statements, the Israeli Knesset proclaimed on January 23, 1950, that Jerusalem had always been the capital of Israel; after that date, Israel treated the New City of Jerusalem as an integral part of its territory.

King 'Abd Allah of Jordan, who was equally opposed to the internationalization of Jerusalem, lost no time in following suit. He arranged for elections to be held for a National Assembly that would be composed of an equal number of Palestinians and Jordanians. It convened in Amman on April 24, 1950, and proclaimed the union of Jordan and Palestine. This union was not, strictly speaking, an annexation and thus cannot be equated with Israel's action in the New City of Jerusalem, which was taken without regard to the wishes and the rights of the Arab inhabitants.

In June 1967 Israel attacked and captured the Old City of Jerusalem. Three weeks later the Israelis proceeded with its annexation. By the "Law and Administration Ordinance" of June 27, 1967, Israeli law, jurisdiction and administration were extended to the Old City and an adjacent area. As in the case of the annexation of the New City, Israel denied that this action meant or amounted to annexation. On June 29, 1967, Abba Eban, Israel's Foreign Minister, told the General Assembly of the United Nations:

Some delegations and Governments have made statements in recent days concerning certain developments in Jerusalem.

12. General Assembly, *Official Records*, Part II (1949), pp. 223 and 286.

54

There seems to me to be a basic misunderstanding about the import of yesterday's administrative legislation. This, as the General Assembly will be aware, contained no new political statement, and concerned itself exclusively with the urgent necessities of repairing the ravages and dislocations arising from the division of the city's life ... The import of the recent legislation is to assure for the inhabitants of all parts of the city social, municipal and fiscal services.[13]

Moreover, in a letter dated July 10, 1967, addressed to the United Nations, Israel declared that the term "annexation" was improper to describe the action it had taken in Jerusalem because the measures that it introduced concerned the "integration" of Jerusalem on the administrative and municipal levels.[14] However, under general international law and the Fourth Geneva Convention of August 12, 1949, a belligerent occupant is not entitled to undertake expropriations, colonization, construction of settlements, and other modifications of the demographic structure of occupied territory. The Israeli government undertook all these actions, for political purposes, in the Old City.[15]

NULLITY OF ANNEXATION

Israel's annexation of Jerusalem is legally void on three grounds.

First, the annexation of Jerusalem, whether of its modern section or the Old City, violates its international legal status as determined by the United Nations in 1947.

Following the occupation of Jerusalem in May 1948 by Israel and Jordan, and despite this occupation, the General Assembly reaffirmed the international regime of the City by its Resolutions 194 of December 11, 1948 and 303 of December 9, 1949. Such a reaffirmation *after* the City's occupation meant that the General Assembly did not consider that the occupation of Jerusalem

13. 1541st meeting of the General Assembly, June 29, 1967.

14. See Report of Secretary-General U Thant, UN Doc. S./805.

15. Regarding expropriations, settlements and demographic changes made by Israel in Jerusalem, see Henry Cattan, *Jerusalem* (London: Croom Helm, 1981), pp. 79–100.

impaired or abrogated the international regime. In fact, Resolution 303 requested the Trusteeship Council to complete the preparation of the Statute of Jerusalem and to proceed with its implementation without allowing "any actions taken by any interested Governments to divert it from adopting and implementing the Statute of Jerusalem."

Moreover, mindful of the internationalization of Jerusalem by the United Nations in 1947, the world community refused to recognize the annexation of Jerusalem, whether by Israel or by Jordan. This was the attitude of the United States, Britain, and most other states. Despite their recognition of Israel, these states resisted Israeli requests to move their embassies from Tel Aviv to Jerusalem. Thus the Department of State declared in 1953:

> The United States does not plan to transfer its Embassy from Tel Aviv to Jerusalem. It is felt that this would be inconsistent with the UN resolutions dealing with the international nature of Jerusalem.[16]

Secretary of State Dulles stated that "the presently standing UN resolution about Jerusalem contemplates that it should be, to a large extent at least, an international city rather than a purely national city."[17] Similarly, the British government declared in a written reply to the House of Commons on November 27, 1967:

> While Her Majesty's Government have, since 1949, recognized the *de facto* authority of Israel and Jordan in the parts of Jerusalem which they occupied, they, in common with other governments, have not recognized *de jure* Israeli or Jordanian sovereignty over any part of the area defined in General Assembly Resolution 303 (IV) of the 9th December 1949, which called for an international status for a designated area of Jerusalem.

Again in 1967, the U.S. government reaffirmed its non-recognition of the annexation of the Old City:

16. *Department of State Bulletin,* July 20, 1953, p. 82.
17. *Ibid.,* August 10, 1953, p. 177.

The United States has never recognized such unilateral actions by any of the states in the area as governing the international status of Jerusalem.[18]

The United Nations also censured Israel's annexation of the Old City after its capture in 1967 and declared it invalid.[19] The nullity was not limited to the act of annexation alone, but applied to all measures which tended to change the status of Jerusalem. Thus in Resolution 298 of September 25, 1971, the Security Council declared that it:

Confirms in the clearest possible terms that all legislative and administrative actions taken by Israel to change the status of the City of Jerusalem, including expropriations of land and properties, transfer of populations and legislation aimed at the incorporation of the occupied section, are totally invalid and cannot change that status.

The nullity of the measures taken by Israel in Jerusalem was reaffirmed in several subsequent resolutions. It is noteworthy that in Resolution 465 of March 1, 1980, the Security Council referred specifically to another of those measures by calling upon Israel "to dismantle the settlements" that it had established in Jerusalem and the occupied territories.

Again, the Security Council declared in its Resolution 476 of June 30, 1980, that it:

Reiterates that all such measures which have altered the geographic, demographic and historical character and status of the Holy City of Jerusalem are null and void and must be rescinded in compliance with the relevant resolutions of the Security Council.

18. Ibid., June 28, 1967, p. 57.
19. See, inter alia, General Assembly Resolutions 2253 of July 4, 1967, 2254 of July 14, 1967, 31/106 of December 16, 1976, 32/5 of October 28, 1977, 33/113 of December 18, 1978, ES/72 of July 29, 1980 and Security Council Resolutions 252 of May 21, 1968, 267 of July 3, 1969, 271 of September 15, 1969, 298 of September 25, 1971, 446 of March 22, 1979, 465 of March 1, 1980, 476 of June 30, 1980 and 478 of August 20, 1980.

Finally, in Resolution 478 adopted on August 20, 1980, following the proclamation of Jerusalem as the eternal capital of Israel, the Security Council:

- reaffirmed again that the acquisition of territory by force is inadmissible;
- expressed its concern over the enactment of a "basic law" in the Israeli Knesset proclaiming a change in the character and status of the Holy City, with its implications for peace and security;
- censured in the strongest terms the enactment by Israel of the "basic law" on Jerusalem;
- affirmed that the enactment of the "basic law" by Israel constitutes a violation of international law and does not affect the continued application of the Fourth Geneva Convention of August 12, 1949, in the Palestinian and other Arab territories occupied since June 1967, including Jerusalem;
- determined that all legislation and administrative measures taken by Israel, the occupying power, which have altered or purported to alter the character and status of the Holy City of Jerusalem, and, in particular, the recent "basic law" on Jerusalem, are null and void and must be rescinded forthwith; and
- called upon states that have established diplomatic missions in Jerusalem to withdraw them from the Holy City.

As a result of this directive and also a warning by the Arab states that they would break off diplomatic and economic relations with any country recognizing Jerusalem as Israel's capital or maintaining its embassy in the City, all thirteen states that maintained diplomatic missions in Jerusalem—the Netherlands and twelve Latin American countries—withdrew them from the City and moved them to Tel Aviv.[20]

20. The condemnation by the Arab States of Israel's annexation of Jerusalem was endorsed by the Islamic Foreign Ministers' Conference held at Fez (September 18–20, 1980), and by the Islamic Summit held at Ta'if (January 25–28, 1981) and attended by 37 Arab and Muslim states and the Palestine Liberation Organization. The Islamic Summit called for a mobilization of the military, political and economic potential of the

The preceding resolution of the Security Council was also endorsed by 144 states of the General Assembly in its Resolution 35/169E dated December 15, 1980. The universal character of this endorsement is hardly affected by the solitary negative vote of Israel or by the four absentions of the Dominican Republic, Guatemala, Malawi, and the United States.

Of great significance also is the preamble to Resolution 35/169A, which was adopted by the General Assembly on December 15, 1980. In this preamble, the General Assembly recalled and reaffirmed its Resolutions 181(II) of November 29, 1947, 194(III) of December 11, 1948, 3236(XXIX) of November 22, 1974, and other resolutions. This reaffirmation can only mean that the General Assembly is pointing the way to the solution: confirmation of the boundaries of the Arab and Jewish states as defined in 1947, implementation of the international regime of Jerusalem, and repatriation of the Palestinian refugees.

It is noteworthy that in all the resolutions adopted by the United Nations on Jerusalem since 1967, the legal status of the City is invoked in order to condemn Israel's actions and proclaim their nullity. Although some resolutions simply refer to "the status of Jerusalem," others speak of "the legal status of Jerusalem" (Security Council Resolution 252 of May 21, 1968, and General Assembly Resolution 32/5 of October 28, 1977), or of "the specific status of Jerusalem" (Security Council Resolutions 452 of July 20, 1979, 465 of March 1, 1980, and 476 of June 30, 1980). The only "status" or "legal status" or "specific status" which Jerusalem possesses is that laid down in Resolution 181 of November 29, 1947. Resolutions of the Security Council, such as 267 of July 3, 1969, 271 of September 15, 1969, and 298 of September 25, 1971, and General Assembly Resolution 2253 of July 4, 1967, refer to the status of "the City of Jerusalem." The appellation "City of Jerusalem" is derived from Resolution 181 and demarcates the area and boundaries of the *corpus separatum* of Jerusalem as defined in that resolution. It is thus clear that the gradual annexation of Jerusalem by Israel in 1948–1950, 1967, and 1980 and all the measures that it has taken in the *corpus*

Arab and Islamic world for the liberation of Jerusalem and the realization of the rights of the people of Palestine.

separatum of the City of Jerusalem are void under United Nations resolutions.

Second, the annexation of Jerusalem is void under general international law. The modern law of nations holds that conquest is not grounds for the acquisition of territory. H. Lauterpacht observes that "title by conquest has been abolished."[21] The rule is also stated in these terms:

> Conquest has ceased to constitute a mode of acquisition of territory since the general prohibition on recourse to force (Pact of Paris of 1928, Charter of the United Nations, Art. 2, para. 4).[22]

Following the Napoleonic wars a distinction came to be made between annexation and belligerent occupation of foreign territory. It is now universally established that an occupying power does not acquire sovereignty over the occupied territory,[23] nor does occupation destroy or extinguish the sovereignty of the legitimate sovereign. The occupier merely acquires a temporary right of administration.[24]

The rule of international law that conquest does not give title has been affirmed in numerous resolutions adopted by the United Nations—with respect to the Arab-Israeli conflict and Israel's annexation of Jerusalem—which have proclaimed "the inadmissibility of the acquisition of territory by war" or "by military conquest."[25] These resolutions have also recognized that Israel's

---

21. *Private Law Sources and Analogies of International Law* (London: Longman, 1927), p. 107.

22. N. Dinh, P. Dailler, and A. Pellet, *Droit International Public*, 2nd ed. (Paris: Librairie Générale de Droit et de Jurisprudence, 1980), p. 406.

23. L. Oppenheim, *International Law*, 7th ed. (London: Longman, 1952), vol. 2, p. 436.

24. *Ibid.*, pp. 433, 434, and 436.

25. See Security Council Resolutions 242 of November 22, 1967, 252 of May 21, 1968, 267 of July 3, 1969, 271 of September 15, 1969, 298 of September 25, 1971, 476 of June 30, 1980, 478 of August 20, 1980 and General Assembly Resolutions 2628 of November 4, 1970, 2799 of

status in the occupied territories, including Jerusalem, is that of an occupying power and that it is bound by the Fourth Geneva Convention of August 12, 1949, which lays down the obligations of the occupying power.

No doubt exists, therefore, that in accordance with general international law, Israel's annexation of Jerusalem is null and void and has not affected either the international legal status of the City or the sovereignty of the Palestinians.

Third, the annexation of Jerusalem is invalid on the ground of estoppel. "Estoppel" is the legal doctrine whereby a party is precluded, by its own conduct, from claiming a right that would harm another party which was entitled to expect only lawful conduct in the first place. Having accepted the international regime of Jerusalem, Israel cannot contest the international legal status of the City as laid down by Resolution 181. Such estoppel is established by the following:

(1) The Jews formally accepted in 1947 Resolution 181, including its provisions for an international regime for Jerusalem. Walter Eytan, Director General of the Israeli Foreign Ministry, states: "The Jewish Agency accepted internationalization, albeit under protest. Internationalization formed an integral part of the partition plan whose general advantages, notably the establishment of an independent Jewish state, outweighed the bitter sacrifice involved in relinquishing the ancient capital of Israel."[26]

But Israel's acceptance of internationalization, whether reluctant or not, was binding and irrevocable.

(2) The Jews proclaimed the State of Israel on May 14, 1948, "by virtue of the natural and historic right of the Jewish people and of the Resolution of the General Assembly of the United Nations." The Proclamation declared that "the State

December 13, 1971, 2949 of December 8, 1972, 34/70 of December 6, 1979, ES/72 of July 29, 1980, and 35/169E of December 15, 1980.

26. Walter Eytan, *The First Ten Years* (London: Weidenfeld and Nicolson, 1958), p. 65.

of Israel will be ready to cooperate with organs and representatives of the United Nations in implementation of the
Resolution of the General Assembly of November 29, 1947."

(3) Israel gave formal assurances in support of its application
for admission to United Nations membership in 1949 that it
would implement Resolutions 181 and 194 on the repatriation of the Palestine refugees and internationalization of
Jerusalem.[27] In its Resolution 273 of May 11, 1949, which
accepted Israel's membership, the General Assembly expressly took note of "the declarations and explanations made
by the representative of the Government of Israel before the
Ad Hoc Political Committee in respect of the implementation of its Resolutions dated 29 November 1947 and 11
December 1948."[28]

(4) During the debate on Israel's application for admission to
United Nations membership in 1949, Abba Eban, Israel's
Foreign Minister, declared that "the legal status of Jerusalem
is different from that of the territory in which Israel is
sovereign."[29] Equally significant is his statement that "Israel
had cooperated to the fullest extent with the Statute [of
Jerusalem] drawn up in November 1947"[30] and that the
transfer of certain ministries to Jerusalem was not intended
to create "juridical" or "political" facts.[31]

In conclusion, it should be clear from what I have argued that
Jerusalem possesses an international legal status which coexists
with Palestinian sovereignty and applies to the entire *corpus
separatum* of the City of Jerusalem as defined by the General
Assembly of the United Nations in its Resolution 181 of November 29, 1947. Neither the legal status of Jerusalem nor Palestinian

27. See the reports of the meetings held in connection with Israel's
application for admission to United Nations membership in General
Assembly, *Official Records*, Ad Hoc Political Committee, Part II (1949),
pp. 179–360.
28. See Cattan, *Palestine and International Law*, pp. 252–254.
29. See General Assembly, *Official Records*, Part II (1949), p. 286.
30. *Ibid.*, p. 235.
31. *Ibid.*, p. 233.

sovereignty has been impaired or abrogated by Israel's occupation and annexation of the City. The usurpation of Jerusalem and all other measures taken by Israel in order to alter its status are thus invalid under international law and United Nations resolutions.

CHAPTER FIVE

Saudi Arabia, Culture Change, and the International Legal Order

JAMES PISCATORI

Most international lawyers aspire to a law of universal validity and enforceability; some feel this aim is close to realization. All agree that an order universally composed of equally sovereign states already exists. But they also recognize that divisions of belief and value complicate the drive for a law which operates beyond the nation-state level. This recognition that the world is one of sovereign uniformity but polycultural diversity has led jurisprudents to accept culture as an integral component of law's evolution. Yet two lines of thought compete with each other on the subject.

One line holds that as culture gradually becomes universal, it will support a new form of world law. C. Wilfred Jenks argued that if a common law of mankind is to emerge, there must be a convergence of values among the world's major cultural regions.[1] F. S. C. Northrop gave a broader theoretical foundation to his conclusion that the future of world order is dependent on a

---

1. *The Common Law of Mankind* (London: Stevens & Sons Limited, 1958).

reconciliation of Eastern and Western values. Rejecting the predominant view that understanding sense-objects entails the interaction of the object, the observer, and the senses, he believed that only two matters count in knowledge—intuition and postulation. His study of great cultural zones led him to the conclusion that Eastern civilization is mainly intuitive and aesthetic, whereas Western civilization has been primarily postulative and theoretical. The central point of his analysis is that these two ways of knowing are inherently connected as well as compatible because an "epistemic correlation" holds between them. A world society would thus be possible to attain if it were based on a human nature developed by both aesthetic intuition and the theoretical insights of the natural sciences. Once we understood the correct epistemology, he thought, universal law would follow the development of this comprehensive nature.[2]

The second line of thought maintains that culture is more likely to serve as an obstacle to the emergence of effective international law. Its most prominent proponent is Adda Bozeman, who in her important work, *The Future of Law in a Multicultural World*, argues that the largely rhetorical uniformity of international law masks the incompatible values of nations. Instead of finding similar traits in various cultures, she discovers fundamental cultural differences of view on the role of the individual, the importance of the future, and the desirability of peace, and she suspects that the international lawyers' adoption of uniform—and Western—terminology is an attempt to impose a conceptual superstructure on an intricate and ephemeral reality. In fact, she maintains that in the absence of common meanings, legal terms will remain empty expressions of the underlying political and social realities. The final break with the advocates of the first line of thought comes in her conclusion

2. *The Meeting of East and West: An Inquiry Concerning World Understanding* (New York: Collier Books, 1972), pp. x, 3–4, 440–458; "Naturalistic and Cultural Foundations for a More Effective International Law," *Yale Law Review*, 59, No. 8 (December 1950), pp. 1430, 1444. Also see: *The Taming of the Nations; A Study of the Cultural Bases of International Policy* (New York: The Macmillan Company, 1954).

that, because of the probable persistence of cultural diversity, hopes of a universal order are completely unfounded. Whereas Jenks and Northrop saw at least the potential for cultural harmony, which would support a common legal order, Bozeman thinks the legal future is grim because a monistic law cannot rest on pluralistic foundations.[3] I propose to focus on her work because of the thought-provoking stand which it takes and the attention which it has received since its publication in 1971.

BOZEMAN'S ISLAM

Part of the evidence that Bozeman cites for her conclusions is the experience of Islam. But her examination is seriously flawed on two counts. First, her review of Islamic political theory distorts the nature of the Islamic polity, making it seem incapable of organizing structures and hostile to individual liberty. Part of her misconception derives from her slight understanding of non-Western values as compared with prevailing Western ones.

We will better appreciate Islam's philosophical contributions by comparing it to what preceded it. In this sense, Muhammad's revelatory experiences represent the definitive break with the closed, pre-Islamic society. The world in which the Prophet was born was one where Arabs worshipped idols singly or in combination with some overarching deity. In distinct contrast, Islam adheres to an uncompromising monotheism. Unreflective custom, which had allowed infanticide and blood revenge, governed pre-Islamic social relations. In the Islamic community and according to Islamic philosophy, however, Allah's revealed law governs all interactions, and men are expected to live according to the divine scriptures and not merely according to passion and expediency. In addition, the tribal members of pre-Islamic society organized themselves according to the cohesive bonds of blood relationships; 'asabiyya or group solidarity assured the integrity of tribal unity. Yet Muhammad's community of believers is based on the bonds of morality, which involve the acceptance of responsibilities toward God and men and of the mutual rights of

---

3. *The Future of Law in a Multicultural World* (Princeton: Princeton University Press, 1971), pp. xii, 26, 29, 164, 181.

all believers. Finally, government in the *jahiliyya* or pre-Islamic "era of ignorance" was the creation of human hands and built on means-ends calculations which were designed to gain worldly success. There is a clear difference between that and the Islamic community, which is also concerned with earthly happiness but the primary focus of which is on the transcendent.[4]

In philosophical terms, Allah's revelation to Muhammad marked, to use the terminology of Mircea Eliade, the opening of the archaic society. It is probable that prior to Muhammad the Arabs worshipped several deities, including one paramount god. Yet not until the Prophet's receipt of the Qur'an did acknowledgement of Allah's supremacy rule out the existence of other, lesser, divinities. It is the contribution of Muhammad that he taught the Arabs that Allah is without equal or competitor, and, in doing so, initiated a break in Arab society between the past of polytheism and "the open horizon of its future."[5] In symbolic terms, the Prophet's *hijra* or exodus from Mecca to Medina rivals the philosophical ascent from the Platonic cave and Moses' departure from Egypt as the archetypal act of openness. Von Grunebaum said much the same thing when he argued that Islam brings political theory to the area for the first time.[6]

But Bozeman, in her search for the differences between Western and Islamic values, fails to appreciate that the standard of a "reliable secular order" is so different that, when readily invoked, it obscures the achievements Islamic political thought has made. Indeed, she points to the absence of such concepts as those of the corporation, the juristic person, and legislation to explain "why Mohammedan society, rich in cosmopolitan industrious cities, could not bring forth the polis, the commune, the

4. This discussion is suggested by that found in Albert Hourani, *Arabic Thought in the Liberal Age, 1798–1939* (London: Oxford University Press, 1970), pp. 6–7.

5. The phrase is Eric Voegelin's. See his *Order and History* (Baton Rouge: Louisiana State University Press, 1957), vol. 2, pp. 1, 3.

6. Von Grunebaum's chapter in Gustave E. von Grunebaum (ed.), *Unity and Variety in Muslim Civilization* (Chicago: The University of Chicago Press, 1955), p. 21.

chartered town, or leagues of self-governing cities . . ."[7] Islam, rather, yields only a vaguely defined polity whose regime has unspecified authority and whose institutional character seems "illegitimate and coercive" to those who must suffer its arbitrary ways.[8] Completely unlike the West, then, Islam embodies a divergence of law and government that is likely to persist.[9]

Bozeman's account, however, is based on too literal a reading of Islamic civilization. For example, the fact that legislation was "officially" absent [10] should not obscure the long and rich record of legislative innovation that Muslims have widely accepted and admired. Joseph Schacht, to whom she refers but whose point she misses, reminded us that "the popular and administrative practice of the last Umayyad period was transformed into the religious law of Islam."[11] Moreover, Muslim jurists have long recognized juristic persons. According to them, the *musta'min* (one granted safe passage) and the *dhimmi* (a scriptuary) are non-Muslims who gain legal status for various periods of time in the Islamic realm and whom the Caliph is bound to protect. Their specific civil rights, however, differ from those of the believers, whom jurists have always regarded as legal individuals with rights and duties.[12]

More importantly, Bozeman distorts the spirit of the Islamic state by concentrating on the lack of exact conceptual equivalents and identical individual rights to those found in the West. This is seen in her discussion of illegitimate and coercive government in Islam. She does not take into account that the Qur'an, repeatedly urging men to submit to those in authority, is clear in enjoining rulers to be fair as well as firm. Moreover, the widely-held belief that the *umma* or Islamic community is both religious and political assures, at least, an acceptance of the inherent worth

7. Bozeman, *The Future of Law in a Multicultural World*, pp. 66–67.

8. *Ibid.*, pp. 75–76.

9. *Ibid.*, pp. 75, 78.

10. *Ibid.*, p. 66.

11. "The Law," in von Grunebaum (ed.), *Unity and Variety in Muslim Civilization*, p. 72.

12. See Majid Khadduri, *The Islamic Law of Nations: Shaybani's Siyar* (Baltimore: The Johns Hopkins Press, 1966), pp. 10–11, 51.

of political or governmental activity. Indeed, Muslims have argued that government is essential for the salvation of the individual soul because of the order, protection, and good example that it provides for the believer in a hostile world. It is thus an exaggeration to conclude that Muslim jurisprudents regarded governing as a dishonorable endeavor. In legal theory, furthermore, there is no divergence, as Bozeman suggests, between law and government, but an intimate association: the *shari'a* limits the government, while the government executes the *shari'a*. The two concepts have coexisted in history as well, for Muslim governments have developed an entire set of laws and administrative courts that are, or have been rationalized as, consonant with the *shari'a*.

My first main point, then, is that legal scholars in Islam, and thus Islamic legal theory, have viewed government as neither evil nor separate from the norms of God. Bozeman's description is a generalization that belies Islamic reality—as it would even the Augustinian-medieval Christian thinking on politics.

Second, in addition to its treatment of classical theory, Bozeman's discussion is seriously flawed because it ignores culture change within Islam. She argues that despite the prevalence of Western rhetoric, the traditional values of Islam retain today their essential vigor. In fact, she says, there is a sense of disillusionment in the Arab-Muslim world which leads to a yearning for the "good old medieval days." Traditionalists and modernists agree that alien liberal institutions are the basic cause of their common malady and that the panacea is a return to the hallowed political organization of the exemplary political community.[13] On this point, however, Bozeman would have been more correct to argue that there is a widespread respect for the classical period covering the time of the Prophet through the first four "rightly guided" leaders or *al-khulafa' al-rashidun*—a period extending until roughly 661 AD. This era, rather than the medieval period *per se*, represents the paradigm for most Muslims.

But this is quibbling. Far more disturbing about Bozeman's conclusion that there is a convergence of opinions among Muslims is that it simplifies a complex process of culture change that

13. *The Future of Law in a Multicultural World*, pp. 57–58.

has been developing since at least the Napoleonic invasion of Egypt in 1798. As a harbinger of developments in the Arab-Muslim world generally, Muhammad 'Ali introduced a number of wide-ranging reforms in response to this brief European incursion: centralization of the administration and economy, development of modern armed forces, agricultural reform, and industrial promotion. His most significant contributions were the far-sighted adoption of the printing press at home and the sending of students abroad. Another factor in inducing change was the humiliation of foreign occupation—e.g., at the hands of the British after the defeat of al-'Urabi's army revolt in 1882. As George Antonius demonstrated, the presence of foreign troops on Arab soil inspired the growth of local nationalisms.[14] It was against this background of incipient modernization, foreign penetration, access to Western civilization, local misrule (such as that of Khedive Isma'il which led to bankruptcy), and European occupation that Arab Muslims began to agitate for reform and to reexamine their beliefs and place in the modern world.

Yet the reappraisal has failed to yield a uniform Muslim response. The many response, rather, fall into loose groupings whose cohesion and importance vary with the observer. Louis Milliot, for instance, enumerated four categories in a 1949 article on the caliphate: the conservatives who argued for a return to a spiritual caliphate; the Arab "racists" who sought unity about the Hashimites or about the Al Sa'ud; the reformists who followed either the *salafiyya*, inspired by the elders of Islam, or the secularists, encouraged by the Turkish example; and the nationalists who were interested less in Arab or Islamic unity than in the integrity of the individual territorial unit.[15] Majid Khadduri

14. *The Arab Awakening: The Story of the Arab National Movements* (London: Hamish Hamilton, 1938), p. 100. For the background of events in Egypt, see Ibrahim Amin Ghali, *L'Egypte nationaliste et libérale, Mustapha Kemal à Saad Zagloul (1892–1927)* (Le Havre: Martinus Nijhoff, 1969) and Christina Phelps Harris, *Nationalism and Revolution in Egypt: The Role of the Muslim Brotherhood* (The Hague: Mouton and Co., 1964).

15. "La conception de l'état et de l'ordre légal dans l'Islam," *Recueil des Cours*, 75, II (1949), pp. 677–678.

also sees distinct schools that fit into three historical periods: the Islamic and Western schools interacted in the later eighteenth to nineteenth centuries; after the First World War and through the inter-war period, the debate centered around particular movements, such as those of the nationalists, constitutionalists, and secularists, in which little concern was given to their Islamic validity; and since the Second World War, contention exists among such groups as the Ba'thists, Nasirists, and social democrats, but it is generally a period of the creative synthesis of Islamic and Western perspectives.[16] R. Stephen Humphreys has elucidated the three standard categories: the modernists who seek inspiration from, but also reevaluate, the past in order to justify innovations within Islam; the secularists who find the traditional religion a barrier to progress; and the fundamentalists who, like the modernists, look to the Islamic past but, unlike them, find most of its values relevant still.[17]

Regardless of the categorization, Milliot's early conclusion retains its validity: the responses are too numerous and divergent for real unity among Muslims to emerge. Yet it is in this melange and even clash of perspectives that culture change within Islam is occurring—a process that Bozeman does not probe or consider. No definitive consensus has yet developed, but I suspect that the following key ideas have emerged as part of the present stock of values of both the traditional and the reform-minded, though not necessarily of the secularists, who remain a small minority: (1) the desirability of progress (even the Islamic conservatives accept the progressive character of their faith, although progress is measured in terms of recapturing the spirit of the original *umma*); (2) the compatibility of reason, science, and Islam and the importance of rational investigation; (3) the need for constitutional limitations on government; (4) the duty of Muslims in the realm of social security and the implied acceptance that government has positive functions to perform; (5) the acceptability of some measure of legislation in the public interest; and (6) an

16. *Political Trends in the Arab World: The Role of Ideas and Ideals in Politics* (Baltimore: The Johns Hopkins Press, 1970), pp. 5–6.

17. "Islam and Political Values in Saudi Arabia, Egypt and Syria," *The Middle East Journal*, 33, No. 1 (Winter 1979), pp. 1–19.

implicit recognition that the nation-state is compatible with Islam.

Bozeman came closer to recognizing the possibilities of change in her earlier contrasting, but equally overstated, observation in *Politics and Culture in International History:* "It is a paradoxical yet obvious fact that the new Muslim nations are more nearly in accord today in claiming the political legacy of Western Europe than in demanding a resuscitation of the political traditions of Islam."[18] Perhaps this thought accounts for the odd reference in her later work to the argument that reform has irreversibly destroyed the traditional law. But for one who mainly finds the persistence of varying deeply cherished beliefs and the traditional law a hindrance to international legal development, it is incumbent at least to clarify, as she does not, how deep traditional Islamic values are and to what extent and where they constitute the "mainspring" of politics.[19]

SAUDI CULTURE

Saudi Arabia seems to be a favorite example, for non-Muslims at least, of the Islamic state where traditional values are profoundly entrenched in every phase of life, including public life. Proud of their Bedouin heritage of tribal solidarity, hospitality, independence, and personal and familial honor, Saudis are almost chauvinistic about their religious roots. Their country is the holy land where, according to legend, Eve's tomb is found, where God tested Abraham, the sanctuary of the Ka'ba is located, the Prophet and his companions made their home, and from where Islam spread to vast areas of the world. The intensity of their faith, it would seem, is related to proximity to the primordial Islamic community. Jurisprudentially as well, Saudis insist on closeness to the original sources and thus rely on the Hanbali school, perhaps the most conservative of the orthodox legal schools in its

18. *Politics and Culture in International History* (Princeton: Princeton University Press, 1960), p. 359. The willingness to borrow "foreign ideals" is also affirmed in fn. 1, p. 371.

19. *The Future of Law in a Multicultural World*, fn. 12, p. 54; p. 53.

strong dependence on the Qur'an and *sunna* (traditions of the Prophet) as the primary sources of law.

This conservatism is directly traceable to the reforms of Muhammad ibn 'Abd al-Wahhab in the mid-eighteenth century. Self-consciously following Ibn Hanbal and Ibn Taymiyya, who emphasized the importance of the authoritative text over that of even the *ijma'* or agreement of scholars, Ibn 'Abd al-Wahhab set out to purify the sacred peninsula of false innovations (*bid'a*) that the Umayyads had introduced. His dedication to uncompromising monotheism was intense: any veneration of the Prophet or saints was strongly enjoined. Followers of Ibn 'Abd al-Wahhab and the Al Sa'ud, first linked in 1744, were responsible for the destruction of many religious shrines and tombs of the Hijaz in the early years of this century; the Prophet's tomb itself barely missed razing.

These *muwahhidun*, believers in the absolute unity of God, ironically, introduced their own innovations in the name of rigid orthodoxy. These included mandatory prayer, a prohibition on smoking, and the confirmation of the believer's faith based on an investigation of his character that went beyond proof of the repetition of the *shahada* (the profession of faith and the usual standard of one's adherence to Islam). In general historical terms, the *muwahhid* influence has led to the austerity of present day Saudi Arabia—simple, unadorned architecture, the absence of theatrical centers, and the *muttawwi'yun* or "religious police" whose tasks are to enforce mosque attendance and *suq* or market closing during prayer times and to guard against improper dress. What many have wrongly called "the Wahhabi faith" is, in short, a puritanical movement whose professed aim is to recapture the piety of the early *umma*; at the least it has offered a strict code of conduct for the individual believer.

But codes and belief patterns change out of necessity, and Saudi Arabia is no exception. By 1959, H. St. John Philby had occasion to lament the passing of traditional mores and the introduction of Western ways in Najd and the capital of Riyadh: believers no longer recited their prayers at precisely the time of the *mu'adhdhan's* call; automobiles had disturbed the traditional city calm; Western dress was visible on the streets; restaurants had opened; and military uniforms had become standard.[20] In the realm of ideas too, cultural change had begun to set in.

A combination of external and internal stimuli has prompted such changes. Saudi Arabia, spared the ignominy of military defeat which spurred reforms in the cases of Egypt and the Ottoman Empire, endured a jolting invasion—that of the American employees of the Arabian American Oil Company (ARAMCO). Two results ensued: the wealth that was produced stimulated the desire for Western goods; the technicians and teachers who were introduced created the demand for new skills and education. Ahmad Zaki al-Yamani, former Minister of Petroleum, has presented a variant of this argument that change follows on external stimulus. He has argued that the universities must revise and strengthen their curricula if the country is to meet the Zionists on equal terms.[21]

An internal stimulus for change, certainly, has been the vast oil revenues. Opulence has allowed increasingly greater numbers of Saudi students to pursue higher education in the United States and Western Europe. The contact has bred a certain dissatisfaction with prevailing ways at home, though criticism has tended to be muted. 'Abd Allah 'Abd al-'Aziz al-Munifi, a legal adviser to the Saudi government, for instance, in his law school dissertation does not question the monarchy, but he does suggest that the Islamic polity is better governed by a democratic, presidential or parliamentary system, and that the 'ulama' or religious scholars are not always representative of the people.[22]

The process of culture change has not been simple or smooth. Rather, intense debates over the ends, rate, and means of change persist. In the early days of the kingdom, the king confronted the 'ulama', who attempted to resist changes of any significance. These religious leaders voiced strong opposition to 'Abd al-'Aziz's

20. "Riyadh: Ancient and Modern," The Middle East Journal, 13, No. 2 (Spring 1959), pp. 138–141.

21. Comments of Shaykh Ahmad Zaki al-Yamani at "Mission of the University" Conference, University of Riyadh, November 18, 1974.

22. "The Islamic Constitutional Theory" (unpublished doctoral dissertation, Law School, University of Virginia, 1973), pp. 303, 317, 356, 373, 378–379.

introduction of foreigners, photography, and radio, all thought to be contrary to the Islamic teachings which warn against consorting with the infidel and the devil. More recently, the debate has not been as shrill, but members of the intelligentsia continue to argue, often against the traditional religious people, that more changes in thought are necessary if Islam is to have vigor. Zaki al-Yamani, for example, criticizes Muslim reactionaries for inducing stagnation. 'Abd al-Hamid Abu Sulayman, formerly on the faculty of the University of Riyadh and now president of the International Institute of Islamic Thought in Washington, D.C., also argues that scholars cannot freeze Islam at the period of the Prophetic experience; and Hamad Sa'dun al-Hamad, a Saudi academic, has rejected the complete reliance on *fiqh* or jurisprudential texts as inhibiting.[23]

Although all three of these Western-educated intellectuals make the argument that Muslims and, by inference, Saudis need progress in social and legal affairs, they reject secularism as exceeding the limits of permissable change. Al-Hamad argues that such a move would undermine the traditional culture, destabilize the political structure, and sow confusion among the people. Abu Sulayman similarly rejects non-religious modernism because of its intellectual immaturity, imitative rather than innovative quality, and inability to gain popular acceptance. Al-Yamani refers to the distinction between "religious" and "secular" elements in Islam in order to exemplify its progressive nature. Yet even this ostensibly unorthodox bifurcation of the religious and secular realms does not detract from his basic point that the "religious" background of Islam is a renewable source of strength.[24]

23. Abdul-Hamid Abu Sulayman, "The Islamic Theory of International Relations: Its Relevance, Past and Present" (unpublished doctoral dissertation, University of Pennsylvania, 1973), fn. 57, p. 74; Hamad Sadun al-Hamad, "The Legislative Process and the Development of Saudi Arabia" (unpublished doctoral dissertation, University of Southern California, 1973), p. 183.

24. Al-Hamad, "The Legislative Process and the Development of Saudi Arabia," p. 183; Abu Sulayman, "The Islamic Theory of International Relations," p. 199; Ahmad Zaki Yamani, *Islamic Law and*

There is also general agreement that the traditional frame-work is inherently able to adapt to changing demands. Al-Yamani finds that the *shari'a* is capable of changing because of jurispru-dents' reliance on analogy, reason, and the concept of public interest. Al-Hamad points out that both Kings 'Abd al-'Aziz and Faysal used the right of *ijtihad* (independent judgment) to intro-duce change. He says that Faysal institutionalized the reliance by creating "the Judicial Council" in order to reconcile the con-flicting demands of modern life and traditional thought.[25] Stories of 'Abd al-'Aziz's ingenuity are in fact legion, the general thrust of which is his reliance on the spirit of the Qur'an and fundamental texts to justify innovation. He legitimated photography, for example, by stressing that it joins the divine creations of light and shadow, and radio by demonstrating that it transmits God's words accurately. For these reasons, I think some observers miss the point when they argue that the Saudis do not rely on deductive reasoning as a means of inducing legal and other changes.

In the course of debating the possibilities and dimensions of change, a remarkable measure of agreement on which values are acceptable has emerged. As in other Muslim societies, these values include the desirability of progress and reform, the com-patibility of Islam and reason, and the need to serve the public welfare *(maslaha)*. There is even growing acceptance that some form of legislation is permissible and beneficial. Al-Yamani, in speaking of God as the "prime" legislator, implies that others are possible. He is also explicit in arguing that the law can develop by following the public good "as a source of legislation." Al-Hamad agrees that legislation is important, but that it is the prerogative of the king and his Council of Ministers.[26]

Contemporary Issues (Jidda: The Saudi Publishing House, 1388/1969), pp. 13–14.

25. Yamani, *Islamic Law and Contemporary Issues*, pp. 8–9; al-Hamad, "The Legislative Process and the Development of Saudi Arabia," p. 187.

26. Yamani, *Islamic Law and Contemporary Issues*, pp. 9, 47. Discussion with Hamad Sa'dun al-Hamad, then Chairman of the Depart-ment of Political Science, University of Riyadh, January 16, 1975.

The Saudis have also adopted constitutionalism and democracy as convenient and apparently interchangeable symbols, even if their commitment to these ideas does not go as far as the will to implement them. Few are as explicit as al-Munifi in calling for American-style constitutionalism, but the Ministry of Justice defends the monarchy as a constitutional arrangement which guarantees the king's subservience to the *shari'a* and his ultimate responsibility to God and the people.[27] The Saudi participants in a joint Saudi-European colloquium on Islamic law specifically defended the idea that sovereignty flows from the people and argued that Islam rejects theocracy as incompatible with democracy.[28] Fahd also has promised several times that the government will establish a Consultative Assembly *(majlis al-shura)* in keeping with the Islamic principle of consultation. There is thus widespread acknowledgement that some kind of democracy is a positive value and that government, while necessary to restrain sinful men, is even a good thing if it is subject to law. The latter point is made by Shaykh ibn Matrak, formerly a Deputy Minister of Justice,[29] and stands in contrast to Bozeman's conclusion that Muslims view government *per se* as evil.

Saudis also endorse the principle of social security. Al-Yamani writes at length of the practice of social security which, he says, was begun by the Prophet and the pious *khulafa'*. The system is especially designed to care for individuals who have a physical disability, are the victims of job accidents, or suffer severe family difficulties. The *zakat* tax is the concrete expression of the entire community's obligation to provide this care. Arguing that because of its comprehensiveness Islam always had a better system than that of Western countries, al-Yamani laments the lapse in adherence to this order, "which, if practiced by subsequent Muslim societies [i.e, to the original Islamic order of

27. Ministry of Justice, *The Saudi Report on the Legal System in the Kingdom of Saudi Arabia*, mimeographed paper (n.d.), p. 1.

28. *Nadwat 'Ilmiyya Hawla al-Shari'a al-Islamiyya wa Haquq al-Insan fi'l-Islam* (Beirut: Dar al-Kitab al-Lubnani, 1973), pp. 111, 177–178.

29. Discussion with 'Umar ibn Matrak, Deputy Minister for Judicial Affairs, Ministry of Justice, Riyadh, July 11, 1975.

the seventh century], would have made our present situation other than it now is."[30] Whether inspired by the Islamic or by the Western-*cum*-Islamic notion of social security, the *Labor and Workmen Law* is concerned with rectifying part of the situation by providing for guaranteed safe and healthy working conditions.[31]

Although the Saudis have gone far towards accepting ideas which we normally think of as Western, they retain key traditional values. Among these is Islamic brotherhood. The pull of the *umma* is sufficiently strong to evoke repeated appeals by leaders for the oneness of all Muslims and the need for greater harmony on economic, social, political, and diplomatic lines. Somewhat related to, though not necessarily derivative of, this broader framework is condescension, if not hostility, to the non-Muslim world. Saudi leaders are often patronizing toward Westerners, particularly for their resistance to the influence of morality. There is an uncompromising opposition to communists, as evidenced by almost daily media attacks on their atheism and by the kingdom's vigorous participation in the World Anti-Communist League. The Saudis link their antagonism toward communists with their antagonism toward Zionists; King Faysal believed that the two were in league and posed the greatest danger to world peace today.

The Saudis also tenaciously hold to the traditional idea of religious law governing social relations. All private and many public areas of Saudi life have been subjected to the principles of the *shari'a*. At times private life is seen to be a public affair, and at these times the law governing society is thought of as best framed in Islamic terms. For example, a royal decree outlaws contraceptives because the advocates of birth control are "the enemy of Islam."[32] It is to be admitted that the government is concerned about the relatively small national population, but the religious sentiment also runs deep and is important.

30. *Islamic Law and Contemporary Issues*, p. 45.

31. *Nizam al-'Amal wa'l-'Ummal*, issued under Royal Decree No. M/21 of Ramadan 1389 (1st printing; Mecca: Matba'at al-Hukuma, 1389/1970).

32. *Arab News*, May 7, 1975; May 16, 1975.

Such intimate connections between religion, politics, and law lead Saudis to conclude that their legal order is superior to others. In fact, Saudi jurists have emphasized that the *shari'a* is effective in protecting the dignity and well-being of individuals and societies, whereas international law is nugatory.[33] Some also suggest that the traditional order is responsible for the fact that Saudi Arabia has the lowest crime rate in the world.

There is, furthermore, a strong emphasis on the past glory of the peninsula to which the present order ought to aspire. Although looking back to the Prophet's community for inspiration is not unique among Muslims, the presence of the two holiest cities of Islam in the Saudi kingdom creates among the Saudis a particularly intense feeling, even among the Western-educated. Al-Yamani, for instance, relies heavily in his *Islamic Law and Contemporary Issues* on examples of the Prophet and his immediate successors, particularly 'Umar, to legitimate his arguments. Abu Sulayman, who is critical of classical jurists, is insistent that Muslims should discard the methodological distortions which have crept in so that the fundamentals of the faith can resume their central place in current thought. And al-Munifi pleads for a return to the original theory, freed of the encrustations of the fourth Islamic century and beyond.[34]

In general, a cultural mosaic emerges in which the values of progress, reason, social security, and public interest coexist with the more traditional values of Islamic solidarity, supremacy of the religious law, and esteem of the past. It is dangerous, to be sure, to conclude that Saudis have fully internalized all these values, or even that they agree on the existence of a mosaic. While no one would expect the uneducated Saudi to understand the implications of the concepts of progress and rationality, the emergence of these values and others among the elite, both traditionally and foreign educated, suggests that these are being introduced at the effective, policy-making and policy-influencing levels of the society. Bozeman denies that the usage of key words

33. *Nadwat 'Ilmiyya*, p. 132.

34. Yamani, *Islamic Law and Contemporary Issues*, p. 39; Abu Sulayman, "The Islamic Theory of International Relations," pp. 135–138; Al-Munifi, "The Islamic Constitutional Theory," pp. 480–481.

is more than symbolic, but her argument underestimates both the socialization of Western-trained leaders and the dynamics of culture change itself. Contrary to what we would expect of Saudi Arabia on the basis of this argument, then, even that stereotypically tradition-bound country is making conceptual adaptations to modernity.

SAUDI INTERNATIONAL LEGAL RELATIONS

Bozeman seems unaware that countries like Saudi Arabia are also adept at conforming to the present standards of international law. The Realist critic of her position would say that her failure to appreciate this conformity is not due to the fact that she ignores cultural change, but stems from neglect of the requirements of interstate diplomacy. From the perspective of *realpolitik*, indeed, it matters very little in diplomacy what values a people hold; what count, rather, are the circumstances which condition the decision makers' choice of means to fulfill national interests. Thus, according to the Realists, Saudi statesmen operate in the same manner as other statesmen, unmoved by cultural standards and responding to the realities of power. Bozeman's admission that "personalism and pragmatism rather than principle and system provide the norms for the conduct of foreign affairs in this civilization"[35] does not seem far removed from her general cultural stereotyping and is, thus, unlikely to satisfy the Realists.

The Law of the Sea

Saudi Arabia, of course, brings the same pragmatism to bear as any nation-state does when it comes to deal with questions on which Islam is silent. A notable example is the law of the sea, in which the Saudi government has had an interest since the fishing and Coast Guard regulations of 1932. This is a subject which does not clash with or relate to the *shari'a* at all. Like most states, Saudi Arabia gradually extended its territorial limits from six miles, decreed in 1949, to twelve miles, decreed in 1958. It also followed the lead of the United States in claiming sovereignty

35. Bozeman, *The Future of Law in a Multicultural World*, p. 83.

over the subsoil and seabed of its adjacent, continental shelf-type areas.[36] Moreover, the kingdom has fully deliberated in the various sessions of the 1958, 1960, and current multilateral negotiations on the law of the sea, although it has steadfastly refused to sign any of the Geneva conventions that have come into effect. The reason, however, has nothing to do with Islam but, rather, with the fact that these texts do not specify the breadth of the territorial sea and that one of them, the Convention on the Territorial Sea and Contiguous Zone, provides, in Article 16(4), for the free passage of all ships through all straits— including Israeli ships through the Straits of Tiran.

The debates in general reveal several points. First, time and again Saudi Arabia has displayed that raw kind of sensitivity to the prerogatives of sovereignty which has become a hallmark of the "new" states. It has stressed the need for coastal state control in questions of warship passage, fishing rights, and scientific exploration; and in the 1960 Conference on the Law of the Sea, it carried the preoccupation with state interest to what might seem an odd conclusion. In effect, it argued that sovereignty restrains conflict; that is, if states extend their sovereignty into the sea, there will be a lesser amount of the high seas where states are free to conduct military operations.[37] The realm of state control is

36. *Fishing and Shell Fishing Regulations Applicable to the Coasts of the Red Sea, Umm al-Qura*, No. 397, 18 Rabi'I 1351 (July 22, 1932), translated by J. C. Stewart (Dhahran: Arabian-American Oil Company, September 29, 1948); Decree No. 6/4/5/3711, *Umm al-Qura*, No. 1263, 2 Sha'ban 1368 (May 29, 1949), translated in *The American Journal of International Law*, 43, No. 3 (July 1949), *Official Documents*, Supplement 3, pp. 154–156; text of decree in Mohamed Zayyan al-Jazairi, "Saudi Arabia: A Diplomatic History, 1924–1964" (unpublished doctoral dissertation, University of Utah, 1970), pp. 274–278; *Royal Pronouncement Concerning the Policy of the Kingdom of Saudi Arabia with Respect to the Subsoil and Sea Bed of Areas in the Persian Gulf Contiguous to the Coasts of the Kingdom of Saudi Arabia, Umm al-Qura*, No. 1263, 2 Sha'ban 1368 (May 29, 1949), translated in *The American Journal of International Law*, 43, No. 3 (July 1949), *Official Documents*, Supplement 3, pp. 156–157.

37. United Nations, Second Conference on the Law of the Sea, *Official Records*, Committee of the Whole (Geneva: March 17–April 26,

thus a realm of peace. If nothing else, this manner of argumentation should refute Bozeman's belief that Muslims are unable to accept the nation-state system because of the notional division of the world into *dar al-Islam* (realm of Islam) and *dar al-harb* (realm of war).[38]

Second, the debates reveal that the Saudis have mainly justified their positions by reference to the sources listed in the Statute of the International Court of Justice. They have invoked state practice expressed in treaties and diplomatic notes, Anglo-American and Continental court cases, and the writings of Western scholars and jurists, such as Burtolus, Sarpi, Oppenheim, and Jessup. In regard to the Saudi 1949 decree on the continental shelf, it also relied on the evolving customary behavior of states. The lack of references to the Qur'an and *hadith* (sayings of the Prophet) and to Islam as a comprehensive symbol is noteworthy, but only to be expected given that no *shari'a* regulations bear directly on the subject.

Third, although Saudi Arabia is not a signatory of the Geneva conventions and says it will not be until they are enforceable, it does accept, in theory and in its decrees and regulations, a number of specific principles accepted by most states. These include the rights of a state to proclaim sovereignty over its territorial sea and the subsurface and air above it; to exercise control over its contiguous zone; to extend sovereignty over the adjacent submarine area or continental shelf and its natural resources; to invoke in interstate negotiations the concepts of the median line and equidistance in order to delineate marine boundaries; to move on the high seas beyond the territorial sea and above the continental shelf; and to share in the exploitation of the resources of the deep seabed as the "common heritage of mankind."

The Law of Human Rights

But before I leave the impression that culture is irrelevant, I must note that Saudi Arabia has strongly dissented from the

1960), pp. 399–400.

38. Bozeman, *The Future of Law in a Multicultural World*, pp. 53–56, 79–82.

developing consensus on the law of human rights. Referring almost exclusively to Islam and their own version of individual rights guaranteed under the *shari'a*, the Saudis have expressed opposition to the specific endorsement of the right to change religion and of the equality of women. Strong feelings are apparent on these subjects because of clear *shari'a* guidance on them. In the Saudi view, equality of women ignores the different treatment of men and women prescribed by the Qur'an. More generally, Saudi jurists have objected to the existing legal texts, the Covenants on Civil and Political Rights and on Economic, Social, and Cultural Rights, both because they refer only to the materialistic side of man's nature and because they are mere "pious sermons" without the vigor and effectiveness of the *shari'a*.[39]

With specific reference to the draft Declaration on Religious Intolerance in 1973, long-time delegate Jamil al-Barudi expressed the general Saudi belief that international law is incapable of codifying norms which are rooted in religion: "Rules and regulations could be formulated for tangible things but not for religion. Their utopian initiative would only result in an ineffective declaration which could never become an effective convention because of the divergence of conscience, norms, observance and even moral codes in different religions."[40] In view of the fact that Islam presents a distinctive moral code on the rights of the individual, it would be unfair, I think, to criticize Bozeman—as some have—for mixing the "apples" of domestic legal concepts with the "oranges" of international legal attitudes. Sometimes, as the human rights example indicates, domestic legal ideas *are* relevant to international law, particularly in its newer areas of codification.

The Law of Treatment of Aliens

The law on the treatment of aliens is an older area where cultural values seem to play a part, but it is a mixture of

---

39. *Nadwat 'Ilmiyya*, pp. 93–95, 123.

40. United Nations, General Assembly, *Official Records*, Third Committee, 29th Session (New York, 1973).

traditional Arab and Islamic legal values. A long list of adventurers has testified to the willingness of the desert Bedouin to share food and lodging and to offer protection to the innocent traveler. Lady Ann Blunt, for instance, wrote approvingly of Arabian hospitality during her nineteenth century journey to Najd. She became so accustomed to the lavish treatment, in fact, that she and her husband complained when they failed to continue receiving it owing to a servant's chicanery in passing the distinguished travelers off as his assistants. W. B. Seabrook related how he escaped the thievery of a raiding party of Bedouin in the 1920s by placing himself in their hands as a guest. Once reminded of their solemn obligation, the bandits left his goods and person untouched. An American cleric who had angered King 'Abd al-'Aziz by his tactless questioning on Islam also escaped unkind treatment because he was a guest.[41]

Other travelers, however, have demonstrated that among the devout suspicion of the infidel is at times the weightier part of their social code. Classical theory allows for non-Muslims to live among the believers provided that they pay a special tax and accept certain limitations on their freedom of action, including the prohibition on travel to the holy areas of the Arabian peninsula. The great explorer Richard Burton, understanding the dangers of a Christian traveling in the vicinity of Mecca and Medina, assumed the disguise of a Persian nobleman, becoming non-Western in appearance and seemingly Muslim in faith.[42] By way of contrast, when Charles M. Doughty was detained in the Hijaz, he honestly admitted that he was Christian and, more significantly, English. To the Muslims who were agitated over his religion, his defense based on nationality must have seemed weak and his protest irrelevant: " 'What is this! I am an Engleysy and being of a friendly nation, why am I dealt with thus?' " But a more

41. Lady Anne Blunt, *A Pilgrimage to Nejd* (London: John Murray, 1881), vol. 2, pp. 18–21; W. B. Seabrook, *Adventures in Arabia* (New York: Harcourt, Brace and Company, Inc., 1927), pp. 22–24; reported in St. John Philby, *Forty Years in the Wilderness* (London: Robert Hale Limited, 1957), pp. 221–222.

42. Richard F. Burton, *Personal Narrative of a Pilgrimage to al-Madinah & Mecca* (London: George Bell & Sons, 1907), vol. 1, pp. 3–5.

discerning Arab prudently pointed out to his naive colleagues that this Christian's land was, if not friendly, then mighty, able to despatch a mobile, practiced fleet:

'What, he said, are these Nasara [Christians]—listen all of you! It is a strong nation: were not two or three Nasranies murdered some years ago in Jidda?—well, what followed? There came great war-ships of their nation and bombarded the place . . . And who were those that fought against Jidda? I tell you the Engleys, the people of this Khalil [Doughty]: the Engleys are high-handed, ay wellah, jababara!'[43]

This typical linkage of religion and nationality, as influenced by the Islamic legal view that the Muslim is a citizen, is a notable deviation from the clear separation of the two in the West since the eighteenth century. The identification of religion and nationality in the Arabian Peninsula in the early part of the present century is understandable given the high degree of isolation and the low degree of national integration. Since the formation of the united Saudi kingdom, a gradual evolution in thinking has emerged, with religion and nationality no longer automatically tied together. Although an Hijazi law of 1926 specified that citizens must be Muslim, current nationality law does not make adherence to Islam a condition of citizenship.[44] Nevertheless, considerable confusion seems to exist among jurists as to whether the modern concept of the alien entirely supersedes the classical idea of the protected non-believer, the *dhimmi*. Some Saudis feel that, like any modern nation-state, Saudi Arabia does not discriminate between non-Muslim foreigners and nationals; others believe that the traditional distinction still holds because of the special juridical nature of the Arabian peninsula; and others argue that the law enjoins equal protection of foreigner and

43. Charles M. Doughty, *Travels in Arabia Deserta*, One volume ed. (New York: Random House, 1937), pp. 81–82, 86.

44. For the 1926 law, see Jean S. Saba, *L'Islam et la nationalité* (Paris: Librairie de jurisprudence ancienne et moderne, Eduouard Duchemin, 1931), pp. 118–119; *Nizam al-Jinsiyya al-'Arabiyya al-Sa'udiyya*, issued under Royal Decree No. 8/20/5604 of 22 Safar 1374 (October 20, 1954) (Dammam: Arabian American Oil Company, February 1955).

national but does not confer equal rights. Whatever the currents of legal thought, 'Abd al-'Aziz's wish that foreigners "were on the far shore of a sea of flame and fire"[45] is disconcertingly at times still a discernible attitude among some Saudis.

An examination of Saudi Arabia's treaties, however, reveals its acceptance of the duty to protect aliens, though these instruments do not indicate to what extent this must be done. At the same time, the Saudis insist that aliens adhere to local law. The Saudi position thus straddles the Latin American and Soviet positions by guaranteeing equal protection of the law for both citizens and aliens, as the Latin American position holds, and by seeking protection for itself from outside interference, as does the Soviet position. For example, a 1968 cultural agreement with the United States calls for each country to facilitate entry and customs for professors, students, and technicians of the other country, but only in line with local rules. There is, moreover, a strongly worded disclaimer that the accord does not affect domestic law and that all activities are to be in strict conformity with the laws of the two countries.[46]

Even in the area of foreign business the same dual emphasis, on protection of the "foreigner" as Islam requires and on the supremacy of local law as national sovereignty demands, may be noted. 'Abd al-'Aziz told the chairman of the Board of Directors of ARAMCO in 1950: "You walk in the length and breadth of my land and enjoy the same protection as my own subjects."[47] Explicit reference to the trade-off of protection for respect for local regulations is seen in the Getty, Japan Petroleum Trading Company, and French Auxirab oil concessions. The model *Contract for the Employment of Foreigners* requires that foreign workmen be subject to all the laws of the kingdom at present or in the future in return for the privilege of operating in the

45. Gerald de Gaury, *Arabian Journey and Other Desert Travels* (London: George O. Harrap & Co., Ltd., 1950), p. 58.

46. *Agreement for Cultural Exchange Between the United States and Saudi Arabia*, Jidda, July 25, 1968, in United Nations, *Treaty Series*, 723, No. 10401 (1970), pp. 143–144.

47. Quoted in J. N. D. Anderson, *Islamic Law in the Modern World* (New York: New York University Press, 1959), p. xii.

kingdom. The *Foreign Capital Investments Regulations* of 1964 state in Article 9: "It is not permissible for persons in charge of such projects to concern themselves in any way with the country's religious or political affairs, or to interfere in such affairs."[48]

The combination of respect for moral responsibilities and pursuit of self-interest is seen in the lengthy negotiations over the complete take-over of ARAMCO. It is obvious that it would not have been in the interest of the Saudis to expropriate the oil consortium overnight in order to affirm national pride or to stave off criticism from more adventuresome oil-producing states. The lack of native skilled management and technical services would have compounded the inevitable problems of any sudden disruptions in production. But the Saudis have also repeatedly referred to Islamic principles, not only because they want to legitimate their position but also because they believe that some ways of doing things are more correct than others.

Shaykh al-Yamani, arguing that Islam enshrines the principle of private property, points out that there are limitations imposed by considerations of individual rights and communal good; that is, the property owner is obligated to give food from his fields to the hungry, and valuable wealth cannot be held at the expense of the community as a whole. Classical jurists disagreed on the extent of public ownership allowable, but he appears to agree with the Maliki position that the state owns the minerals which are found in its land. This position reflects the Saudi *Mining Code's* Article 1,[49] which proclaims state possession of minerals in the soil and subsoil, and it puts Saudi Arabia in line with the widely-endorsed United Nations Resolution on the Permanent Sovereignty over Natural Resources.

48. *Contract for the Employment of Foreigners,* Sanctioned and Enforced by Virtue of Royal Decree No. 3/11/5846, Dated 1/3/1374 (Mecca: Government Press, 1394), p. 9; *Foreign Capital Investments Regulation,* 1383/1964, mimeographed copy (Riyadh: Industrial and Development Centre, Ministry of Commerce and Industry, n.d.), p. 3.

49. *Nizam al-Ta'din,* issued under Royal Decree No. 40, 11 Ramadan 1384 (February 5, 1963) (1st printing; Mecca: Matba'at al-Hukuma, 1384/1964), pp. 5, 23–26.

But the grant of surface ownership, while preserving state ownership of the real wealth, creates an undeniable obligation toward the individual possessor.

Once the right of private ownership is created, it cannot be revoked by he who is in authority except for a well-specified public interest consideration and for prompt and adequate compensation. Therefore, the concept of political national-ization which is being followed as a general policy nowadays is an alien element to the principles of Islam.[50]

Consistent with these obligations, al-Yamani proposed in 1972 the alternative concept of participation as an intermediate stage between outright nationalization and complete company ownership. As he himself recognized, it was an idea that fulfilled Saudi moral responsibilities while at the same time assuring the continued influx of foreign investments and technical skills.[51] But he has also pointed to ample flexibility in Islam that allows the ruler to decide which individuals are to develop mineral wealth in return for profits. Muhammad Madani also refers to the discretion of the *imam* to decide whether individuals or the community are to control resources and under what circum-stances.[52] Doubtless grateful for this flexibility when it moved for one hundred per cent control of ARAMCO, the Saudi government pursued this goal neither precipitately nor without regard to its solemn contractual obligations.

CONCLUSION
    Despite Saudi Arabia's reputation as the most traditional and

50. Yamani, *Islamic Law and Contemporary Issues*, p. 31; also see pp. 26–29.

51. *Middle East Economic Digest* (September 29, 1972), pp. 1125–1127.

52. Yamani, *Islamic Law and Contemporary Issues*, pp. 29–31; Muhammad O. Madani, "The Relationship Between Saudi Arabian Domestic Law and International Law: A Study of the Oil Agreements with Foreign Companies" (unpublished doctoral dissertation, Law School, The George Washington University, 1970), p. 38.

self-consciously "Islamic" state,[53] it is undergoing cultural changes—of ideas as well as lifestyles. It is not chained to the static version of Islam that Bozeman describes. Indeed, cultures are not stiff and fixed phenomena; they are not insurmountable obstacles to social, political, and legal innovations. The Saudi example shows, rather, that collectivities of Muslims are capable of adapting their perceptions and policies to new circumstances.

Often, however, culture has nothing to do with those perceptions and policies. Werner Levi reminds us that recent history testifies to the irrelevance of polyculturalism and to the relevance of national power in international legal dealings.[54] Surely no one could seriously propose that Saudi statesmen would engage routinely in national self-abnegation for the sake of fidelity to principle. Even the Prophet provided ample precedent of the compromises required by prudence in the affairs of state. Yet it would be unwise to conclude that statesmen in their international legal relations never bother with what the people—and some of themselves—cherish and wish to promote. At times, especially when the guidance of the *shari'a* is clear, these cultural values seem to dominate official thinking, as in the Saudi reaction to the law of human rights, and at other times, especially when the guidance of the *shari'a* is not as direct, they support what seems prudent, as in questions of the treatment of aliens. Values do indeed sometimes help to explain why a state observes international law—either because they enter into shaping a view of what is right and wrong, or because they legitimate what obviously seems to be the national interest.

But the cultural influence on international law is uncertain and variable. Although they are right to argue against the Realists that power is not the only factor that counts in world affairs, the proponents of the relevance of culture go off the track in making it seem that virtual certainties exist in the search for universal

---

53. Of course, it is entirely open to question whether Saudi Arabia constitutes an Islamic state; many Muslims are vociferous in their denunciations of Saudi Islamic pretensions.

54. See Werner Levi, "International Law in a Multicultural World," *International Studies Quarterly*, 18, No. 4 (December 1974), pp. 417–449.

order. Northrop and Jenks, for example, over-estimated the ease with which people will abandon some beliefs, modify others, and accept foreign ideas, whereas Bozeman has underestimated the dynamics of culture change. The reality is mixed, as the Saudi case shows: some values persist, while others change in content. With respect to international law, although Saudi Arabia is not of the post-Westphalian nation-state system and disagrees with some of its values from time to time, it accepts nonetheless that it is in the system.

PART III

Ideas and Personalities in the Arab World

CHAPTER SIX

Ameen Rihani and the Hijaz-Najd Conflict: An Abortive Peace Mission

HERMANN FREDERICK EILTS

In September 1924, the storm broke over the Hijaz. It had long been brewing. The expulsion of the Turks from most of that province during the Arab Revolt of 1916–1918, Medina excepted,[1] in support of British military operations against the Turks in Palestine and Syria, had brought but transient calm. In its place, heightened political and military confrontation had emerged between 'Abd al-'Aziz ibn 'Abd al-Rahman ibn Faysal Al Sa'ud, the ruler of Najd, and the sharifian King Husayn ibn 'Ali of the Hijaz for preeminence in the Arabian Peninsula. A Syrian-American, Ameen Rihani,[2] acting in a purely private capacity, would involve himself in the penultimate stages of that conflict as putative peace maker.

RIHANI

Ameen Faris Rihani was born in Frayka, Mount Lebanon, on November 24, 1876. Brought to the United States by his parents

---

1. The besieged Turkish garrison in Medina, under Fakhriddin Pasha, held out until January 1919, more than two months after Turkey had signed the armistice of Mudros.

2. Jarring though it may be to transliteration purists, Rihani spelled his given name "Ameen." His preference is respected here.

at the age of twelve, he became a naturalized American citizen in 1903. A Unitarian Christian, he studied law, but soon found literary pursuits more to his liking. By 1920 his reputation as poet, author and philosopher had already been established through a series of books. His interest in the emerging Arab world remained strong, and in adulthood he lived for extended periods of time in Lebanon, where he became known as the "Hermit of Frayka."[3] An introvert, who found it difficult to socialize, he nevertheless enjoyed wide respect as an intellectual and was an elected member of the Arab Academy of Damascus. He was also a visionary and an incurable romantic. In 1922–1923, he had toured the Arabian Peninsula visiting King Husayn, the Idrisi of 'Asir, Imam Yahya of Yemen, and other Arab leaders. His by then already recognized literary standing, including his Arabic prose and poetry, afforded him ready entrée to Arab nationalist political circles. He had heard the bitter recriminations of each ruler against the others, but had judiciously avoided taking sides.

To all he preached a single, earnest theme: only through Arab unity would the Arabs be able to resist European pressures. Above all others, Husayn and 'Abd al-'Aziz (Ibn Sa'ud) impressed him most as statesmen of the Arab cause. From this tour there also followed, in time, a series of books on the rulers of Arabia—some in Arabic, some in English—which remain valuable time pieces of Arabian history.[4] While engaged in writing some of these volumes in Frayka in 1924, his restless mind pondered a multiplicity of ideas on how he might help to resolve the seemingly irreconcilable intra-Arab quarrels and to further that pan-Arabism of which he had become the self-appointed apostle.

Since his return from Arabia in 1923, Rihani had kept in touch with 'Abd al-'Aziz, urging him to conclude peace treaties with Imam Yahya, with King Faysal of Iraq and the King of the Hijaz. Husayn's assumption of the caliphal title in the spring of

3. On Rihani, see *Who Was Who in America, 1897–1942* (Chicago: Marquis, 1943), vol. 1, p. 1035. He died in 1940.

4. See his *Maluk al-'Arab* (Beirut: Dar al-Rihani, 1950), 2 vols; *Ibn Sa'oud of Arabia* (London: Constable & Co., 1928), a work obviously intended to reingratiate himself with its subject. Also see his *Around the Coasts of Arabia* (London: Constable & Co., 1930).

1924 did not disturb him in the least. This, in his view, had taken place through "the suffrage of the majority of Muslims of Palestine, a minority of the Muslims of Iraq, and of those in Syria who did not heed the wishes of the French authorities to the contrary."[5] In other words, Rihani believed, indigenous Syrian Muslims had welcomed Husayn's action and had genuinely supported it.

Aware of growing Hijaz-Najd tensions, and anxious to keep these in check, a novel thought had struck him. 'Abd al-'Aziz, Rihani was persuaded, did not covet the caliphate; the Sultan of Najd's ambition was purely temporal, to be "the ruler of all Arabia." This was a prescient judgment. Husayn, on the other hand, "who might have been elected Khalif by the majority of the Muslims of the world, had given up hope of ever becoming King of the Arabs." This estimate was more doubtful. Might not peace in Arabia be restored, Rihani reflected, by a mutually agreeable division of temporal and spiritual authority between the two contenders? He might have drawn the analogy of the first Saudi state (1747–1819), in which political and religious authority had indeed been divided between Al Sa'ud and what came to be called

5. National Archives, Foreign Affairs Section (hereinafter NA/FA), "Bearer of (U.S.) Passport No. 354536" (Rihani), report entitled, "My Peace Mission in al-Hijaz," September 5, 1925, sent to the American Consul in Beirut who transmitted it to the Department of State under cover of Beirut's despatch No. 1985, September 23, 1925, File 8906.000 [hereinafter Rihani Report—quotations, unless otherwise indicated, are taken from it]. Although Rihani had told the consul of his mission shortly after his return to Beirut, and had promised a written report, his literary pursuits allegedly prevented him from producing such a document until almost seven months later. There is no indication of Washington reaction, but the report probably was a factor in the United States Government's long delay in recognizing Saudi Arabia.

Rihani's report has been published, without editing and replete with marring typographical errors, in Ibrahim al-Rashid, ed., *Documents on the History of Saudi Arabia* (Salisbury, North Carolina: Documentary Publications, 1976), vol. 2, pp. 24–43. Rihani later recounted many of the details of his abortive peace effort in his *Tarikh Najd al-Hadith wa Mulhaqatihi* (Beirut: al-Matba' al-'Ilmiyya, 1928), pp. 355–426. He clearly remained sensitive to his failure.

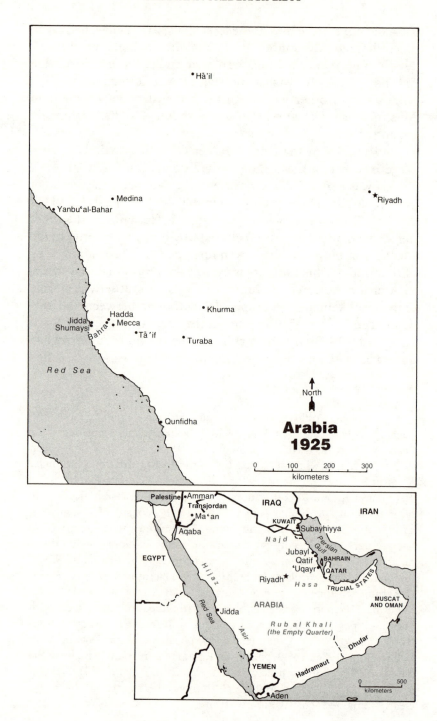

Al Shaykh, or of 'Abd al-'Aziz's own similar divisive action in designating his father as Imam, while he remained secular leader. But there is no evidence that either of these precedents influenced his thinking. Not being an authority on Islam, Rihani assumed a simplistic Christian dichotomy—God and Caesar, the religious and the political.

FIRST EXCHANGE WITH 'ABD AL-'AZIZ—THE UNSIGNED MISSIVE

In a flush of enthusiasm, Rihani wrote a long letter to 'Abd al-'Aziz to broach the subject. After first speaking of a book he was then writing on the Arab rulers, Rihani inquired of 'Abd al-'Aziz "if he would give his suffrage and that of the people of Najd to Husein as Khalif on condition that Husein recognize Ibn Sa'oud as the political leader of Arabia."[6] Rihani wrote in ignorance of the militant Riyadh congress and of Amir Faysal's subsequent circular letter denouncing Husayn's assumption of the caliphate. Two months later, a reply, dated 10 Safar 1343/September 11, 1923, arrived. In a formal answer, the Sultan of Najd simply wrote that the question was one requiring the consensus of the Islamic world.

Yet an air of suspense hung about the laconic epistle, and the matter did not end there. "Pinned," to use Rihani's term, to the formal letter was a confidential note, unsigned, but which Rihani believed had been written by 'Abd al-'Aziz personally, expressing cautious interest in the proposal. He might be willing to concur, the writer confided, if Husayn's acquiescence were first obtained. Moreover, the writer cautioned, any such arrangement would

6. Letter of Rihani to 'Abd al-'Aziz, Frayke, undated (but probably sometime in early July 1923), *Rihani Report*. Through the kindness of the late Shaykh Hafiz Wahba, long-time royal counselor to various Saudi monarchs, the writer was shown copies of this letter and of subsequent correspondence between Rihani and 'Abd al-'Aziz in the Royal Saudi Archives. Not the originals, these copies, Wahba explained, had been presented to the Saudi Arabian Government shortly after the Second World War by Rihani's son. Asked where the original Saudi copies might be, Wahba shrugged his shoulders. Interviews with Shaykh Hafiz Wahba, Jidda, July 19, 26 and August 5, 1967.

have to be supported by a majority of Syrian Muslims—Indians, Egyptians, and Iraqis were not mentioned—before there could be any intimation, public or private, that he, presumably 'Abd al-Aziz, was privy to it.[7]

Along with 'Abd al-'Aziz's letter, the news of the fall of Ta'if was received. This, Rihani mused, had occurred six days before the Sultan's letter had been penned. Although speculating that the ruler of Najd had probably been unaware of the fall of Ta'if when writing his note—Riyadh being a ten-day camel ride from Ta'if—Rihani concluded that the conquest had been consciously planned in order to coerce Husayn into acknowledging 'Abd al-'Aziz's political leadership. For the moment, therefore, pending further developments in the Hijaz, he shelved his religious-political dyarchy concept.

KHATIB'S PLEA

Early in October, Rihani, still in Frayka, received a telegram from Shaykh Fu'ad al-Khatib, a distinguished Arab poet, long-time Foreign Minister of the Kingdom of the Hijaz, nominal editor of *al-Qibla*, and an acquaintance from Rihani's earlier visit

---

7. Although 'Abd al-'Aziz's reply was included among the documents produced by Shaykh Hafiz Wahba, there was nothing even resembling the "penned" note of which Rihani speaks. When queried about this, Wahba expressed puzzlement. Observing that he had written the letter for 'Abd al-'Aziz, he insisted there had been no attachment of any kind. Interview with Shaykh Hafiz Wahba, Jidda, July 26, 1967. The late King Faysal, when also asked by the writer about the alleged "penned" note, knew of the correspondence, but denied there had been any additional communication, as Rihani avers. Interview with King Faysal, Jidda, August 11, 1968. Faysal had a photographic memory. There was no reason for him to dissimulate with the writer with whom he had over the years discussed numerous points of Saudi political and family history. Yet Rihani is categoric on the subject, and there is also no reason to doubt his veracity. Someone, we may never know who, attached the confidential, unsigned probatory note to 'Abd al-'Aziz's reply. Whoever that was clearly did not wish anyone else to know about it. It could have been 'Abd al-'Aziz, determined to leave no options unexplored, but unwilling to tell his advisors of his probe.

to Jidda, expressing an urgent desire to see him and inviting him to come to Amman for this purpose. Khatib, disillusioned with what had become a purely titular role in the Hijaz, had prevailed on Husayn to name him ambassador to Persia. After arriving in Amman, on his way to Tehran, he received news of the fall of Ta'if and of Husayn's abdication, along with a request from King 'Ali to return and to resume his former position. Khatib had accepted and at once sought ways to assuage the Hijaz-Najd confrontation. Among others, Rihani seemed an ideal mediator, if he could be prevailed upon to try. Since Khatib had been refused Syrian transit privileges by the French mandatory authorities, a meeting in Lebanon was not possible. It was finally arranged that they meet in Haifa, readily accessible as it was to both men.

At that meeting, Rihani was asked as a friend of 'Abd al-'Aziz to go to Jidda in order to mediate the sharifian-Sa'udi dispute. Initially hesitant to do so, Rihani subsequently accompanied the reappointed Hijazi Foreign Minister to a meeting in Amman with Amir 'Abd Allah, who had four years earlier, much to his father's displeasure, accepted a British offer to become *amir* of that part of the Palestine mandate known as Transjordan. Assuring Rihani that he spoke for his elder brother, King 'Ali, Amir 'Abd Allah stressed the sharifian desire for an "honorable peace" with 'Abd al-'Aziz. The very next day a telegram arrived from 'Ali, who had immediately been apprised of the meeting, warmly welcoming a visit to Jidda by Rihani, to whom he referred as "peace messenger" *(rasul salam)*.[8]

In the face of these pressing solicitations, still anxious to promote harmony among the Arabs, and bolstered by the curious message he had received a month earlier from 'Abd al-'Aziz, about which he told no one, Rihani decided to accede to the request. He arranged to accompany Shaykh Fu'ad al-Khatib to Jidda, but before doing so armed himself with two self-drafted petitions, signed by Muslim notables of Beirut, one addressed to King 'Ali, the other to 'Abd al-'Aziz, urging peace between them and an amicable settlement of Arab affairs by the Arabs themselves if European interference was to be forestalled.

8. Rihani, *Tarikh Najd*, p. 355.

ARRIVAL IN JIDDA

Arriving in Jidda on November 6, just over a month after 'Ali's nominal takeover, Rihani found a badly confused situation. Husayn, ever the royal kibitzer, was in exile near Aqaba, but was constantly bombarding his son and successor with gratuitous advice. The sharifian treasury was bare and loans requested from various foreign states had been refused. Mecca was already in the hands of the *ikhwan* (the paramilitary Wahhabi tribesmen of Najd), while most of the remainder of the Hijaz was adrift in its allegiance, anxiously awaiting the outcome of the anticipated military confrontation.

By mid-October, apart from Jidda, only Medina and its port, Yanbu' al-Bahr, remained in sharifian hands. Italy, alone among the foreign powers, had recognized King 'Ali's government. Great Britain, after having persistently been rebuffed by Husayn in urging an Anglo-Hijazi treaty, in its turn refused belated but now urgent Hijazi overtures for such a treaty. Although supplies had earlier been permitted to pass through Jidda to Mecca, such transit privileges had been curtailed on the advice of the Hijazi military, much to the annoyance not only of the Saudi commanders in Mecca, but also of Meccans who angrily felt that they had been deceived and turned upon by their erstwhile Hashimite rulers. 'Abd al-'Aziz was still in Riyadh, and his intentions remained unknown.

At the time of the fall of Mecca, Jidda's defenses had been virtually nonexistent. Had the *ikhwan* moved on Jidda immediately after taking Mecca, Rihani and other observers believed, the city would have fallen to them at once. About 500 soldiers, mainly Syrian and Palestinian mercenaries, hastily recruited in Transjordan at Husayn's behest, had arrived in Jidda in late October. They were busily digging trenches and stringing barbed wire around the defense perimeter, a short distance outside the town walls. As Jidda's defense posture seemed to improve, so did the ascendancy of King 'Ali's military counselors, headed by Tahsin Pasha and his deputy, Naurus Bey, an able former Turkish engineer.

Not only could Jidda be held, the military insisted, but the *ikhwan* forces could in fact be defeated. Four (Rihani wrongly says three) decrepit DH-9 aircraft had been purchased through the Italian Disposal Board, along with a few old bombs bought separately from British authorities. Britain subsequently forbade the export of additional ordnance to the Hijaz as inconsistent with announced British neutrality. Jiddawis were divided among themselves, as the National Party, which had forced Husayn's departure, collapsed because of disagreement on objectives. Though all Jiddawis favored peace, there were differences on how this might be achieved. Some were willing to obtain it through a complete renunciation of the sharifian regime; others wished 'Ali's position guaranteed; still others had formulae in-between. Few wanted *ikhwan* control, but the existing situation was equally intolerable. With no end in sight, there were those willing to risk any possibilities.

FELLOW MEDIATORS

Three weeks before Rihani's arrival, H. St. John B. Philby had appeared. Shortly before, he had resigned his position as Political Advisor to Amir 'Abd Allah in Transjordan, in something of a huff, because of incompatibility of views with the ruler of that British-controlled principality and with his London superiors. Philby was still nominally an Indian Government official until his terminal leave expired. During the First World War, he had visited 'Abd al-'Aziz in Riyadh and, subsequently, had traveled across the Arabian Peninsula to Ta'if and to the vicinity of Mecca, much to the annoyance of Husayn. Philby had gone on his own initiative, but had obtained the recommendation of Dr. Naji al-'Asil, the unofficial and discredited Hijazi representative in London, with the ostensible purpose of mediating the Hijaz-Najd dispute. He also had personal objectives. Among these were schemes to obtain 'Abd al-'Aziz's support to cross the Empty Quarter and, separately, to talk about the possibility of an oil concession.

Philby proceeded to Jidda against the express wishes of the British authorities. Both King 'Ali and 'Abd al-'Aziz—and, subsequently Rihani—were formally advised by the British Consul in Jidda, Reader Bullard, that Philby's presence had nothing to do with the British government and that the latter had forbidden him to travel inland. Nevertheless, it was widely believed in Jidda that Philby was a British agent.

101

Shortly after his arrival in Jidda, Philby had written to 'Abd al-'Aziz and to Khalid ibn Luway', then military governor of Mecca, suggesting a meeting at a convenient place to discuss the situation. Ibn Luway' coldly replied that the letter to 'Abd al-'Aziz had been forwarded, but ignored the suggestion for a meeting. He also transmitted a letter of his own to the foreign consuls in Jidda, demanding 'Ali's ouster from the Hijaz and warning that their subjects in Jidda should leave the city. The British, French, Dutch, Italian, and Persian consuls had collectively replied that they would hold 'Abd al-'Aziz responsible for the safety of their subjects and announced their neutrality. To lend weight to their counter warning, a British, a French, and an Italian warship appeared shortly afterwards in Jidda and remained in port.[9]

On November 25, 1924, Sayyid Talib al-Naqib arrived at Jidda to join the two peacemakers. An Iraqi from Basra, who was a direct descendant of the collateral branch of the Prophet's family, it was believed that he had good credentials with 'Abd al-'Aziz. The Naqib family, and especially its Kuwait branch, claimed to have cooperated with Shaykh Mubarak of Kuwait in assisting 'Abd al-'Aziz when he embarked in 1902 on what was to prove a successful mission to recapture Riyadh. Shaykh Mubarak, according to Naqib family tradition, provided arms; the Naqib family provided money. Although long considered an Arab nationalist, Sayyid Talib had on a number of occasions served the Turkish government in earlier negotiations with 'Abd al-'Aziz. Thus, after the latter's expulsion of the Turks from Hasa province in December 1913, Talib, at Turkish behest, had met with 'Abd al-'Aziz at Subayhiyya, on Kuwait territory, and had obtained an oral understanding that he would formally recognize Turkish suzerainty. That oral agreement had led to 'Abd al-'Aziz's signing of the treaty of Basra with the Turkish governor of that province in 1914. Talib had been present at the signing and had played a significant part in persuading 'Abd al-'Aziz to agree to accept the

9. Text of foreign consuls' declaration was published by the Saudi authorities in *Umm al-Qura* [Mecca], No. 2, 22 Jumada I 1343/December 19, 1924.

position of Turkish *qaimaqam* (district governor) of Najd and Hasa.

In May 1917, Talib undertook another mission on behalf of the Turkish government, nominally to negotiate a peace between Ibn Rashid of Ha'il and 'Abd al-'Aziz in which the border between the two Arabian principalities would be delimited. His effort was unsuccessful, aborted as it transpired by the Kuwaiti leadership, but it brought him into renewed contact with 'Abd al-'Aziz.[10]

In the immediate years after the First World War, Talib became Minister of the Interior of the provincial government of Iraq, but subsequently opposed the installation by the British of Sharif Faysal ibn Husayn as King of Iraq. Suspecting that Talib might have monarchical ambitions of his own, the British High Commissioner in Baghdad shamefully kidnapped and exiled him to Ceylon, an act condemned by friends and even some foes as perfidious. He was eventually allowed to go to Europe and spent some time living in Germany.[11] During his exile in Germany, Sayyid Talib, descendant of the Prophet though he was, acquired a reputation for amorous dalliance and high living. He also remained in constant touch with Philby, first while the latter was in Iraq, and later in Trans-Jordan. They were fellow critics of British policy in the Middle East and could commiserate with one another on this score. Philby had throughout sought to obtain redress in London for the injustice done Sayyid Talib by the British authorities in Iraq, but to no avail.

In 1924 Henry Cox, Philby's successor as Political Advisor to the ruler of Transjordan, offered Talib the position of Prime Minister of that principality. Talib rejected the offer, but was subsequently approached by Colonel Stewart Symes, then Acting

10. Arabian American Oil Company Library, Dhahran, Memorandum 2, Chief Political Officer in Charge of Iraqi Section, Arab Bureau to Director, Arab Bureau, Cairo, January 12, 1917. Enclosure 1, *H. St. John Philby Papers*, Section II-A, Microfilm, Frame 203.

11. Haifa Ahmad al-Nakib, "A Critical Study of Sayyid Talib Pasha al-Nakib" (unpublished M.A. thesis, University of Leeds, 1973), pp. 33–106. The writer is indebted to Miss al-Naqib and to her uncle, Sayyid Ahmad al-Naqib, both of Kuwait, for their generosity in making available to him a copy of this unique study of Sayyid Talib.

Chief Secretary of Palestine, and by Frederick Peake Pasha, the British commander of the Transjordanian Arab Legion, who sounded him out on accepting the throne of Transjordan. The British, they explained, were seriously considering removing Amir 'Abd Allah because of French opposition to his alleged clandestine support of anti-French dissidents in Syria.

'Abd Allah, however, got wind of the rumored British design. In order to circumvent it, he telegraphed his elder brother, 'Ali, suggesting that Sayyid Talib might be a suitable Prime Minister in the Hijaz to replace the aging and by now ineffective Shaykh 'Abd Allah Siraj. 'Abd Allah also arranged that Shaykh Fu'ad al-Khatib, who was preparing to return to Jidda from Amman in order to resume his Foreign Ministry portfolio, invite Sayyid Talib to accompany him to Jidda and work with his friend Philby, already there, to mediate peace.[12] Philby, when apprised of this possibility, warmly endorsed the idea that Talib join in the peace effort and himself wrote to the *sayyid* to urge him to come.

Although the British authorities in Egypt and Transjordan pressed Talib not to accept the Hijazi invitation, Talib consented to do so. Before departing, he visited Damascus and was well received there by Syrian nationalists, although the French mandatory authorities broadly hinted that the shorter his stay, the better! Upon arrival, he was given lodgings at Qandara Palace, the government guest house, where Philby and Rihani were also housed.

Like Philby, Talib had an ulterior motive for going to Jidda. He was indeed interested in replacing Amir 'Abd Allah on the Transjordanian throne and hoped to obtain 'Abd al-'Aziz's endorsement. It was his hope that 'Abd al-'Aziz could be prevailed upon to inform the British government that 'Abd Allah on the Transjordanian throne was anathema to him and that Sayyid Talib would be a more acceptable candidate. If 'Abd al-'Aziz was

---

12. *Ibid.*, p. 111; Philby, *Forty Years in the Wilderness* (London: R. Hale, 1957), p. 119; 'Abd Allah, according to Haifa al-Nakib, "vaguely" offered Sayyid Talib the Prime Ministership of Trans-Jordan to succeed Rikabi, but Talib refused. Her source was Naqib family tradition and unpublished Philby reminiscences collected by Professor Elizabeth Monroe of Oxford.

prepared to do this, Talib confided to Philby, he, once ruler of Transjordan, would be prepared to cede to 'Abd al-'Aziz the disputed Wadi Sirhan area.[13]

Philby, an inveterate opponent of 'Abd Allah, sympathized with Talib's aspirations and saw him as a useful addition to the body of would-be mediators. On his part, Rihani, although accepting Philby, had little use for Sayyid Talib. The latter's view of Rihani is unrecorded, but can hardly have been warm. Traditional Syrian-Iraqi antipathy was doubtless one factor. So were their different life styles. The gregarious *dolce vita* devotee, Talib, had little in common with the introspective, slightly prudish Rihani. To some extent, Philby was the bridge between them, but his close personal friendship with Sayyid Talib aroused Rihani's innate suspicions.

It was indeed a curious trio. Two of the three so-called mediators, Philby and Sayyid Talib, had well-known records opposing Hashimite aspirations. That they should even have been accepted as mediators by 'Ali was already a reflection of the King's desperate situation. Neither Philby nor Sayyid Talib ever spelled out his concept of what a Najd-Hijaz peace settlement might entail. Indeed, both seemed more concerned with form than with substance. Only Rihani, despite Philby's belief that he favored 'Abd al-'Aziz,[14] could make a reasonable claim to be a neutral mediator and one with definite ideas about the substance of a possible negotiated settlement.

SECOND EXCHANGE WITH 'ABD AL-'AZIZ

The immediate problem confronting the peacemakers was how to get in touch with 'Abd al-'Aziz. Prior to his departure for the Hijaz, Rihani had sent a cable from Haifa, dated October 23, 1924, indicating his intention to proceed to Jidda and asking 'Abd al-'Aziz to stop his advance and all hostilities until they could meet. Sent through the Qusaybi firm of Bahrain, 'Abd al-'Aziz's agents there, the cable elicited no reply. It was in fact received by

13. Al-Nakib, "A Critical Study of Sayyid Talib Pasha al-Nakib," p. 112; Philby, *Forty Years in the Wilderness*, pp. 130–131.
14. Philby, *Forty Years in the Wilderness*, p. 118.

'Abd al-'Aziz in Riyadh only two or three days before his departure for the Hijaz.[15] Immediately after his arrival in Jidda, Rihani
sent a second, similar cable message to 'Abd al-'Aziz in Riyadh.
Letters were also sent by him to Sultan Ibn Bijad, the *ikhwan*
leader, whom Rihani had met the previous year, and to Khalid Ibn
Luway', proposing a meeting with them outside the precincts of
Mecca. These, too, remained unanswered. Undeterred, Rihani
again wrote to Sultan Ibn Bijad, requesting an escort to conduct
him to Riyadh in order to meet with 'Abd al-'Aziz there. Although the letter appears to have been delivered, Rihani subsequently learned that his courier had not been permitted by the
ikhwan to return to Jidda.

Toward mid-November, the situation clarified somewhat,
though hardly auspiciously. On November 16—i.e., before Sayyid
Talib's appearance—Rihani received a one-line telegram from
'Abd al-'Aziz's agent in Bahrain stating that the Sultan was
already en route to the Hijaz. A day later King 'Ali received a
telegram from 'Abd al-'Aziz himself. It was simply addressed to
"Sharif 'Ali ibn Husayn" without other customary honorifics.
Though expressing respect for 'Ali's person, 'Abd al-'Aziz called
on him to leave the Hijaz forthwith. The administration of the
Holy Places, the message insisted, should be for the Islamic world
to decide. If it chose 'Ali, he, 'Abd al-'Aziz, would gladly accept.[16]
But the clear implication was it would not do so. Another cable
message, sent by 'Abd al-'Aziz to the Muslim countries, and
published in various newspapers outside Arabia, invited the
Muslim world to send delegations to meet with him in Mecca in
order to discuss the future administration of the Holy Places. He
was, or at least seemed to be, responding to Egyptian and Indian
Khilafat Congress urgings that all Muslims be guaranteed access
to the Holy Places.

On December 1, through the British consul in Jidda, Philby
received a reply from 'Abd al-'Aziz to his earlier message. While
insisting that the matter of mediation was one for the Islamic
world to decide, 'Abd al-'Aziz's message held out hope for a

15. Interview with Shaykh Hafiz Wahba, Jidda, July 19, 1967.
16. Text in Philby, *Forty Years in the Wilderness*, p. 126. Rihani's
account of 'Abd al-'Aziz's telegram generally tallies with that of Philby.

meeting with Philby once the Sultan had arrived in Mecca.[17] At the same time, a letter was addressed by 'Abd al-'Aziz to the "people of Jidda," offering them peace and security on condition that they leave Jidda, either for Mecca or elsewhere, or alternatively, that they expel "Sharif 'Ali ibn Hussayn" from the city. Failing this, 'Abd al-'Aziz ominously disclaimed responsibility for any consequences. Not surprisingly, the letter did not appear in the official Jidda newspaper, *Barid al-Hijaz*. Word of it was widespread, however, even before the Mecca newspaper, *Umm al-Qura*, edited by the Syrian Shaykh Yusuf Yassin, published it a week later.[18] In still a third letter, this one addressed to the foreign consuls in Jidda, 'Abd al-'Aziz reiterated the warning that their nationals should be removed to a place of safety.

These warnings, implying that an attack on Jidda might shortly be launched, hardly boded well for the peace effort. Nevertheless, all three of the peacemakers at once wrote letters to 'Abd al-'Aziz in a renewed effort to preempt hostilities. Rihani and Philby, as Christians,[19] could not hope to go to Mecca to meet with the Sultan there. Accordingly, in separate letters, each dated December 4, they asked 'Abd al-'Aziz to designate a place outside the holy precincts where they might confer with him. Sayyid Talib, as a Muslim and a descendant of the Prophet, wrote requesting an *ikhwan* escort to meet him halfway between Jidda and Mecca and to escort him to Mecca in order to meet with 'Abd al-'Aziz.

On the morning of December 9, the trio was summoned to the palace in Jidda, where King 'Ali delivered to each a sealed reply. They were read by the recipients and exchanged amongst themselves. The letter to Philby, according to Rihani, announced that 'Abd al-'Aziz had arrived in Mecca only a few days earlier (December 5) and was still in need of rest. It acknowledged receipt of Philby's previous letter and pointedly alluded to the earlier communication from the British Consul to the effect that Philby's visit to Jidda had no official standing. If Philby wished to discuss personal matters, a meeting might be arranged, perhaps at

---

17. *Ibid.*, p. 131. Rihani's account is silent on this letter to Philby.

18. Text in *Umm al-Qura*, No. 1, 15 Jumada I 1343/December 12, 1924; see also Philby, *Forty Years in the Wilderness*, p. 132.

19. Philby was not formally admitted to Islam until August 7, 1930.

the village of Bahra, midway between Mecca and Jidda. But if the affairs of the Hijaz were the object of the proposed talk, any such meeting was pointless; 'Abd al-'Aziz's sole purpose in moving into the Hijaz was to rid the people of Husayn and his sons. The Muslim world could then settle the problems of the Hijaz. 'Abd al-'Aziz cautioned that it was in neither his nor Philby's interest that the latter, as a non-Muslim, attempt to mediate a purely Islamic question. As the Sultan of Najd now professed to view the issue, it was religious and global, no longer political and merely peninsular, in scope. The letter to Sayyid Talib was similar except that it expressed willingness to see his "old friend" in Mecca, but in a purely personal capacity.

In his letter to Rihani, dated December 6, 'Abd al-'Aziz acknowledged receipt of two previous telegrams which, he explained, had reached him in the desert on the way to Mecca. While thanking Rihani for the latter's services to the Arabs, 'Abd al-'Aziz reiterated what he had said to Philby and Sayyid Talib about the Hijaz. He wished Rihani to know that before they met, he wanted both Husayn and 'Ali out of the Hijaz. The decision on the "Hijaz question" was one for the Muslims alone to make. He had received letters from Muslims all over the world, he asserted, demanding that the rule of Husayn and his sons be terminated in the Hijaz. He could not go against the wishes of the Islamic world on a matter of such importance to Islam and Arabia. Therefore, while welcoming Rihani in principle, he wanted a clearer statement about his purposes before agreeing to any meeting.[20] A letter from 'Abd al-'Aziz to the foreign consuls, received in the same mail, assured them that their nationals and the people of Jidda had nothing to fear in the event of a Saudi attack on the city, provided they remained indoors. This was intended to ameliorate the earlier threat, but still left open the possibility of attack.

20. *Rihani Report.* For Philby's account of these letters, see Philby, *Forty Years in the Wilderness*, p. 135. Though Philby's recital is similar to Rihani's version, it dismisses the letter to Rihani as a refusal by 'Abd al-'Aziz to see him in prevailing circumstances.

THIRD EXCHANGE WITH 'ABD AL-'AZIZ

Despite the rebuff and the only slightly less worrisome sound of 'Abd al-'Aziz's letter to the foreign consuls, the three peace-makers again set to work. Their replies were sent to the palace in Jidda on December 10 and were again carried across the lines by special courier. Philby—who, Rihani claims, was already preparing to leave Jidda in discouragement—wrote that his principal reason for wishing to see 'Abd al-'Aziz was to fulfill a promise made long before and, incidentally, to discuss certain economic matters, including the possibility of arranging an oil concession in Hasa province. Disclaiming any desire to intervene in purely Muslim affairs, Philby averred that his sole purpose was "to serve the cause of the Arabs to the best of my ability."[21] Sayyid Talib unconditionally accepted the invitation to visit 'Abd al-'Aziz in Mecca and asked that arrangements be made to escort him there.

By then, Rihani had lost all confidence in his Iraqi confrere, fearing that Sayyid Talib's personal ambitions and propensity for intrigue would undermine the high cause that Rihani had set for himself. In the circumstance, realizing that 'Abd al-'Aziz's reluctance to allow him to travel to Mecca probably precluded an early meeting, Rihani set about to devise an alternative means of conveying confidentially to 'Abd al-'Aziz the essential part of his message. Secrecy would have to be maintained, even should Sayyid Talib meet directly with the Sultan or his intermediaries. He was unprepared to confide his ideas to the *sayyid*, lest he preempt or distort them. In his message to 'Abd al-'Aziz, therefore, Rihani also disclaimed any intention of interfering in purely Islamic questions, but explained that he had come to Jidda to impart some "very important matters" to the Sultan. These could not be put into writing. He proposed, therefore, to send a confidential friend, a prominent merchant of Jidda with business associations in Mecca, for whom he would obtain permission to pass through the lines.

---

21. *Rihani Report.* Philby says nothing about planning to leave Jidda at that time. Elsewhere, however, he notes that Sayyid Talib had begun to reproach him for persuading the *sayyid* to come on a futile mission. Philby, *Forty Years in the Wilderness*, p. 139.

Jidda's defenses had by then been completed and, in consequence, the military group around King 'Ali had become more
bellicose. Tahsin Pasha wished to take an immediate initiative by
despatching aircraft to harass 'Abd al-'Aziz. In support of their
hard line, the military could point to the enunciation of 'Abd
al-'Aziz's war aims as expressed in his strong letters and procla-
mations. Indeed, in an official proclamation to the people of
Mecca, dated 12 Jumada I 1343/December 9, 1924, 'Abd al-'Aziz
had publicly listed his purposes as (a) the removal of Husayn, his
sons, and their followers from the Holy Places; and (b) the
convening of a general Islamic conference to determine the
administration of these places in a manner consonant with
Qur'anic precepts. Concurrently, the Sultan let it be known that
he stood ready to pay the salaries of government employees of the
sharifian regime and to treat all people equally.[22] This was a
clever ploy, since the Hijazi military and civil servants were
considerably in arrears in governmental payments due them and
were showing restiveness.

HIJAZI BELLICOSITY

Under pressure from his military advisors, King 'Ali on
December 16 (Philby says 15) summoned the peacemakers to
assess latest developments and to review what might be done.
'Abd al-'Aziz, 'Ali noted, had been actively recruiting among the
Hijazi tribes and appeared to be preparing to move on Jidda.
Already certain neighboring coastal villages had been prevented
by the *ikhwan* from sending charcoal and fodder to Jidda. Almost
a week had passed since the trio's last letters to the Sultan, but no
reply had been received. 'Ali announced that he was considering
the desirability of sending an aircraft to fly over Mecca the next
day in order to drop a warning message. It had been proposed that
a day later all four aircraft in the Hijazi air force would be sent to
bomb 'Abta, the square on the northeast end of Mecca. He
solicited the advice of his three "friends" on this plan, which he
acknowledged had been suggested to him by his military advisors.

22. Text in *Umm al-Qura*, No. 1, 15 Jumada I 1343/December 12,
1924.

Sayyid Talib spoke first. As Rihani understood him, he approved in principle the harassing concept, but sought to defer implementation. Could King 'Ali be sure, he asked, that the old bombs would in fact explode? If they failed to do so, the effect would be the reverse of that intended. Might it not be wise, therefore, to try out the bombs somewhere before despatching aircraft for a military operation? On his part, Philby strongly opposed any such design and forthrightly argued for a delay in any hostile action until 'Abd al-'Aziz's replies had been received. Somewhat testily, King 'Ali observed to Philby that he could not wait indefinitely. The last to speak, Rihani sided with Philby. Bombing Mecca, he asserted, was certain to have an adverse psychological effect on the entire Islamic world. (It is hard to believe, as Rihani's account implies through omission, that Sayyid Talib, as a Muslim, would not also have pressed this critical point.) Nor would it bring the Sultan out, as 'Ali's military faction seemed to believe. Instead, Rihani proposed, all reconnoitering and military movements by sharifian forces should be postponed for three days to give more time for a reply to be received. The meeting took place on Sunday; King 'Ali agreed to postpone any decision until the following Wednesday.

Two days later (Philby says on the day after the meeting), however, Tahsin Pasha sent one of the Hijazi aircraft to bomb Bahra, where advance *ikhwan* forces were reported to do be. When angrily questioned by Rihani about this attack, the Pasha blandly responded that he had received intelligence on a force of 500 *ikhwan* already moving toward Jidda. Chernikoff, the Russian pilot who had flown the aircraft, and his Syrian observer later told Rihani that they had seen no military activities whatsoever, either at Bahra or elsewhere en route.[23] Others scoffed that they had flown so high in order to avoid ground fire that they could see nothing and had dropped their bombs aimlessly in flight.

Rihani was by now deeply perturbed. Though it had done no physical damage, the ill-advised bombing of Bahra, he feared, would ring the death knell of any hope for a peaceful settlement. It was tantamount to a declaration of war. The prospect that 'Abd

---

23. *Rihani Report.* For Tahsin Pasha's reply to Philby's similar remonstrance, see Philby, *Forty Years in the Wilderness*, pp. 137–138.

al-'Aziz might still consent to receive him or Philby seemed slim. In a desperate effort to try to redress whatever psychological damage the bombing had done, Rihani urged King 'Ali to send another courier, with copies of the earlier letters and a request for an immediate reply. Sayyid Talib and Philby, who in the light of the bombing incident had concluded that their mission was now hopeless, simply wrote to 'Abd al-'Aziz announcing their intention to depart. Rihani's letter alone indicated his desire to continue the mediation effort.

Three days later replies from 'Abd al-'Aziz were received. To Philby, the Sultan expressed regret at his inability to see him in the immediate future because of the pressure of work.[24] To Sayyid Talib, he expressed regret at the *sayyid's* intended departure and the hope that he might correspond with him in Egypt or elsewhere. The people of Mecca, he explained, had asked him to defer the proposed meeting.[25] To Rihani, he also expressed regret at his inability to meet with him, but agreed to receive the special messenger whom Rihani had earlier suggested. "Charge him to be careful," he enjoined, "in conveying to us your view and ideas." Henceforth, although both Philby and Sayyid Talib would still be in Jidda until January 3, 1925, they played no further role in the peace talks.

RIHANI'S MEMORANDUM

Chosen by Rihani for the role of confidential messenger was Haj Husayn al-'Uwayni, then a Lebanese merchant acting as business agent for the firm 'Abd al-Ghani Idlibi in both Jidda and Mecca.[26] On December 23, 1924, 'Uwayni, garbed as a pilgrim,

---

24. *Ibid.*

25. Philby once asserted, obviously erroneously, that Sayyid Talib did visit 'Abd al-'Aziz in Mecca and, following his return, reported unfavorably on prospects of a settlement. H. St. John Philby, *Arabian Days* (London: R. Hale, 1948), p. 244. He must have had a lapse of memory when writing this and did not repeat the error in later pertinent accounts.

26. Husayn 'Uwayni later became a leading Lebanese political figure and served as Prime Minister and Foreign Minister of that country. He retained important business interests in Saudi Arabia into the early

i.e., wearing the *ihram*, making the little pilgrimage, left Jidda by mule with an escort of two men. There was no prohibition from either side to doing so. In addition to a verbal message from Rihani, and a copy of the petition of the Muslim notables of Beirut, he carried with him a fifteen-point expository memorandum. Written by Rihani in response to 'Abd al-'Aziz's specific request, the memorandum explained the author's views on the importance of a peaceful settlement of the existing Sa'udi-sharifian dispute. The thrust of Rihani's arguments, to which some exception might reasonably have been taken, was as follows:

Save for 'Abd al-'Aziz's own Hasa coastal towns of 'Uqayr, Qatif, and Jubayl, and for Jidda and the ports of the Hijaz, no Arab seaports on either the Persian Gulf or the Red Sea could be said to be free of foreign influence and control. Should the *ikhwan* occupy the Hijaz, the likely ensuing disorders would afford a pretext for foreign intervention. The British and the French, in his view, were simply waiting for such a pretext. Already war vessels of Great Britain, France, and Italy lay in the Jidda harbor. 'Abd al-'Aziz's reputation would be irreparably harmed were he to become responsible for "a foreign occupation" of any Arabian seaport.

The Kingdom of the Hijaz, Rihani continued, had been recognized by the Allied Powers. Yet, he ominously intoned, "certain European governments" had a "tacit understanding" to oppose collectively the independence of Muslim states in Asia and Africa. Had not England, France, and Italy, he asked, recently come to an understanding about Egypt? England and France, Rihani asserted, would be only too pleased to see the independence of the Hijaz lost. Should the Hijazi government fall, a pillar of the Arab movement would collapse and any hope of an Arab federation to be achieved in 'Abd al-'Aziz's reign and under his leadership would virtually vanish.

Independence for Syria and Palestine, Rihani contended, were the goals of the pan-Arab movement. 'Abd al-'Aziz should heed the mistake Husayn had made and not allow a single enemy or rival prince to remain on the Arabian Peninsula. "A complete

1950s under the commercial names of (Ibrahim) Shakir and Husayn 'Uwayni.

accord in southern and western Arabia is the foundation of absolute authority in its northern parts (Syria and Palestine)," he stressed.

French benevolence toward 'Abd al-'Aziz, the Francophobe Rihani warned, was suspect. It was prompted primarily by opposition to England and desire to stifle the pan-Arab movement. 'Abd al-'Aziz ought to avoid both a complete break with Britain and overly close ties with France. Should the independence of the Hijaz be destroyed, the policies of a dubious friend, France, and a selfish one, England, would only be furthered. Politically, these states sought solely to weaken indigenous rulers and to interpose obstacles to cooperation and union in the Arab world. A defensive and offensive alliance between Najd and the Hijaz, if this could be achieved, Rihani was convinced, would force the British government to change its policy in Arabia. Such an alliance would also be the "cornerstone" of an eventual Arab federation. That, in turn, would lead to an Arab empire of the future. Any such treaty with the Hijaz would, moreover, guarantee 'Abd al-'Aziz a considerable source of revenue. (Orally, 'Uwayni was asked to convey to 'Abd al-'Aziz, that 30 percent of Jidda customs receipts might be turned over to Najd along with retention of the Red Sea port of Qunfidha, which had previously been seized by the Saudi forces.[27]) It would also augment 'Abd al-'Aziz's power and prestige and preclude European governments from playing off 'Ali against the Sultan.

'Abd al-'Aziz's vociferous supporters in India, particularly Muhammad and Shawkat 'Ali of the Khilafat Congress, Rihani branded as unreliable. They fulminated much, but did little. The Arabs alone were the only reliable friends of Arabia; no one else had its interests at heart. Any administration of the Holy Places by a multinational Islamic commission, as the Indian Khilafat Congress proposed, would surely spell "foreign rule" for the Hijaz. For was not most of the Islamic world already subject to foreign domination in one form or another? (India, he might have

---

27. *Rihani Report.* Such customs revenue sharing, plus putative Saudi retention of the Red Sea port of Qunfidha, had previously been accepted by King 'Ali, Rihani claims—if so, doubtless on Rihani's urgings.

said but did not, was a case in point.) Peace rather than war in the Hijaz, Rihani averred, was better for 'Abd al-'Aziz's own interests and for the overall Arab cause.

Adverting to the contentious caliphate issue, Rihani emphasized that King 'Ali, unlike his father, made no claim to the caliphate and did not seek it. He had in fact expressly renounced it. "An agreement with him would be more advantageous than with someone else [whom] you might set up in his place because he is of a mild nature; is pious and honest; has a sense of justice; is satisfied with Hijaz; and he sincerely desires peace as well as the success of the Arab movement. As your ally, he would prove more serviceable, it is my belief, than any other *ameer.*" And 'Ali was certainly better than any mixed commission, as the Indian Khilafat Congress wanted, for the administration of the Hijaz. Any such commission, Rihani cautioned, might subsequently seek to interfere in 'Abd al-'Aziz's own affairs in Najd.

Wisdom and justice, Rihani's memorandum went on, required that the views of the Arabs of Syria and Palestine not be ignored. In his view, they supported 'Ali as Husayn's rightful successor in the Hijaz. Any "understanding" between 'Abd al-'Aziz and the Islamic world should be "balanced" by one between 'Abd al-'Aziz and Syria. Syria, at least the Syrian people, supported King 'Ali in the Hijaz and wanted peace in Arabia.

Adverting to 'Abd al-'Aziz's earlier expressed willingness to accept 'Ali, should the latter be chosen by the Islamic world, Rihani argued that 'Abd al-'Aziz had more to gain from a peace agreement directly negotiated with 'Ali. Outsiders should not be allowed to interfere. Only if peace were immediately concluded with the Hijaz, would 'Abd al-'Aziz have the time and the resources to turn toward Transjordan. There, Rihani suggested, the prevailing state of affairs demanded a "change of administration." He concluded by asking for an urgent reply. He was encountering difficulty in restraining the military party in Jidda, which, he lamented, was becoming increasingly strong and impatient.

A curious document, Rihani's memorandum reflects the ingrained bitterness and distrust of Syrian-oriented intellectuals over the French and British failure to honor the pledges of the First World War to the Arabs and their suspicion of the continued political designs of these powers. Some of his judgments were patently based on personal prejudices and beliefs, and Rihani would later not be above trying to play off the French against the British and *vice versa*. Still, it must be assumed that his ideas were advanced in all sincerity.

With the memorandum, in a sealed envelope, whose contents were supposedly unknown even to Rihani's confidential messenger, was a separate note to 'Abd al-'Aziz which said, "If there is any hope for peace, please tell my messenger ['Uwayni] when he comes to leave, to say to me 'Mecca'. If there is no hope at all and you propose to pursue your war policy to the end, please tell him to say to me 'Ta'if.' " In the latter event, Rihani, already suffering from recurrent malaria bouts, proposed to leave Jidda at once for more salubrious climes.

'ABD AL-'AZIZ'S RESPONSE

'Uwayni was gone for three days. Returning on Christmas eve (27 Jumada I), he carried 'Abd al-'Aziz's written reply. His policy, the Sultan insisted, was "one of peace—peace with those who desire peace and wish to be in accord with us." Only to those who wished evil for him and his people would it be one of war. The Sultan had considered Rihani's advice. Before considering Rihani's suggestion further, 'Abd al-'Aziz sought his views on three questions: (a) What was 'Ali's position in the Hijaz? (b) What status would the Government of Najd have in the Hijaz under Rihani's proposal, and what rights would it enjoy there? and (c) What were 'Ali's relations with his father and brothers?

On its surface, the reply seemed promising. Even more so was the messenger's oral report. When leaving 'Abd al-'Aziz the latter had asked 'Uwayni to convey greetings to Rihani and the word, "Mecca!" In the palace in Jidda, spirits quickened "for this no doubt foreshadowed peace," exulted Rihani. "This was a fine Christmas present from Ibn Sa'ud." Even Philby later recalled, somewhat ruefully, the virtual exclusion of Sayyid Talib and himself from further palace consultations as "peace was believed to be imminent as the result of Ameen Rihani's message to 'Abd al-'Aziz."[28]

28. *Rihani Report;* Philby, *Forty Years in the Wilderness,* p. 141.

RIHANI'S SUPPLEMENTARY EXPOSITION

On the following day, in consultation with Shaykh Fu'ad al-Khatib, answers were drafted by Rihani to 'Abd al-'Aziz's several queries. These were submitted in draft form to King 'Ali who, whatever personal doubts he may have had about some of them, resignedly left the matter to Rihani's judgment. 'Ali, Rihani wrote, "is the King of Hijaz by election—the King of Hijaz only." Unlike his father, Husayn, he sought neither the caliphate nor sovereignty outside of the Hijaz. Peace with all the rulers of Arabia, especially with 'Abd al-'Aziz, was his objective. He was a fine, just man, who could be counted upon to introduce progress into the country. He was generally liked by the people. Those who opposed him, as 'Abd al-'Aziz must know, did so for "personal reasons."

On the future relationship between Najd and the Hijaz, Rihani acknowledged that this would require a political and an economic understanding, but was vague on details. As he envisioned such cooperation, its purpose would be to improve the economies of both the Hijaz and Najd and to encourage trade between them. This would require a customs agreement between the two polities, especially for goods transitting the Hijaz en route to Najd. On the political front, the objective of any such bilateral agreement should be to further the "Arab cause" both within and without the peninsula.

Rihani opined that Husayn, still in Aqaba, would not return to Jidda. The people of Jidda and the Hijaz did not want him. True, Husayn continued to send messages to certain officials of the Hijaz government, but they were ignored. As Rihani understood it, presumably from British sources, negotiations were already underway to arrange for Husayn's departure from Aqaba. 'Ali's relations with his brothers were at most fraternal and correct. "I have heard King 'Ali say," Rihani claimed, "that if his brother 'Abd Allah or his brother Faysal were at war with an Arab tribe or an Arab state, he is not obliged to help them. Nor would he permit any interference on their part in his own affairs and the affairs of his country. . . ." Clearly as an afterthought, Rihani assured 'Abd al-'Aziz that no treaty had been signed between King 'Ali and Great Britain, as had sometimes been mooted. He had himself seen specific instructions sent to the Hijazi representative in London, in King 'Ali's name, to discontinue all further treaty negotiations with the British. These supplementary observations, Rihani hoped, would respond satisfactorily to 'Abd al-'Aziz's queries.

HIJAZI MILITARY OUT OF HAND

By now, however, intrigue was rife in Jidda. Those Jiddawis favoring peace, and feeling the economic pinch, spoke more and more openly for 'Abd al-'Aziz. Concurrently, the military party, seemingly a law unto itself, continued to do everything possible to scuttle peace talks. The messenger taking back Rihani's reply to 'Abd al-'Aziz was searched for two hours by military guards at the palace, lest he also be carrying messages to 'Abd al-'Aziz from covert supporters in Jidda.[29] Aircraft of the Royal Hijazi Air Force, piloted by hired White Russian pilots, continued to be sent out for reconnoitering purposes. It was even alleged, though unconfirmed, that a few bombs had been dropped in the vicinity of Mecca.

Still more damaging to the cause of peace, on the day prior to Rihani's receipt of 'Abd al-'Aziz's reply, a proclamation had been prepared by King 'Ali's government, addressed to the people of Mecca, stating that sharifian forces would shortly march on the Holy City and exhorting its people to be of good heart. At such time as sharifian aircraft bombed the invaders, as the proclamation warned might soon be expected, the *ikhwan* forces should be denied shelter, and every effort should be made by the populace to drive them out. The proclamation was published in 'Ali's official newspaper, *Barid al-Hijaz*.[30] Such braggadocio was as self-destructive as it was empty.

When taxed with the proclamation, King 'Ali explained to Philby that it had been published without his assent. Whether published with or without 'Ali's foreknowledge, copies were sent to the Citadel in Jidda to be dropped by Hijazi aircraft on Mecca. On Rihani's urgent representations, 'Ali now instructed Tahsin Pasha to hold them until further notice. The delay was but

---

29. *Ibid.* Rihani's account makes no mention of this incident.

30. Text in *Barid al-Hijaz* [Jidda], No. 7, 20 Jumada II 1343/December 17, 1924; see also Philby, *Forty Years in the Wilderness*, p. 139.

temporary. On December 29, copies were indeed dropped from Hijazi aircraft on Mecca and on 'Abd al-'Aziz's camp at Shumaysi, some fifteen miles southwest of the city. Not until two days later did Rihani hear of this. In response to his indignant protest, 'Ali, after conferring with Tahsin Pasha, ordered the aircraft's Syrian observer to be imprisoned for one week on the charge of disobeying instructions. The latter subsequently insisted to Rihani that he had only followed the orders of his superiors. He could not have acted on his own. It was all a sorry farce. 'Ali, sincere though he might be, was but a figurehead; Tahsin Pasha and his military colleagues were in the saddle.

REJECTION

The new year opened with no further word from 'Abd al-'Aziz. On January 2, however, King 'Ali received a secret communication from Mecca, which seemed to undermine any residual prospect for Rihani's peace effort. 'Abd al-'Aziz, the message reported, had met with various disillusioned *ashraf* in Mecca to discuss the putative election of "Sharif Adnan," of the Dhu Zayd branch of the Hashimite family, as King of the Hijaz.[31] It was reported, moreover, that *ikhwan* contingents, hitherto camped at 'Abta on the outskirts of Mecca, had moved and were deploying toward Jidda. 'Ali and his advisors assumed that these actions signalled 'Abd al-'Aziz's intention to continue to wage war. Accordingly, on the morning of January 3, a sharifian aircraft dropped two bombs on the outskirts of Mecca.

That same evening a war council was held at the palace in Jidda, which Rihani was invited to attend. There had by then already been firing on the city's outskirts. Deep concern existed

---

31. Probably intended was Sharif 'Ali Haydar of the Dhu Zayd branch of the *ashraf*. He had long been an arch-competitor of Husayn for the position of Sharif of Mecca. For an account that 'Ali Haydar was at the time 'Abd al-'Aziz's preference to replace 'Ali as King of the Hijaz, see George Stitt, *A Prince of Arabia* (London: Allen & Unwin, 1948), pp. 280–283; see also the abbreviated account of 'Ali Haydar's daughter, Princess Musbah Haidar, *Arabesque* (London: Sphere, 1968), p. 367. The scheme, if ever seriously considered, came to naught.

that the *ikhwan* might attack Jidda that same night. Once more the military pressed for preemptive action. And once more Rihani pleaded for a little more time. Perhaps the courier had not gotten through to 'Abd al-'Aziz; Rihani urged that another be sent and a reply awaited before further hostilities were undertaken. "The King, calm and thoughtful, unlike his little warlords, supported me," Rihani later wrote of the meeting. Another courier was found and sent with a message to 'Abd al-'Aziz appealing for an immediate reply to Rihani's last message. 'Abd al-'Aziz, it was learned, had already advanced as far as Hadda on the Mecca-Jidda road.

About noon the following day the courier returned. He had met 'Abd al-'Aziz at Bahra, halfway between Mecca and Jidda. In answer to Rihani's latest appeal, the Sultan insisted that he had replied to the previous message and sent a copy of that reply. (It was later ascertained that Rihani's earlier courier had joined the *ikhwan* and had been fearful of returning to Jidda.) 'Abd al-'Aziz's letter, after adverting to Rihani's answers to his questions, read in part: "I do not think that you really anticipate such a settlement, or the purpose behind it has escaped you. For 'Ali desires to meet us in combat. He says so in his proclamation to the people of Makkah. We have therefore responded . . . let 'Ali come out to meet us."

The die was cast. A half hour later, an *ikhwan* cavalry detachment galloped across the plain before Jidda firing their weapons. "It was a declaration of war," Rihani sadly admitted. In a final, desperate try, Rihani sent one more letter, dated 16 Jumada II/January 12, 1925, to 'Abd al-'Aziz, touting the strength of 'Ali's forces. Three days later, 'Abd al-'Aziz replied, scoffing at 'Ali's alleged military strength and welcoming any trial of arms between the two sides.[32] Rihani's effort at peace-making had failed.

32. This exchange of letters is omitted from Rihani's report to the American consul in Beirut, probably because it reflects poorly on Rihani's political acumen and tact. Copies of the exchange were included in the letters shown to the writer by Shaykh Hafiz Wahba. Wahba commented that 'Abd al-'Aziz and those around him, including himself, had allowed himself to be duped. Interview with Shaykh Hafiz Wahba, Jidda, July 26, 1967.

EPILOGUE

In the difficult weeks that followed, a despondent Rihani made no further efforts to mediate between the disputants. 'Abd al-'Aziz, he regretfully surmised, had concluded that Rihani was being used or misled by the sharifians. The bombings, King 'Ali's proclamation, and the generally bellicose posture of the Hijazi authorities all lent credence to such a belief. The military was out of 'Ali's control and spoiling for a fight.

There were also other reasons for the failure, as Rihani was now forced to admit. Husayn's anomalous position and continued presence at Aqaba had given rise to suspicions. Aqaba, along with nearby Ma'an, was coveted by Amir 'Abd Allah of Transjordan, should Hashimite rule in the Hijaz be extinguished. Hijazi tribal elements, moreover, who regularly drifted between the two camps and were conscious of the comparative strength of each, tended increasingly to find it prudent to support the Saudi cause. Rihani might have added that much of Jidda's population, which had lost hope that a sharifian reassertion of authority in the Hijaz could be achieved from the tiny Jidda enclave, became increasingly opposed to 'Ali's continuation in office. The Syrians around 'Ali were arrogant, resented, and despised. Even as Rihani was desperately striving to arrange some negotiated accommodation between the King and 'Abd al-'Aziz which might somehow allow the former to remain, notables of Jidda were in secret communication with the Sultan of Najd promising their support to oust the sharifian rulers. Curiously enough, Rihani, intellectual that he was, seemed blind to this public opinion, although he later acknowledged its importance in his writings.

And what of 'Abd al-'Aziz? Why, after an initial rebuff, did he appear to encourage Rihani's peace efforts over those of Sayyid Talib and Philby? Was the Sultan of Najd dissimulating from the outset or was he serious in his apparent willingness as late as December 24, 1924, to explore negotiating possibilities? One can only speculate on these matters. Ever cautious, 'Abd al-'Aziz had at the Riyadh conference of June 25, 1924, under pressure from the *ikhwan* and his father, temporized in meeting the demand of his followers. To be sure, he had sanctioned *ikhwan* preparations for military probing based on their hold on the towns of Khurma and Turaba. But he had not given orders for an all-out invasion of the Hijaz. By mid-1924, he could be certain neither of the *ikhwan's* military capability and staying power in the mountains of the Hijaz, nor of the possible reaction of concerned European powers, especially the British, to any full-scale effort to conquer the Holy Cities of Islam. Indeed, he ran the risk of provoking British military reaction in behalf of protected Indian nationals killed or despoiled by intolerant *ikhwan* tribesmen.

Even after the fall of Mecca, 'Abd al-'Aziz could not be sure but that foreign intervention might yet take place. Foreign warships remained anchored in Jidda harbor, and 'Abd al-'Aziz had no way of knowing how forces aboard them might be used. In this context, Rihani's efforts were both welcomed and suspect. On the one hand, they still offered the option of a negotiated settlement, if this should prove necessary. On the other, Rihani's repeated warnings of possible foreign involvement in Arab affairs fueled 'Abd al-'Aziz's nagging concern of this danger. He and those around him suspected, moreover, that Rihani, no less than Philby, was in fact a British agent. The shortsighted provocations of 'Ali and the sharifian military undoubtedly roiled him and strengthened the hand of those advisors pressing for all-out action. The combination of these factors, together with *ikhwan* pressure on 'Abd al-'Aziz, vitiated Rihani's effort. Finally, Rihani's last letter, speaking of the sharifian military strength when 'Ali's weakness was only too apparent, was tactless. Not surprisingly, it had precisely the opposite effect on 'Abd al-'Aziz from that which Rihani intended.

Toward the end of January, Rihani made several more efforts to communicate with 'Abd al-'Aziz. His purpose was no longer to achieve a peace settlement, but to persuade the Sultan of Najd of his own sincerity in conducting the peace correspondence. An Egyptian doctor who had seen 'Abd al-'Aziz at Hadda, Rihani wrote on January 23, had reported to him the Sultan's alleged annoyance with Rihani's peace efforts and messages. Apologizing for any annoyance that his letters may have caused, Rihani noted that he had sent them through "good Syrians." Their sole purpose had been, he insisted, to achieve peace between two Arab leaders. Were 'Abd al-'Aziz aware of the difficulties Rihani had experienced in Jidda, he would think more charitably of Rihani's labors. He remained in Jidda awaiting the Sultan's orders.

Four days later, on January 27, 1925, a reply was received. 'Abd al-'Aziz, while acknowledging Rihani's sincerity and disinterestedness, advised him to leave Jidda forthwith.[33] There was nothing to negotiate and there was no purpose in his remaining. Ten days later, on February 6, a sadder and wiser Rihani left Jidda. His peace mission had proved abortive. On the very day of his departure, almost symbolically, a shell from an *ikhwan* artillery piece fell in front of the house in Jidda where he had made his residence. By the end of that year—by December 1925 in fact—'Abd al-'Aziz was undisputed master of Jidda and all the Hijaz.

33. This final exchange is also not mentioned in Rihani's report, but was among the documents provided by Shaykh Hafiz Wahba.

CHAPTER SEVEN

Arab Nationalism and the Idealist Politician: The Career of Sulayman al-Baruni

J. E. PETERSON

The career of the Tripolitanian resistance leader and Ibadi author, Sulayman al-Baruni (1870–1940), took place during a critical period in the evolutionary process of modern political thought in the Arab world. Al-Baruni was raised in a traditional and heavily religious atmosphere, yet during his lifetime he displayed a strong commitment to secular politics and acquired military experience as a guerrilla commander in Tripolitania against the Italians. The combination of religious upbringing with involvement in political and military affairs may seem paradoxical at first glance, but this ambiguous role formation was a logical result of the intellectual and political climate prevailing in the Arab world during the early part of the twentieth century. At that time, Arab response to the direct challenge of European culture and politics had not yet been clearly articulated.

That the reaction of Middle Eastern society in the nineteenth and early twentieth centuries to modern European encroachment was frequently in terms of a pan-Islamic ideology is not surprising. The subsequent development of an indigenous secular Arab nationalism over the twentieth century follows rather directly

124

from the example of secular nationalism (based on linguistic, ethnic or similar foundations) in Europe. Nevertheless, between the pan-Islamist antecedents and the secular, ethnically oriented nationalism of the present era lay a transitional phase incorporating ideological elements from both.

> [In the nineteenth century] the distinction between religion and nationhood was somewhat blurred: in any case, for the broad masses nationalism and Islam were indistinguishable. The secret of Islam's hold on the political realm ... lay precisely in its capacity to see the sacred and the profane interchangeably, in terms of the same scale of values.[1]

Early resistance to European penetration of Islamic territory was led by religious figures turned military commanders. Three such individuals who waged unsuccessful campaigns against the invaders in the first half of the nineteenth century were Ahmad Brilwi (fighting against the Sikhs and British influence in northern India); Imam Shamil (fighting against the Russians in Daghistan); and 'Abd al-Qadr (fighting against the French in Algeria).[2] Later, expressions of pan-Islamist response relied increasingly on secular notions of nationalism without, however, giving up the underlying idea that opposition to existing regimes could be legitimated by appeals to Islam. The mid-nineteenth century variety of pan-Islamism espoused by the Young Ottomans regarded the Ottoman Empire as the primary political unit, thus linking nationalist aims to a geographical territory rather than totally relying on the amorphous concept of *dar al-Islam*. Over the following century, the goals of pan-Islamism and pan-Arabism became increasingly incompatible without, however, becoming completely severed.

The development of a clearly observable schism between pan-Islamism and pan-Arabism occurred first in the Arab East. Before the First World War, most Muslim intellectuals and

---

1. Hisham Sharabi, *Arab Intellectuals and the West: The Formative Years, 1875–1914* (Baltimore: The Johns Hopkins Press, 1970), pp. 106–107.
2. These examples are drawn from Bernard Lewis, *The Middle East and the West* (New York: Harper Torchbooks, 1964), pp. 99–100.

political activists of the Mashriq still shared a similar orientation in "opposition to European culture and domination . . . To them Ottomanism, Islam, and nationalism constituted basic if often mutually exclusive terms of reference.[3] The war and especially the Arab revolt, however, severed the remaining links between pan-Islamism, and its ideological cousin pan-Ottomanism in particular, and pan-Arabism. In the Maghreb, though, the links had always been much stronger. There, the prominence of European culture was reinforced by political domination, i.e., colonialism.

> Nationalism in . . . North African countries was linked with religion. For, unlike the Arab nationalists in the Eastern Arab world, the primary object of their nationalism was not to attack the leading Muslim Power and Islam as a basis of the state, but to enlist Ottoman support and make use of Islam to enforce North Africa's resistance to Christian encroachments. While the nationalist in Eastern Arab countries was clearly distinguished from, if not always opposed to, the Pan-Islamist, the two were hardly distinguishable in North Africa. Religion was indeed one of the most potent factors in the rise and development of nationalism in North Africa, and the sacred authority of the sultan-caliph was often invoked to bolster up the national cause.[4]

This then was the intellectual and political environment which shaped the thoughts and actions of Sulayman al-Baruni. In the guise of an incipient Arab nationalist, he aroused the antipathy of such colonial powers as Italy, France, and Great Britain. Nevertheless, during his years in Istanbul, he was on good terms with various leaders of the Young Turk movement and served as an Ottoman governor. Although the product of a traditional Ibadi environment and education, and recognized as a prominent Ibadi scholar, al-Baruni seemed more successful in non-Ibadi milieux and he spent much of his life in non-Ibadi countries. While he is identified with the Arab nationalist cause of the first part of the

---

3. Sharabi, *Arab Intellectuals and the West*, p. 3.
4. Majid Khadduri, *Modern Libya: A Study in Political Development* (Baltimore: The Johns Hopkins Press, 1963), p. 10.

twentieth century, he was at the same time not only a Berber but a Berber "nationalist," as indicated by his efforts to secure autonomy for the Berber areas of overwhelmingly Arab Tripolitania, following the Italian conquest. He is still revered as a great Libyan patriot, yet he spent most of his life outside Libya in both Arab and non-Arab countries.

Two basic elements in al-Baruni's background, i.e., Berber origins and Ibadi faith, would seem to have played fundamental roles in the direction of his life. The Berbers of Tripolitania have formed a closed, defensive society which has been largely looked down upon by their surrounding Arab neighbors.[5] In addition, Tripolitanian Berbers are nearly always Ibadi. This sect began as a relatively moderate outgrowth from Kharijism, the first separatist movement in Islam. Although the movement arose in Basra and the first Ibadi states were established in eastern and southern Arabia, the spread of the sect to North Africa was in large part due to its appeal to the Berber population as an acceptable expression of opposition to the dominant Arab leadership. At the present time, North Africa is one of the two major areas of Ibadi concentration, with significant communities in the Jabal al-Nafusa and Zuwara regions of Tripolitania, the island of Jarba in Tunisia, and the cities of the Mizab in Algeria. The other large Ibadi community is in the central region of Oman.[6] At various stages of his life, al-Baruni established ties with all of these centers.

AL-BARUNI'S CAREER

Sulayman bin 'Abd Allah bin Yahya bin Zakariyya al-Baruni was born in 1870 into an old and respected Ibadi family of the

5. More information on Libyan Berbers is contained in Louis Dupree, "The Non-Arab Ethnic Groups of Libya," *Middle East Journal*, 12, No. 1 (1958), pp. 33–44.

6. Representative studies on Ibadism include Tadeusz Lewiski, "al-Ibadiyya," *Encyclopaedia of Islam* (new ed.), vol. 3, pp. 648–660; Roberto Rubinacci, "The Ibadis," in A. J. Arberry (ed.), *Religion in the Middle East* (Cambridge: Cambridge University Press, 1969), vol. 2, pp. 302–317; and J.C. Wilkinson, "The Ibadi imami," *Bulletin of the School of Oriental and African Studies*, 39, Pt. 3 (1976), pp. 535–551. The latter is concerned principally with Ibadism within the Omani community.

Jabal al-Nafusa, with his birthplace being at Jadaw.[7] His father enjoyed a reputation as a religious scholar, poet, and teacher in an Ibadi *zawiyya* (a combination of mosque and religious school). Not surprisingly, Sulayman followed in his father's footsteps, studying theology in Tunis, Algeria, and at al-Azhar in Cairo. His mentors in Algeria apparently included Abu Ishaq Ibrahim Atfiyash and his apparent uncle, Muhammad bin Yusuf Atfiyash, a noted Ibadi scholar and author who died in 1914.[8] While in Cairo, al-Baruni also founded a newspaper *(al-Asad al-Islami)* and began a printing press (Matba'at al-Azhar al-Baruniyya) which served to disseminate Ibadi religious works.

Despite his religious background, he apparently engaged in political activity from an early age. Indeed, his sojourn in Cairo seems to have been prompted in part by the haven it offered from Ottoman authorities' suspicions of his efforts toward achieving Berber autonomy. Nevertheless, following the institution of the Ottoman constitution in the wake of the Young Turk revolt of 1908, al-Baruni journeyed to Istanbul as an elected deputy representing the western Jabal region of Tripolitania. There he made important contacts with various leading Arab figures—among them Sayyid Talib Pasha and Faysal bin Husayn al-Hashimi.

In 1911, al-Baruni returned to Tripolitania to participate in the armed struggle against the Italians and eventually became the principal leader of resistance forces following Ottoman withdrawal as a consequence of their peace treaty with Italy in October 1912.[9] The Tripolitanians by themselves, however, were

7. Details of his early life and family background are given in Laura Veccia Vaglieri, "Sulayman al-Baruni," *Encyclopaedia of Islam* (new ed.), vol. 1, pp. 1070–1071; and Abu'l-Qasim al-Baruni, *Hayat Sulayman Basha al-Baruni: Za'im al-Mujahidin al-Tarabulusiyyin*, 2nd ed. (n.p., 1367/1948).

8. For a biography of Muhammad b. Yusuf, see the article under his name by Joseph Schacht in the *Encyclopaedia of Islam* (new ed.), vol. 1, p. 736. Another article on Muhammad states that his brother, Ibrahim b. Yusuf traveled in Oman. Pierre Cuperly, "Muhammad Atfayyas et sa Risala safiya fi ba'd tawarih ahl wadi Mizab," *IBLA, Révue de l'Institut des Belles Lettres Arabes*, 35, No. 130 (1972), p. 262.

9. For first-hand, although anecdotal, accounts of resistance efforts in the Tripolitarian mountains during this period, including glimpses of

no match for the Italians, and al-Baruni's forces were soon driven across the Tunisian border at the beginning of 1913. He there-upon returned to Istanbul by Turkish steamer in March, where he was appointed a Senator by the Sultan and received the title of "Pasha." "Sulayman Pasha" was sent back to Tripoli by the Ottoman government following the outbreak of the First World War to organize further resistance to the Italians. While there, he was named Governor of Tripoli and entrusted with military command of combined Ottoman and local military forces. He also received regular military aid and other supplies via German submarines.[10] Nevertheless, the Tripolitanian forces were de-feated in battle by the Italians in 1917 and al-Baruni was replaced as military commander by Nuri Pasha, brother of prominent Young Turk Enver Pasha.

In November 1918, a nationalist convention established the Tripolitanian Republic (al-Jumhuriyya al-Tarabulusiyya), to be headed by a Council of Four, including al-Baruni.[11] Although Italy

Baruni's role, see Ernest Griffin, *Adventures in Tripoli: A Doctor in the Desert* (London: Philip Allan, 1924); and George F. Abbott, *The Holy War in Tripoli* (London: Edward Arnold, 1912; New York: Longmans, Green, 1912). The latter contains a somewhat fanciful biographical sketch of al-Baruni on pp. 117–119.

10. Raffaele Ciasca, *Storia Coloniale dell'Italia Contemporanea*, 2nd rev. ed. (Milan: Ulrico Hoepli, 1940), p. 442. For greater detail on the First World War as it affected Libya and al-Baruni's role there, see also Laura Veccia Vaglieri, "La partecipazione di Suleimàn el-Baruni alla guerra di Libia," *L'Oltremare*, 8, No. 2 (February 1934), pp. 70–73; Abu'l-Qasim al-Baruni, *Hayat Sulayman Basha al-Baruni*; and Za'ima bint Sulayman al-Baruni (ed.), *Safahat Khalida min al-Jihad li'l-Mujahid al-Libi, Sulayman al-Baruni* (Tripoli: al-Istiqlal al-Kubra, 1964). Other accounts of the Italian conquest of Libya and its subsequent effects include Claudio G. Segrè, *The Fourth Shore: The Italian Colonization of Libya* (Chicago: University of Chicago Press, 1974); W. C. Askew, *Europe and Italy's Acquisition of Libya, 1911–1912* (Durham, N. C.: Duke University Press, 1942); Cesare Causa, *La Guerra Italo-Turca e la conquista della Tripolitania e della Cirenaica*, new ed. (Florence: Adriano Salani, 1935); and Jean Depois, *La colonisation italienne en Libye: Problèmes et méthodes* (Paris: Larose, 1935).

11. Khadduri, *Modern Libya*, p. 21.

recognized the republic in a statute of June 1919, Rome meant to retain full control of Tripolitania and spent the next decade subduing a fitful resistance to its rule. Al-Baruni apparently entered into cooperation with the Italians at this time in hopes of promoting Berber autonomy within the framework of the republic. The Italians, however, suspected him, as had the Ottomans in pre-war days, of nurturing plans for a Berber amirate or Ibadi imamate and consequently banished him from Tripolitania.[12] He spent the next several years secluded in European hotels, principally in Marseilles and Paris. Decidedly ill at ease in Europe, yet forbidden entry to North Africa, al-Baruni also found the atmosphere of Istanbul considerably less congenial than in pre-war days: his visits there in *ca.* 1919 and 1923 lasted for only short lengths of time. The impression that he gave the British High Commissioner in Istanbul on one of these trips was definitely negative:

> Suleiman-el-Baruni, though a person of consequence in his own part of Northern Africa, enjoys little consideration in this country. He was a member of the Turkish Senate until late November when it, with the Constantinople Government, ceased to exist. His role in Turkey, such as it is, is that of a busy-body with pan-Islamic leanings. He is by no means lacking in intelligence, but is something of an adventurer, intriguer and charlatan. Though he need not be taken very seriously anywhere outside Africa, I do not think he should be encouraged to travel in British Moslem dependencies.[13]

Eventually, his former colleague from the Ottoman Senate, Sharif Husayn al-Hashimi provided the means for al-Baruni to join the 1924 *hajj*, and while in Mecca he was appointed a member of the preparations committee for the Second Congress of the Hajj.[14] During his stay in the Hijaz, al-Baruni had engaged

12. For more information on Libyan resistance after the war, see Raffaele Rapex, *L'affermazione della sovranità italiana in Tripolitania* (Tientsin: Chihli Press, 1937).

13. Foreign Office, 1357/1307/23, Horace Rumbold to Marquess Curzon, April 14, 1923, No. 222; copy in India Office Records in London (hereinafter cited as "IOR"), R/15/3/449.

14. *Oriente Moderno*, 9, No. 10 (October 1924), p. 601; translated

in correspondence with Sultan Taymur bin Faysal Al Bu Sa'id of the Sultanate of Muscat and Oman. As a consequence, he joined a group of Omani and Gulf pilgrims returning to their homes and arrived in Muscat in August 1924. There he contracted malaria and allegedly refused British permission to travel to Karachi for treatment.

Instead, he responded to an invitation from Muhammad ibn 'Abd Allah al-Khalili, Imam of the autonomous Ibadi Imamate of inner Oman, and a few months later journeyed inland in Oman to the settlement of Sama'il.[15] There he married and became a confidant of the Imam and a respected addition to the ranks of Ibadi *'ulama';* over the next few years, his stature continued to grow and he eventually received a position of leadership within the community *(ri'asat hay'at kibar al-'ulama' wa'l-ru'asa').*[16] He was invested with responsibility for the Imamate treasury *(bayt al-mal)* and was involved in the collection of *zakat.* It seems probable that his inflexible standards of financial account-ability led him into disputes with a number of Ibadi Omanis; and

from *Alif-Ba* (Damascus), August 1, 1924. Among other responsibilities, the committee was to deal with such matters as the possibility of Arab unity, discussions on various matters among all Muslim *'ulama',* the creation of a permanent secretariat for the congress along with the means of financing it, and the promotion of the Arabic language. He was later appointed by the Ibadi Imam of Oman as the latter's representative to the 1925 congress of the caliphate but never attended.

15. Following the Agreement of al-Sib (signed in 1920 between the Sultan and various tribal leaders), the interior of Oman had attained a measure of autonomy from the British-supported Sultanate of the coast. For the next fifty-five years, an elected Ibadi Imam exercised a tenuous secular authority, as well as spiritual guidance, over the various tribes of the interior and their powerful leaders. For more information on the creation of the twentieth-century Imamate and the background to the Agreement of al-Sib, see the present author's article, "The Revival of the Ibadi Imamate in Oman and the Threat to Muscat, 1913–20," *Arabian Studies,* 3 (1976), pp. 165–188.

16. Information on the Oman period of al-Baruni's life is drawn from various materials in the India Office Records and from Muhammad b. 'Abd Allah al-Salimi, *Nahdat al-A'yan bi-Hurriyat 'Uman* (Cairo: Dar al-Kitab al-'Arabi, 1380/1961), pp. 379–384; as well as Abu'l-Qasim al-Baruni, *Hayat Sulayman Basha al-Baruni.*

his departure from the service of the Imam Muhammad may have been at least partially the result of antagonisms aroused by his manner.[17]

In 1927, al-Baruni returned to Muscat, once again suffering from malaria. On seeing his condition, the Sultan prevailed upon the British Political Agent and Consul in Muscat to notify King Faysal of Iraq of al-Baruni's predicament. In reply, the King extended a personal invitation for Sulayman to join him in Baghdad. Al-Baruni was to remain in Iraq as a guest of the royal household until 1938. At that point, he once again returned to Muscat and took up residence under the hospitality extended by the new Sultan, Sa'id bin Taymur, who appointed him his "Adviser on Internal Affairs." Although this post was little more than a sinecure in administrative terms, the respect that Sultan Sa'id undoubtedly felt for al-Baruni was genuine. It seems probable that al-Baruni provided an important channel of communication between the Sultan and Imam Muhammad in the interior.[18]

Despite al-Baruni's residence in what was then an isolated corner of the Arab world, he continued to take an active interest in world affairs and particularly in events taking place in the rest of the Arab world and Tripolitania. In 1925, Cairo's *al-Ahram* reported that the Imam had given him the task of mediating between the Hijaz and Najd, then the respective regimes of the Hashimis and the Al Sa'ud, although there is no evidence of his

17. It is interesting to note that his close associate in these duties was Shaykh Nasir b. Rashid al-Kharusi, the brother of the Omani Imam from 1913 to 1920, Salim b. Rashid. Nasir also shared a reputation for intractability and likewise left the service of the Imam in the late 1920s. For more on the administration of the Imamate, see J.E. Peterson, *Oman in the Twentieth Century: Political Foundations of an Emerging State* (London: Croom Helm, 1978), pp. 101–103.

18. Although the two figures never met and were unable to visit each other's domains, the Sultan and the Imam corresponded frequently and the latter was always regarded as a religious scholar (*'allama*) by the secular ruling family. It is possible also that Sultan Sa'id, who long harbored undefined hopes of regaining control of the interior, saw his patronage of al-Baruni as a means of increasing his legitimacy in the eyes of the religious notables of the interior.

actual involvement.[19] Representative of his continuing concern for his homeland was the letter he wrote in 1927 to the Algerian newspaper, *Wadi Mizab*, protesting Mussolini's abolition of the Statute of Tripolitania.[20]

Although his overt political activity had virtually ceased (except for local matters) following his final departure from Tripoli, he continued to keep in contact with fellow Tripolitanian *mujahidun* (freedom-fighters) and bided an opportunity to return to his homeland and once again participate in the struggle for its liberation from foreign domination. While in Oman and Iraq, he contributed frequently to such Arabic newspapers as *al-Ahram, Wadi al-Nil, al-Akhbar, al-Fath* and *al-Rabita al-'Arabiyya* (all in Cairo), *Fatta' al-'Arab* (Damascus), *al-Bilad* (Baghdad), and even the Arabic section of *Tribune d'Orient* (Geneva).[21]

The British authorities in the Persian Gulf and elsewhere, aware of al-Baruni's newspaper articles and uneasy over the possibility of anti-British agitation traceable to nationalist sentiment, were distinctly suspicious of al-Baruni; they viewed him as a potential instigator of anti-British feelings. These suspicions had been given fuel by the visit in the late 1920s of an American observer, long resident in Iraq, to Sama'il, where he had several discussions with al-Baruni.

Short, slightly grey, with beard greyer on the right side than on the left and trimmed to a blunt point and not allowed to grow as a long and ragged fringe in the fashion of the country,

19. *Al-Ahram,* May 20, 1925; article translated in *Oriente Moderno,* 5, No. 6 (June 1925), p. 311. The report also states that al-Baruni had left Muscat for the Hijaz in this connection, which seems inaccurate.

20. *Wadi al-Nil,* August 8, 1927; article translated in *Oriente Moderno,* 7, No. 9 (September 1927), p. 413.

21. Numerous articles concerning him were noted and/or translated into Italian and published in *Oriente Moderno, e.g.:* 2, No. 7 (December 1922), p. 408; 5, No. 6 (June 1925), p. 311; 6, No. 10 (October 1926), p. 544; 7, No. 9 (September 1927), p. 413; 14, No. 8 (August 1934), pp. 392–396; 18, No. 10 (October 1938), pp. 563–564; 18, No. 11 (November 1938), pp. 623; and finally the report of his death, 20, No. 7 (July 1940); p. 326. Other articles have been reproduced in Abu al-Qasim al-Baruni, *Hayat Sulayman Basha al-Baruni.*

his voice low, his speech easy to understand, his manner dignified and courteous, his clothes all white, of the sort worn by a lettered man of Tunis, such is this exile from Tripoli. He came to Uman three years ago, having been refused asylum in French North Africa and in Egypt, so it is said. The climate and the fever of Uman are said to have aged him much, and his beard was jet black when he arrived. He is credited with writing anti-European articles for the Egyptians and other presses. French, Italians, and British he regarded as most undesirable people. Americans he regarded only with mild suspicion. He had known Saiyid Talib Pasha, when the latter had sat with him in council in Stamboul, before the war, and he was glad of news of his old friend. He was particularly interested in the whereabouts of the Minister of Finance of Muskat and the R.A.F. officers and their widely advertised attempt to get to the Baraimi oasis; and rumor has it that it was al-Baruni himself who has kept them out of that place. The whole subject of airplanes and Imperial Airways was one on which he was anxious for information. The question of Cyprus and a possible new king for that island he discussed for some little time. Judging by the precautions he observed, he must be in some fear of assassination.[22]

Al-Baruni's lifelong interest in pan-Arab affairs and expectations of playing a role in the liberation of Tripolitania continued unabated during his residence in Muscat in the years immediately prior to the Second World War.

This stormy petrel has remained quietly in Muscat. He has lost the confidence of the Sultan and is seldom consulted on Internal Affairs although he is nominally the Sultan's Adviser on this subject and receives an honorarium as such. The outbreak of the war brought new hope to the old man. He expected Italy to side with Germany and he saw visions of Tripoli regaining her independence. He offered his assistance to France and wrote of the influence he could still exert in Tripoli. The course of the war has disappointed him and he

22. IOR, R/15/5/347, "Mr. V.H.W. Dowson's Notes on Smail—Dates, Etc., June 1927–April 1929."

seems to have slipped back into the state of inertia from which he was momentarily awakened.[23]

Ironically, the opportunity for him to realize his ambition and participate in the freeing of his country finally came when it was too late. While accompanying Sultan Sa'id on a trip to Bombay in the spring of 1940, al-Baruni suffered a heart attack and passed away there on April 30.[24] Six weeks after his death, a telegram came from the French forces in North Africa requesting his immediate presence in Algiers to assist in operations in Libya.[25]

AL-BARUNI'S LEGACY

Almost all of his overt political activity, especially that indicating a strong prototypal Arab nationalist ideology, took

23. IOR, R/15/3/338, Annual Muscat Administration Report for 1939.

24. IOR, R/15/3/337, Annual Muscat Administration Report for 1940. His immediate family remained in Muscat until after the war, when Sulayman's nephew (?), 'Umar b. Ahmad al-Baruni, gathered the surviving relatives in May 1947 and departed for Tripoli. IOR, R/15/3/450, Political Agent, Muscat, to Political Resident in the Persian Gulf, Telegram "Q" C/205, May 4, 1947. These included his widow, Amira bint al-Hajj Sa'id; two daughters, Za'ima and 'Aziza; two nieces, Halima bint Ahmad and Maryam bint Ahmad; and two grandsons, Tariq b. Ibrahim and 'Izz al-Din b. Ibrahim. IOR, R/15/3/450, Sultan Sa'id b. Taymur to Political Agent, Muscat, R.I. Hallows, 3 Dhu al-Hijjah 1365/October 29, 1946. Sulayman's niece Maryam was married to Sulayman's son Ibrahim and apparently the mother of the two grandsons mentioned above. The fate of Ibrahim is unclear. He resided in Iraq as late as 1940, when he was accused of threatening the life of the British Ambassador and sent to an asylum. IOR, R/15/3/450, Chancery, Baghdad, to Political Resident in the Persian Gulf, No. 249/5/40, November 22, 1940. Another of Sulayman's sons, 'Isa, had already left Oman and was employed by the British during the Second World War. IOR, R/15/3/450, General Headquarters, Middle East, Political Branch, to Representative of India on Middle East War Council, Cairo, Ref. 10035, February 5, 1942; included as enclosure in Political Resident in the Persian Gulf to Political Agent, Muscat, No. C/71, March 9, 1942.

25. IOR, R/15/3/449, Middle East Intelligence Centre, Cairo, to Political Resident in the Persian Gulf, repeated Political Agent, Muscat, Telegram No. 8657, June 8, 1940.

place during the struggle against the Italians in Tripolitania. With his banishment from North Africa, he shifted into a phase of political quiescence, which undoubtedly served to isolate him from other prominent Arab intellectuals and lessened his impact on the development of Arab nationalism, as well as denying him a reputation as a pan-Arab, and a Libyan, *mujahid*.[26] Indeed, his reputation today rests largely on his contribution to Ibadi theology and culture, as well as poetry, rather than his political activity.[27] In Oman, he is still noted as one of the principal Ibadi religious figures of this century and the large school in Sama'il which he founded bears his name.

As a politician or statesman, al-Baruni would seem to fit in the category of an idealist.[28] But he was also a man of the pen—an intellectual politician—who took up the sword. There are similarities between this military/activist phase of his career and that of another incipient Arab nationalist of the period, 'Aziz 'Ali al-Misri, of Egypt.[29] Both were raised in traditional and religious

26. Even his newspaper articles written in Oman and Iraq were concerned primarily with the war in Tripolitania and possibilities for independence there, and he rarely entered or wrote on Arabian or Iraqi politics. In this connection, it is interesting to note a photograph of al-Baruni wearing shoulder-length hair which he refused to cut until "the enemy quit his country." Abu al-Qasim al-Baruni, *Hayat Sulayman Basha Baruni*, opp. p. 160.

27. Works in this category include *al-Azhar al-Riyadiyya fi A'immat wa-Muluk al-Ibadiyya* (Cairo: n.p., 1906–1907?); *Diwan al-Baruni* (Cairo: Matba'at al-Azhar al-Baruniyya, 1327/1908); *Mukhtasar Tarikh al-Ibadiyya* (Tunis: Maktabat al-Istiqama, 1938; 2nd ed., 1960?); and *Khatirat al-Baruni* (n.p., n.d.).

28. In his book, *Arab Contemporaries: The Role of Personalities in Politics* (Baltimore: The Johns Hopkins University Press, 1973), Majid Khadduri developed three horizontal categories of politicians according to their goals—idealist, realist, and ideological—as well as three vertical categories according to methods used to gain leadership—military, professional, and intellectual.

29. For al-Misri's background, see *ibid.*, pp. 7–18; and Khadduri, " 'Aziz 'Ali al-Misri and the Arab Nationalist Movement," *St. Antony's Papers*, No. 17; Middle Eastern Affairs, No. 4 (ed. by Albert Hourani; Oxford: Oxford University Press, 1964), pp. 140–163.

environments and both were of non-Arab ethnic origin. Both served the Ottoman Empire in Istanbul where they came into close contact with various members of the Young Turk movement. Furthermore, both failed to distinguish themselves on the battlefield and their careers were tainted with suspicions of having "equivocal attitudes."[30] More fundamentally, both men believed in the compatibility of a nationalist expression within the framework of Ottoman unity. Al-Baruni, of course, fought against the Italians as an Ottoman official. While al-Misri was briefly involved with the Arab revolt, apparently he withdrew when it became clear that Sharif Husayn's intention was complete independence and not simply the prevention of foreign occupation of the Hijaz.

Although al-Misri spent a certain amount of time immediately after the First World War wandering through the Arab world just as al-Baruni did, he was more fortunate than al-Baruni in being able to reside in his homeland. There he enjoyed a widely-held reputation as an elder nationalist figure. Al-Misri also was fortunate in living to see the liberation of his country from foreign control and the establishment of a regime based on at least some of the ideas that he had shared and pioneered. Al-Baruni, however, was to be denied that fulfillment. In fact, it should be noted generally that the parallel between al-Baruni and al-Misri is not exact, since the latter was trained and commissioned as an army officer. Furthermore, while al-Baruni apparently remained on cordial terms with Young Turk politicians, al-Misri's trial in 1914 was largely the result of a falling-out with Enver Pasha.

30. On learning of Sharif Husayn's intention to attack Ottoman-held Medina in October 1916, al-Misri apparently was prepared to negotiate with the Ottoman commander to replace the Hashimi leadership of the Arab Revolt and seek Arab autonomy within the Ottoman Empire. Khadduri, "al-Misri and the Arab Nationalist Movement," p. 154. In a similar manner, al-Baruni had participated in a mid-1915 plot to force hostilities between the Sanusi leader, Sayyid Ahmad al-Sharif, and the British forces in Egypt. E. E. Evans-Pitchard, *The Sanusi of Cyrenaica* (Oxford: Clarendon Press, 1949), pp. 125–126. Later, of course, came his actions in dealing with the Italians prior to his banishment from Tripolitania.

Because al-Baruni essentially was a man of the pen, his overall role can also be seen as paralleling that of a better-known contemporary idealist, Muhammad Rashid Rida (1865–1935).[31] The period of these men's political activity was one of major transition in Middle East politics: the dissolution of the Ottoman state and the first stirrings of the idea of Arab leadership for the Arab nation. It was the pressure of these compelling circumstances which drew al-Baruni and Rida away from their theological studies and into the arena of politics. Nevertheless, attainment of their goals—i.e., independent Arab Islamic states—eluded them and both retired from active politics to spend the last decade of their lives engaged in religious philosophy and writing.

Rida's opposition to the despotism of Sultan Abdülhamid and his reaction to the gradual appearance of early Turkish nationalist feelings were mirrored in al-Baruni, although he chose to remain aloof from the Committee of Union and Progress (CUP) regime in distinction to al-Baruni's participation as Tripoli's representative to Istanbul and then commander of Ottoman forces against Italy. Both figures were prominent in attempts to create independent Arab regimes out of the wreckage of the Ottoman state—Rida as President of the Syrian Congress in 1920 and al-Baruni as a member of the Council of the Tripolitanian Republic. But al-Baruni's connection with one of the first attempts at a republican state in the Middle East points toward the difference in political thought between the two men.

This difference may derive from religious background, from Rida's Sunnism and al-Baruni's Ibadism. Rida's goal was the unification of the Arabs in a re-established "pure" Islamic state, and his activity in pre-mandate Syria and later role in negotiations toward the unification of Syria and Iraq bear this out. It also is not surprising that Rida in later years became intrigued with

31. For the background and political thought of Rida, see Albert Hourani, *Arabic Thought in the Liberal Age, 1798–1939* (London: Oxford University Press, 1970), pp. 222–244 and 299–307; Majid Khadduri, *Political Trends in the Arab World: The Role of Ideas and Ideals in Politics* (Baltimore: The Johns Hopkins Press, 1970), pp. 65–69; and Malcolm Kerr, *Islamic Reform* (Berkeley: University of California Press, 1966).

the Al Sa'ud state in Arabia, seemingly the closest contemporary resemblance to a truly Islamic state. Moreover, it was a Sunni movement which had wrested the guardianship of the Holy Places from the Hashimis, tainted in Rida's eyes for their moral laxity and cooperation with the British.

Al-Baruni's political outlook seemed less conservative than that of Rida. After all, his pre-First World War policy had been cooperation with the CUP in pursuit of Tripolitanian autonomy, with this stance occurring even prior to the forging of a common alliance against the Italians. His goals, moreover, seemed less absolute and more narrowly—even practically—defined. He came from the Western edge of the Arab world and his goals and activities were focused specifically on securing self-determination for that particular homeland. The small numbers and inward-looking nature of the Ibadi faith also may have played its part in restricting his nationalist endeavors to Tripolitania, as well as directing his attention in later years to Oman.

While Rida's fascination with a contemporary version of the ideal Islamic (Sunni) state went no further than observation from Cairo, al-Baruni actually participated in the administration of a traditional Ibadi state, vacillating between the corrupted Ibadi regime of the Sultanate and the fragile reconstruction of an elected Imamate in the interior. Nevertheless, even from the vantage point of an observer, Rida came to realize the yawning chasm between his concept of an ideal state and the existing political reality, and so pointed out the impossibility of electing a new Caliph. While al-Baruni may have been relatively more pragmatic in his politics, conflict between his ideals and the frustration in attempting the translation of those ideals into practice seemed inevitable. He too found it necessary eventually to give up active politics and return to the pen.

CHAPTER EIGHT

The Intellectual Origins and Ideas of the Ahali Group

MUDHAFAR AMIN
and
EDMUND GHAREEB

INTRODUCTION

It can be argued that, to a significant degree, Iraq's modern political era opened with the foundation of the Jama'at al-Ahali (the People's Group). In January 1932, when this organization burst on the scene with its newpaper, Iraq was still under British mandate; the bulk of the Iraqi population lived in miserable social and economic conditions. Illiteracy was widespread and ethnic and sectarian conflicts commonplace. Political consciousness was minimal and notions of civil rights or liberties confined to the educated few.

Iraq's declaration of independence and entry into the League of Nations in October 1932 did not free the country from the legacy of the Ottoman regime: rising nationalist sentiment among Arabs and Kurds, intensified by centuries of economic and political neglect. British influence over the monarchy continued while Iraq's rulers took little account of the pressing needs and concerns of society at large. Political activity remained generally the preserve of a privileged minority. Even the tiny opposition groups and parties in the late 1920s and early 1930s concentrated on demanding independence from Britain and showed little or no interest in social and economic problems.[1]

In this environment, the Jama'at al-Ahali emerged as the first Iraqi group to articulate a well-developed ideology linked to a strong social conscience and a concept of economic progress. Indeed, the founders of the Ahali group showed a remarkable dedication to raising levels of political and social consciousness— above and beyond any sectarian or ethnic division—rather than seeking to advance their own careers or self-interest in the fashion of many of their contemporaries. Although from relatively well-to-do and educated backgrounds, they preferred, in the face of fierce opposition from entrenched vested interests, to devote themselves to espousing the cause of the deprived majority.[2]

In the beginning, Jama'at al-Ahali consisted of hardly more than four young college graduates—Husayn Jamil, 'Abd al-Qadir Isma'il, 'Abd al-Fattah Ibrahim, and Muhammad Hadid.[3] They were imbued with ideas of political and social reform as well as a profound desire to cure the ills of their society. Their studies at home and abroad and their personal experiences had led them to a keen realization of Iraq's backwardness and to the belief that formal political education could play a vital role in transforming

1. For an account of Iraq's modern history see Majid Khadduri's *Independent Iraq, 1932–1958; A Study in Iraqi Politics,* 2nd ed. (London: Oxford University Press, 1960) and *Republican Iraq: A Study in Iraqi Politics Since the Revolution of 1958* (London: Oxford University Press, 1969). See also Edmund Ghareeb's *The Kurdish Question in Iraq* (Syracuse: Syracuse University Press, 1969) and "Domestic Politics and Development in Iraq" in Z. Michael Szaz (ed.), *Sources of Domestic and Foreign Policy in Iraq* (Washington, D.C.: American Foreign Policy Institute, 1986), pp. 8–29.

2. Fadil Husayn, *Tarikh al-Hizb al-Watani al-Dimuqrati, 1946–1958* (Baghdad: Matba'at al-Sha'b, 1963), p. 3.

3. Mudhafar Amin conducted interviews with these figures between 1975 and 1979 in London and Baghdad for a 1980 Ph.D. thesis on the ideology of the Ahali group at Durham University. Parts of this paper were mainly drawn from this thesis: "Jama'at al-Ahali: Its Origins, Ideology, and Role in Iraqi Politics, 1932–1946".

the country into a modern democratic state. Then, hoping to create a movement which might eventually be transformed into a mass political party, they decided to establish a newspaper. The publication of their newspaper ushered in a new leftist political trend advocating what was, for most Iraqis, new political, social, and economic concepts.[4] Some observers saw in the group and its newspaper the first step toward the foundation of leftist thought in Iraq,[5] and one of the major contributions to leftist movements in the Arab world during the 1930s.[6] And while socialist ideas were not unknown to Iraqi intellectuals, the Ahali was the first group to advocate liberal socialist ideas in a coherent and systematic way.[7]

STUDENT ACTIVISM IN BEIRUT AND BAGHDAD

After Faysal was crowned King of Iraq in 1921, the government, on the advice of the newly appointed Director-General of

4. Khayri al-'Umari, "Jaridat al-Ahali," al-Aqlam, 6 (October 1969), p. 5.

5. Muhammad Anis, "Jama'at al-Ahali wa Nasha'at al-Yasar al-Iraq," Al-Hilal [Cairo] 73 (January 1, 1965), pp. 43–49.

6. Majid Khadduri, Political Trends in the Arab World (Baltimore: The Johns Hopkins University Press, 1970), pp. 104–106. See also Independent Iraq, pp. 96–98, and Arab Contemporaries: The Role of Personalities in Politics (Baltimore: The Johns Hopkins University Press, 1973).

7. For information on Ahali ideas, the principal sources that have been used to define the group's ideology are:
—Ahali newspapers (al-Ahali and Sawt al-Ahali)
—Ahali tracts, entitled Rasa'il al-Ahali ila'l-Shabab, in 3 volumes: 'Ala Tariq al-Hind (Baghdad: Matba'at al-Ahali, 1932); al-Sha-'biyya fi'l-Mabadi' al-Siyasiyya al-Haditha (Baghdad: Matba'at al-Ahali, 1933), vol. 1; and Mutala'at fi'l-Sha'biyya (Baghdad: Matba'at al-Ahali, 1935)
—Minhaj al-Sha'biyya
—Kamil al-Chadirchi, "al-Siyasa wa'l-Dimuqratiyya," al-Bilad, August 28, 1931.
—Min Awraq Kamil al-Chadirchi (Beirut: Dar al-Tali'a, 1971)
—Kamil al-Chadirchi, Mudhakkirati (wa Tarikh al-Hizb al-Watani al-Dimuqrati) (Beirut: Dar al-Tali'a, 1970).

Education Sati' al-Husri (1880–1964), a well-known Syrian educator and secular Arab nationalist thinker, adopted a policy of
granting government scholarships to promising high school graduates to continue their education abroad.[8] In September 1923,
'Abd al-Fattah Ibrahim was sent to the American University of
Beirut (AUB) to study modern history, and Muhammad Hadid
continued his high school education in Beirut at the International
School under the auspices of AUB.[9]

During the academic year 1924–1925 there were over 50 Iraqi
students at AUB. On campus they formed a society whose
president was Yusuf Zaynal, an activist, with 'Abd al-Fattah
Ibrahim as vice-president. According to Ibrahim, the purpose of
the association was to discuss politics in Iraq and other Arab
countries "and to dissuade the students from Beirut's night
life."[10]

Because the university forbade direct political activities,
more significant was the formation of a secret organization off
campus, consisting of several cells that held regular meetings.
The primary cell included Yusuf Zaynal, Nuri Rufa'il, Darwish
al-Haydari, and 'Abd al-Fattah Ibrahim. Ibrahim was responsible,
in turn, for a second cell that included Muhammad Hadid, 'Ali
Haydar Sulayman, and Jamil Tuma. They opposed the Iraqi
government and pledged to work toward the elimination of
British influence and the real independence of Iraq. They also
called for raising the standard of living. Ibrahim recalls the
political association's early admiration for Mussolini, considered
the liberator of his country.

While Iraqi students in Beirut expended their energies in
activities that included political organization, both open and
secret, those who remained in Baghdad engaged in demonstrations. Husayn Jamil and 'Abd al-Qadir Isma'il, who had become
close friends in 1924 while they were pupils at al-Markaziyya

8. Sati' al-Husri, *Mudhakkirati fi'l-'Iraq, 1921–1941* (Beirut: Dar
al-Tali'a, 1967), p. 35.

9. 'Abd al-Ghani al-Mallah, *Tarikh al-Haraka al-Dimuqratiyya
fi'l-'Iraq fi Nisf Qarn* (Baghdad: Wizarat al-I'lam, 1975), p. 123.

10. Interview with Ibrahim.

(Central) Secondary School, were part of a group that was instrumental in the student demonstrations of 1926, 1928, and 1930.

In 1926 opposition arose among Shi'i students to the publication of a book entitled *Al-Dawla al-Umawiyya fi'l-Sham* [*The Umayyad State in Syria*] by a Lebanese history teacher at al-Markaziyya School, Anis al-Nusuli. It was alleged that al-Nusuli betrayed bias in his exposition of the battle of Karbala, in which the Imam Husayn had been killed. The Minister of Education dismissed al-Nusuli and banned his book, thus giving Jamil and Isma'il an opportunity to demonstrate in favor of freedom of thought. They organized a large protest demonstration of students of the Teachers' Training College. Teachers at both the college and the secondary school signed a letter of protest to the government and marched through the streets of Baghdad demanding al-Nusuli's reinstatement.

As a punishment for those involved, the Minister of Education dismissed all Syrian and Lebanese teachers who supported al-Nusuli. In addition, four students, including Jamil, were expelled for leading the demonstration and attacking the police; eighteen students, including Isma'il, were also suspended for varying periods of time. However, when petitions were addressed to the King and the Prime Minister and the matter was discussed in Parliament, a reprieve was granted: all students who had been expelled were allowed to return to their studies within a month.[11]

Anti-British sentiment triggered another incident at the al-Markaziyya School in 1926. An English teacher told his students, who included Jamil and Isma'il, that because the British wanted them to be "civilized," the Iraqi people were "stupid" for not welcoming the Anglo-Iraqi treaty of January 1926 (which legitimated Britain's mandate over Iraq for the next twenty-five years in return for the incorporation of Mosul in the mandate).[12] He said it was their "ignorance" which prevented them from appreciating what Britain was trying to achieve; he castigated the

---

11. Al-Mallah, *Tarikh al-Haraka al-Dimuqratiyya fi'l-'Iraq*, p. 81. Jamil attributes the student return to public pressure while al-Husri attributes it to his influence with the King. See al-Husri, *Mudhakkirati fi'l-'Iraq*, p. 557.

12. Interviews with Husayn and Jamil.

leaders of the opposition as "fools and donkeys." These insults led Isma'il and Jamil to press their classmates to protest to the headmaster and the Ministry of Education. They urged other students to boycott the teacher's class, and, eventually, the students went on strike and refused to attend any classes at all. When Isma'il and Jamil won the support of other faculty members, the headmaster asked the Ministry to remove the offending teacher. He was transferred. This success encouraged Isma'il and Jamil to deepen their involvement in political activities. At the same time, the fact that the government gave way under popular pressure showed the strength of the nationalist movement.

At the end of January 1928, a second round of demonstrations took place, this time against the visit of Sir Alfred Mond, a leading British Zionist who was director of Imperial Chemical Industries and chairman of the Economic Board of Palestine.[13] It was rumored that King Faysal, who had known Mond in England, had invited him to Baghdad to discuss the construction of an oil pipeline to the Mediterranean.[14] Some of those who participated in the al-Nusuli affair were shocked when they learned that such a prominent Zionist would not only visit Iraq but also engage in political and commercial activities; in particular, there were rumors that he intended to promote Zionist activities in Iraq.[15] Husayn Jamil decided to oppose the Mond visit.

Jamil and Isma'il went to work preparing banners and slogans. They recruited fellow students at the Law College, the Teachers' Training College, and al-Markaziyya School. On the day of Mond's arrival, a huge crowd assembled at the Maude Bridge over which Mond's party would presumably pass on its way from the airport to Baghdad. It is said that some twenty thousand people also paraded in the main street; they blocked passing cars and raised anti-Zionist placards while the police tried

13. Colonial Office, *Report by His Britannic Majesty's Government on the Adminstration of Iraq for 1928* (London: HMSO, 1929), p. 21; Khayri al-'Umari, *Hikayat Siyasiyya min Tarikh al-'Iraq al-Hadith* (Cairo: Dar al-Hilal, 1969), p. 175.

14. Talib Mustaq, *Awraq Ayyami, 1900–1958* (Beirut: Dar al-Tali'a, 1968), p. 188.

15. Interview with Jamil.

in vain to disperse them.[16] The British police commissioner, with an armed contingent, met Mond at the airport and escorted him safely over back roads to the residence of the High Commissioner.[17] Although the crowd succeeded in preventing Mond from passing through the heart of the city, they clashed with the police. A number of people were injured and several were arrested, among them 'Abd al-Qadir Isma'il.

Eighteen of the students who had organized the demonstration, including Jamil and Isma'il, were expelled from school while others were suspended. But, once again, appeals to the King and the government by fellow-students and members of Parliament worked their magic: the government reinstated the students in the next academic year. This incident was a landmark in the growth of popular opposition to the political system and a blow against British influence. It also brought students and teachers to the very center of the opposition movement in the country.

The growing influence of these young nationalists was demonstrated in the third round of demonstrations, which expressed their opposition to the Anglo-Iraqi treaty of July 30, 1930. Even though the 1926 treaty allowed for long-term British rule, London now concluded that it was in its interests to exchange the mandate for a treaty relationship and to sponsor Iraq's admission to the League of Nations. However, opposition parties and leaders declared the treaty binding the Iraqi monarchy to Britain unacceptable and sent protests to the King, prominent Arab and world leaders, and the League of Nations.

Iraqis of all stripes—liberals, socialists, communists, Arab nationalists, and some of the more traditional political leaders—believed the treaty compromised Iraq's sovereignty and independence. It allowed the British to establish air bases in important areas of Iraq, called for standardization of tactics and methods between the Iraqi and British armies, and allowed British officers to be used as advisers in all Iraqi military offices. Iraq also was obliged to provide facilities for the passage of British troops

16. Al-'Umari, *Hikayat Siyasiyya*, p. 175. See also 'Abd al-Razzaq al-Hasani, *Tarikh al-Wizarat al-'Iraqiyya* (Sidon: Matba'at al-'Irfan Press, 1970), vol. 2.

17. Al-'Umari, *Hikayat Siyasiyya*, p. 175.

through Iraqi land and airspace and in its waters.[18]

In order to ensure ratification, Prime Minister Nuri al-Sa'id decided to hold new elections between July 10 and November 10. The opposition, led by Ja'far Abu'l-Timman, leader of al-Hizb al-Watani (the National Party), and Yasin al-Hashimi, leader of Hizb al-Ikha' al-Watani (Party of National Brotherhood), decided to boycott the elections. Husayn Jamil, just graduated from Damascus Law School, and 'Abd al-Qadir Isma'il, in his final year at Baghdad Law College, together with many of their student friends, printed leaflets calling for a boycott of the elections because the treaty was a "pseudo-legal" tool in the hands of Britain to serve its interests.[19]

Isma'il joined by Khalil Kanna, Jamil 'Abd al-Wahhab, Yunis al-Sab'awi and Fa'iq al-Samarra'i applied for a permit to hold a protest rally in the center of the city. Despite the government's refusal to grant the permit, a large crowd responded to a second leaflet displayed on walls all over the city. Blaming Britain for all ills, it called on the people to close shop and attend the rally in a peaceful demonstration. The crowd defied the police and marched to the headquarters of Abu'l-Timman's National Party and assembled at the Haydar-Khana Mosque, a center for popular protests.[20] The police tried to disperse the crowd and made many arrests. The leaders who had signed the leaflet, including Isma'il, were sentenced to six months' imprisonment, others to three months'. But once again the government relented. On appeal, the sentences were reduced and, since the defendants had already been held several weeks, they were all released. Opposition leaders such as Abu'l-Timman, al-Hashimi, and Naji al-Suwaydi had taken part in a campaign against the court decision in the press and in Parliament, which bore fruit in the final release of the student leaders.

18. Muhammad Mahdi Kubba, *Mudhakkirati min Samim al-Ahdath, 1918–1940* (Beirut: Dar al-Tali'a, 1965), pp. 38–40. Also see *Sawt al-'Iraq*, July 27, 1930.

19. Al-'Umari, *Hikayat Siyasiyya*, pp. 339–347.

20. 'Abd al-Razzaq 'Abd al-Daraji, *Ja'far Abu'l-Timman wa Dawrahu fi'l-Haraka al-Wataniyya fi'l-'Iraq*, 2nd ed. (Baghdad: Dar al-Hurriyya, 1980), pp. 308–356.

THE EARLY FORMATIVE STAGE

Of the founders of the Ahali group, 'Abd al-Qadir Isma'il was the only one to remain in Iraq until his graduation from Baghdad Law College in June 1931. He soon renewed his friendship with Husayn Jamil when the latter returned from Damascus, where he had taken his law degree. Thereafter, the two met regularly to discuss the political situation in the country and their plans for the future. They seem to have agreed on most major issues and shared the same drive to achieve their ambitions. They felt the need for a newspaper that would be ideological rather than commercial, and, since no existing newspaper represented their political beliefs or even came close, they decided to publish one of their own.[21] They had already helped to edit various journals and periodicals and had written articles and short stories. Because they had no interest in government employment and maintained a continuous and close interest in Iraqi politics, it was natural that they sought to publish a paper that would "lead our countrymen along the road to independence, democracy, freedom, and equality."[22]

Isma'il, who was then employed at the directorate of the Port Authority in Basra, regularly met with 'Abd al-Fattah Ibrahim (recently returned from the United States where he had studied at Columbia University for a year after his graduation from AUB in 1929) and talked about the plan to publish a newspaper.[23] Ibrahim found Isma'il and Jamil, who were three years his junior, somewhat simple and unpolished. They had focused their attention on Iraq's political situation and were obsessed with the British presence to the virtual exclusion of everything else. Despite this, Ibrahim promised the support of his friends and former classmates at AUB, including Nuri Rufa'il, Jamil Tuma, 'Ali Haydar Sulayman, Ibrahim Baythun, and 'Abd Allah Bakr. In particular, Ibrahim eagerly awaited the return from the London School of Economics of Muhammad Hadid, with whom he had formed close ties in Beirut. Ibrahim and Hadid had adopted socialism as

---

21. Al-Chadirchi, *Mudhakkirati*, p. 23. See also Khalil Kanna, *al-'Iraq, Amsuhu wa Ghaduhu* (Beirut: Dar al-Rihani, 1966), p. 53.

22. Interview with Jamil.

23. Husayn, *Tarikh al-Hizb al-Watani al-Dimuqrati*, pp. 3–4.

the "first article of faith" and were more interested in Iraqi affairs than in Arab nationalist ideas and politics, the main focus of most Iraqi students.[24] The two were similar in character and shared the same political ideas. Ibrahim knew that he could work well with Hadid. Indeed, a balanced partnership was envisioned: Ibrahim would be the ideologist, Hadid the strategist, Jamil the journalist, and Isma'il the activist. In fact, Hadid returned to Baghdad in October 1931 and was immediately approached by Ibrahim. Hadid agreed to participate, and the four contacted Khalil Kanna, a lawyer, who also agreed to join; Ibrahim Baythun joined the group one day before the first issue appeared.[25]

In July 1931, Husayn Jamil was granted a permit by the Ministry of Interior to publish the newspaper. As the owner and manager, he chose the name *al-Ahali* for two main reasons. First, because *al-Ahali* means "the people," it implied that the paper took the side of the populace as contrasted with existing newspapers which generally represented the government's point of view. Second, the name conformed with the paper's ideological principles, which they called *al-sha'biyya* or populism. It may have been that they were also influenced by the opposition to tyranny and suppression voiced in the Egyptian Wafdist press, of which *al-Ahali* newspaper was the most prominent.[26] They could not, in any case, have chosen *al-Bilad (Country)* as their name, for that newspaper already existed and, in fact, had the widest circulation of the time.[27]

The first issue of *al-Ahali* appeared on January 2, 1932, only one day before the expiration of the permit to publish. Under the paper's name appeared the words "a universal political daily newspaper, published by a team of young people." A flaming torch appeared next to the motto: "the welfare of all the people above all; our paper is the people's paper, it sees their welfare above all other goals." Although long, somewhat repetitious, and perhaps naive, the paper's definition of "people's welfare" in its first issue bears quotation at length:

24. Khadduri, *Political Trends in the Arab World*, pp. 105–110.
25. Husayn, *Tarikh al-Hizb al-Watani al-Dimuqrati*, pp. 3–4.
26. Al-'Umari, *Hikayat Siyasiyya*, p. 6.
27. *Ibid.*

. . . . everything that is useful and beneficial to the majority of the citizens of this country, such as the improvement of the standard of living, the achievement of material and spiritual security, the establishment of a stable and healthy political and economic order, the utilization of the population's intellectual talents and its economic and other resources for the people's maximum benefit.

In order to bring this about the country needs individuals who are prepared to work unostentatiously and derive their happiness and satisfaction from this struggle rather than from palaces and wealth. These are the young people with firm beliefs and clear objectives who are prepared to devote their lives to the service of their people in all spheres of political, ideological, and economic activity to achieve goals for which the paper has been published.

We at this newspaper do not support any existing political party. We follow our own free will and support what we believe to be beneficial to the majority and the common good. But this in no way implies any hatred or resentment toward other parties . . . we are after the truth wherever it is and we devote this paper to the cause of truth.

We are publishing this paper because we appreciate the importance of journalism and its great influence. We recognize that newspapers can function as a school for society, developing individuals all through their lives, enlightening them and showing them the right way or, alternatively, misleading them. Newspapers can be the means either of building up or of ruining a society.

Hence, the people have the right to demand that newspaper publishers should be unselfish, and believe that their duty is to serve the country, having truth and frankness as the motto of their profession.[28]

In the same issue, on page 3, the paper further clarified its identity and objectives. In seeking to find a cure for the present

28. *Al-Ahali,* January 2, 1932.

150

backward condition of society, the paper declared it intended to publish daily Iraqi and foreign news, to discuss modern thoughts and ideas, and to translate and summarize the works of modern philosophers and contemporary writers.[29] Until the middle of 1937 it consisted of six pages, but from 1942 to 1946, only four. Special sections were devoted to various sectors of society, such as labor, youth, and women.

Another important section, "News From All Parts of Iraq," concentrated on the needs and complaints of the people, particularly in the poverty-stricken country areas. It showed the appalling living conditions of the rural poor and the injustices inflicted upon them by the *shaykhs* and corrupt government officials. Such information was provided by volunteer correspondents from all over Iraq, of whom one of the most famous was the reporter from Nasiriyya, Yusuf Salam Yusuf, who later, under the codename "Fahd," became the Secretary-General of the Iraqi Communist Party.[30] At least one page was devoted to "Latest Telegrams and Cables" which carried the most recent news from around the world, concentrating particularly on the plight of oppressed peoples, revolutionary struggles for independence by national liberation movements against repressive systems such as the Indian struggle against British rule, and the progress, development, and achievements of the Soviet Union.

About half a page was devoted to the Arab countries. This brought news of the fight against Zionism and colonialism in Syria, Egypt, North Africa, and Palestine, and also reported evidence of democratic progress in Egypt and Syria in the context of the development of political parties and parliamentary institutions. Another half page was devoted to "Reformist Turkey and Iran," emphasizing the progress achieved and reforms undertaken by both countries. A further section was devoted to various economic theories, giving an analysis of world economic conditions generally in the context of Iraq's own economic conditions and problems. A concluding section concerned public health matters and common diseases.

29. *Ibid.*
30. Interviews with Husayn Jamil and 'Abd al-Qadir Isma'il.

151

Although the editorial staff of *al-Ahali* worked together on the production of the paper, each member supervised different sections. Because Isma'il lived in the building where the newspaper was published, he became in effect the resident manager. He supervised overall, day-to-day control of the technical side of production and wrote and edited the "Story for Today." His brother, Yusuf Isma'il, was editor of the Telegrams and Cables section, while 'Abd al-Fattah Ibrahim, in addition to contributing to the daily editorial, was responsible for the sociological, historical, and political articles, which focused on ideological interpretations of populism and included the translation of various articles and books. Hadid concentrated on economics and finance, in addition to translations. Jamil helped to manage the paper, acting as an editor, and he also wrote on legal and public affairs. 'Ali Haydar Sulayman, who had known Ibrahim at AUB, contributed historical and political articles and critical commentaries under the pen-name Shamali ("Northerner")—a reference to his Kurdish background—or "The Young Historian."

A significant development was the association of Kamil al-Chadirchi with the newspaper in 1933. A liberal politician from a well-known aristocratic family, he had been a member of the executive committee of Yasin al-Hashimi's Hizb al-Ikha' al-Watani and the editor of the party newspaper. However, disillusioned with several of his colleagues for compromising with the authorities and accepting high positions in government and believing that he no longer fitted the Arab nationalist mold (with its implied acceptance of the *status quo* within Iraqi society), he resigned from Hizb al-Ikha' in 1933 and was attracted to the Ahali group. He contacted first Ibrahim and then Isma'il and began to meet regularly with them at *al-Ahali*'s offices and in his home. By 1934 he had become one of the outstanding editors of the newspaper, although his influence had already been felt with the advocacy of *sha'biyya*.[31]

An unofficial editorial committee was composed of the founders (Ibrahim, Hadid, Isma'il, and Jamil) and later al-Chadirchi. They suggested appropriate topics, which the group as a whole would analyze, with the writing of the main editorial then

31. Al-Chadirchi, *Mudhakkirati*, p. 27.

assigned to one of them. After it was written, it was normally looked over or corrected by one or more of the group. The editorials were always clearly and precisely written according to a method that never changed. A long and obvious title indicated the subject, and then the body of the article analyzed the problem before suggesting a solution. In contrast to most of the writing of the time that favored rhetorical flourish, nothing was superfluous or exaggerated in the writing. Another novel practice was the omission of the names of contributors. This was particularly suited to *al-Ahali*'s purposes; if the writers were anonymous, they would be safe from prosecution. It also encouraged aspiring writers to contribute articles without fear of being found out, losing their jobs, or being transferred to remote parts of the country.

Although fairly sophisticated, *al-Ahali* always remained in contact with popular aspirations. It consistently attempted to explain political systems and ideologies, and to simplify terms in order to make for easier and more digestible reading. The "Story for Today," for example, was sometimes part of the literature and art page and was generally fictional. But these stories accurately reflected social, economic, and political conditions in Iraq, contrasting the suffering of the workers with the idle and unproductive lifestyle of the upper classes. Progressive writers such as 'Abd Allah Jaddu', Lutfi Bakr Sidqi, Husayn al-Rahhal, 'Abd al-Wahhab al-Amin, Qasim Hasan, Mustafa 'Ali, Yusuf Matti, and 'Abd al-Qadir Isma'il wrote many short stories for the newspaper. In addition, it published translations of the works of such international writers as Tolstoy, Maupassant, Shaw, Goethe, Gorki, and Chekhov. From the very start, studies of the development of various schools of political thought and ideology appeared, explaining and analyzing their characteristics, and so too did translations of the biographies of such national leaders as Gandhi, Nehru, Lenin, and Stalin.

THE IDEOLOGY OF THE AHALI GROUP

The ideological beliefs and principles of the group and its members have been variously characterized. Majid Khadduri describes the founders as a circle of young men who keenly felt that political power was in the hands of elderly men who had paid little or no attention to social and economic problems. The group, advocating essentially the principles of the French Revolution, stressed democracy and liberalism in particular.[32] Other observers have described it as a "meeting ground for socialists and liberal reformers"[33] and its ideas as a mixture of liberal principles of the French Revolution and various kinds of socialism.[34] Some Arab nationalists charged that the group's program threatened to undermine the Arab social order,[35] whereas Marxists described members as "Mensheviks" because they called for sweeping social reforms without advocating violent revolution or class struggle.[36]

On October 8, 1932, al-Ahali carried an editorial which pointed out that the ideology of al-sha'biyya was a combination of and derivation from a number of different ideologies:

> It is wrong to follow one single ideology or principle, neglecting useful features of other ideologies. It is our duty to create our own road to follow in dealing with our own political and social conditions.[37]

This eclecticism can be traced back to the early 1920s when a progressive socialist circle first began to meet in Baghdad to discuss Marxism and socialism. The group was known as al-Ruwwad (The Pioneers) and its founder was Husayn al-Rahhal, who had returned to Iraq after spending some six years in Europe between 1913 and 1919, mainly in Germany where he had witnessed the Spartacist uprising.[38] He later visited India, where

32. Khadduri, *Political Trends in the Arab World*, p. 105.

33. Eliezer Be'eri, *Army Officers in Arab Politics and Society* (New York: Praeger, 1970), p. 17.

34. 'Abd al-Rahman al-Bazzaz, *Muhadarat 'an al-'Iraq min al-Ihtilal hatta'l-Istiqlal* (Baghdad: Matba'at al-'Ani, 1967), p. 37.

35. Fadil al-Barrak, *Dawr al-Jaysh al-'Iraqi bi Harakat al-Difa' al-Watani wa'l-Harb ma' Biritaniyya* (Baghdad: Dar al-'Arabiyya, 1979).

36. Al-Daraji, *Ja'far Abu'l-Timman*, pp. 362–363.

37. *Al-Ahali*, October 8, 1932.

38. A.L. al-Rawi, "al-Mukawwinat al-'Ula li'l-Fikr al-Ishtiraki fi'l-'Iraq," *al-Thaqafa al-Jadida* [Baghdad], No. 59 (March 1974), pp. 182–290.

he probably came into contact with Indian communists.[39] He was a firm believer in socialism, and was well-versed in many foreign languages, thus enabling him to translate articles on Marxism and socialism for his friends and followers. Another outstanding figure in this group was Mahmud Ahmad, the cousin of 'Abd al-Fattah Ibrahim and 'Abd al-Qadir Isma'il, who had visited India in 1919 and was influenced by the revolutionary ideas he found there. He was also in contact with leaders of the labor movement and witnessed their strikes and demonstrations.[40] Ahmad was one of the foremost orators of the Iraqi revolt of 1920 against the imposition of the British mandate and was a novelist of note. He was greatly influenced by the writings of a group of Lebanese socialists, particularly Yusuf Ibrahim Yazbuk[41] with whom he corresponded. He told Yazbuk, who was one of the founders of the Syrian-Lebanese Communist Party, in a 1929 letter that he had been spreading socialist thought in Iraq since 1922, and that his novels described social conditions in Iraq and expressed the socialist aspirations of his fellow writers.[42]

Ahmad and al-Rahhal attracted politically conscious young men such as 'Abd Allah Jaddu', Mustafa 'Ali, Muhammad Salim Fattah, 'Awni Bakr Sidqi, and 'Abd al-Hamid Rif'at, who formed the nucleus of al-Ruwwad. They met daily in an old cafe in Baghdad which became a center for young people for discussions on political and social issues; Ibrahim and Jamil attended many of these gatherings.[43] In 1924, al-Ruwwad published the first social-

---

39. Hanna Batatu, *The Old Social Classes and Revolutionary Movement of Iraq: A Study of Iraq's Old Landed and Commercial Classes and of its Communists, Ba'thists and Free Officers* (Princeton: Princeton University Press, 1978), pp. 60–62.

40. Al-Rawi, "al-Mukawwinat al-'Ula li'l-Fikr al-Ishtiraki," p. 187. See also Batatu, *The Old Social Classes and Revolutionary Movements of Iraq*, chapter 12. Batatu seems to concentrate his attention on Husayn al-Rahhal, while Jama'at al-Ahali put him on a par with Mahmud Ahmad. Khadduri points out that Ahmad may have been the first one to be attracted by socialist thought: *Political Trends in the Arab World*, p. 104.

41. Khadduri, *Political Trends in the Arab World*, pp. 101–105.

42. *Ibid*, p. 105.

43. Interviews with Ibrahim and Isma'il; also al-Rawi, "al-Mukawwinat al-'Ula li'l-Fikr al-Ishtiraki fi'l-'Iraq," p. 187.

ist newspaper in Baghdad—*al-Sahifa (The Journal)*. Its editors wrote to Cairo and Paris pleading for literary contributions and for magazines and books that would help to refine their thinking. The Wafd Party of Egypt was also a source of inspiration.[44] The Iraqis drew on the thinking of Egyptian leaders in their revolt of 1919 to help bolster their own thinking in the revolt of 1920.

Two Lebanese intellectuals who had migrated to Egypt were particularly influential. One was Shubli al-Shumayyil (1860–1917), a medical doctor, who drew up the first proposal for an Egyptian socialist party and expounded on socialist principles. He wanted the government to control wages, improve public facilities, manage schools, and provide employment, but to avoid class warfare. He did not advocate state takeover of the means of production or the abolition of private property, but spoke of an eventual world socialist revolution. However, he stressed peaceful change and called for cooperation among nations.[45]

The other important figure was Niqula Haddad (1870–1954), who edited *al-Muqtataf (Selection)* for several years, wrote a book about socialism, and called for political democracy and individual freedoms. He, like al-Shumayyil, had studied pharmacy at AUB and moved to Egypt after 1900, where he published and edited various magazines and newspapers and wrote several articles and novels. In 1920, Haddad authored a book on socialism *(al-Ishtirakiyya)*, following Salama Musa who had published a pamphlet on the same subject in 1913.[46] Haddad advocated democratic socialism and the single tax on property. He held that political democracy was a prerequisite to economic democracy, and that capitalism rather than socialism restricted freedom.[47] In

44. Al-Umari, *Hikayat Siyasiyya*, p. 6.

45. Khadduri, *Political Trends in the Arab World*; pp. 91–92; and Hourani, *Arabic Thought in the Liberal Age, 1798–1939* (London: Oxford University Press, 1970), pp. 248–253.

46. Donald M. Reid, "The Syrian Christians and Early Socialism in the Arab World," *International Journal of Middle Eastern Studies*, 5, No. 2 (April 1974), p. 184; and Kemal Abu Jaber, *The Arab Ba'th Socialist Party: History, Ideology and Organization*, (Syracuse: Syracuse University Press, 1966).

47. Reid, "The Syrian Christians and Early Socialism in the Arab World," p. 186; Abu Jaber, *The Arab Ba'th Socialist Party*, p. 3.

1923, Mahmud Ahmad wrote Haddad asking him to supply his group with socialist literature because "we want to be socialists, educated socialists . . . and we cannot find the books to satisfy our aspirations."[48] He added that he had read the works of Haddad and Musa on socialism, and he urged him to translate recent books on Marxism and asked for copies of *al-Ishtiraki* newspaper, the organ of the Egyptian socialist party.

Al-Shumayyil and Haddad were close associates of Salama Musa, a member of a distinguished Coptic family who helped edit *al-Hilal (The Crescent)* and *al-Mustaqbal (The Future)*. His close contacts with the Fabians in Britain and *l'Humanité* in Paris and his advocacy of a humanist state socialism, as well as his many books and articles, made him one of the most respected and influential thinkers of his time. Khadduri states that "it is Musa who provides the most direct link between the Syrian Christian socialist pioneers of the early twentieth century and the Arab socialists of the 1960s."[49] In 1921, Musa had joined with other Egyptian intellectuals to form the Egyptian Socialist Party. But he resigned a year later in anger when the Executive Committee transformed it to the Egyptian Communist Party. His socialist ideas were "a mixture of Utopian and Marxist Socialism" and "a combination of parliamentary democracy and state socialism."[50]

Egyptian magazines and newspapers, particularly *al-Muqtataf* (it reached Baghdad as early as 1876),[51] *al-Mustaqbal*, *al-Usur*, and *al-Hilal*, which these and other intellectuals contributed to or edited, had immeasurable influence on Iraqi intellectuals who followed them closely. These magazines and their contributors popularized new ideas including free thought, socialism, and the scientific approach, and they promoted secularism. They engaged in open and heated debates on these issues and other modern ideas.

48. Al-Rawi, "al-Mukawwinat al-'Ula li'l-Fikr al-Ishtiraki," pp. 187–188.

49. For more details, see Khadduri, *Political Trends in the Arab World*, pp. 93–94.

50. *Ibid.* See also Hourani, *Arabic Thought in the Liberal Age*, pp. 246–247.

51. *Ibid.*, p. 247.

After the First World War, the Iraqis began to learn about communism and the October revolution in the Soviet Union. They were also influenced by social democracy in Britain, France, and Germany, and, in particular, students who went to the London School of Economics were deeply influenced by Harold Laski and the Fabian Society.[52] The early Fabians were more concerned with positive action as a means of regenerating society than with precise theoretical formulations, and had a spirit of optimism and faith in humanist values, just like the young founders of *al-Ahali*. Other similarities between the Fabians and al-Ahali group include rejection of the notion of class struggle or violent revolution and the belief that social change can be achieved by raising consciousness through programs of mass education. Both groups used publications to promote their ideas, and both restricted membership to selected individuals who pledged to serve their society to the best of their ability, to contribute monthly dues, and to attend the society's meetings.

Al-Ahali's founders were also deeply interested in the progress of the Indian independence struggle, which they likened to the Iraqi struggle for independence. But while Gandhi's idealism made a deep impression, Nehru's more practical vision and aggressive style also influenced the aspiring Iraqis. A comment on Nehru published in the *Guardian* newspaper in 1979 seems appropriate as a comment on the young editors of *al-Ahali* in the 1930s:

Nehru, for all his attachment to Western manners and ideas, was an epitome of Indian, indeed Asian, nationalism. There was no contradiction in his attempt to imbibe all that was good in Western throught while fighting British imperialism nor in his parallel efforts to combine in himself the best values of both Western liberalism and Marxist ideology.[53]

52. Margaret Cole, *The Story of Fabian Socialism* (Stanford: Stanford University Press, 1961), p. 218. For the Fabians' views on anticolonialism, see Martin Kingsley, *Harold Laski, 1893–1950; a Biographical Memoir* (London: Gallencz, 1953), pp. 64–68, 90–91.

53. I. Malhotra, "Nehru," *The Guardian* [London], May 28, 1979.

THE CONCEPT OF AL-SHA'BIYYA

In its manifesto, the Ahali group said of *al-sha'biyya:*

There is no comprehensive definition of *al-sha'biyya.* It is a view of the problems which members of society face in their different walks of life. These problems are divided, according to their nature, into political, economic, and social. *Al-sha'biyya* attempts to ensure security, prosperity, and progress for society.[54]

For years afterwards, the founding fathers tried to elaborate on this statement, but their supplements tended to reflect individual preferences and the basic ideology, by its nature, remained vague.

The term "populism" was adopted to avoid the label of "socialism," *al-ishtirakiyya,* which, at the time, carried a stigma in Iraq and the Arab world. In addition, the fact that some of the members came from conservative and well-to-do families (for example, Hadid came from a wealthy Mosul family), and their concern to avoid any adverse public or family reaction, may have contributed to this caution. Furthermore, the group, and 'Abd al-Fattah Ibrahim in particular, were eager to devise a new ideology which they could call their own.[55]

With the help of others, Ibrahim edited two small volumes in which the ideas of *al-sha'biyya* were discussed. The first volume focused on the history of political thought from the Greeks to the Bolshevik revolution and served as an introduction to the second volume, which outlined the basic principles and became *al-Ahali's* working manifesto.[56] The ideas of the group were also propounded in the various issues of its newspaper and in other tracts, articles, and books by the founders, their colleagues, and al-Chadirchi. One of the earlier articles written in the newspaper under the title, "We are Populists," concluded:

We are populists and what we mean by populism is a common concern for the interests of the majority of the

---

54. *Minhaj al-Sha'biyya.*
55. Khadduri, *Political Trends in the Arab World*, p. 106.
56. *Ibid.*

people, who are the pillar of the structure of the state. We are populists, and the standard by which we judge everything is the interests of the people. Whoever sides with the people, we will support, and whoever opposes the people's interests we will fight.[57]

The doctrine of al-sha'biyya "laid the main stress on the people as a whole rather than the individual, but advocated in the meantime the protection of human rights such as liberty, equality of opportunity, and private property."[58] It rejected the capitalist system of free enterprise and advocated the adoption of a socialist system in which a modern state would guide the economy, pay proper attention to the health and education of the individual and recognize his right to a job, and reduce the economic disparities between social classes.[59] The group also wanted the achievement of complete and full independence of Iraq and of popular sovereignty through the establishment of a democracy by constitutional and gradual methods. But al-sha'biyya, while including democratic as well as socialist principles, was different from both since "in contrast to democracy it advocated a kind of collectivism, and, in contrast to Marxist theory, it did not admit the existence of class struggle or revolutionary process of change."[60] The group also recognized the institutions of religion and family and made patriotism (wataniyya), but not nationalism (qawmiyya), a basic tenet of its whole ideology. It believed nationalism was one of the methods used by the rulers to exploit the people and was responsible for imperialism and the domination of society by one class, whereas patriotism inspired the individual with loyalty to his country.[61] According to al-Ahali's manifesto, "the history of nationalism is full of blood, tyranny, and hypocrisy," whereas the record of

57. Al-Ahali, October 8, 1932.
58. Khadduri, Political Trends in the Arab World, p. 106. Note the striking similarity of these ideas with those of the Kadro movement on Turkey which began publishing a theoretical journal in January 1932 espousing a socialist collectivism that rejected class struggle.
59. Ibid. and interview with Jamil.
60. Ibid.
61. Ibid.

patriotism shows that it does not advocate aggression or social discrimination but recognizes, rather, the equality of all citizens.[62]

Al-Ahali's manifesto emphasized other basic tenents of *al-sha'biyya*. These were "security" (*al-itmi'nan*), which should be political in character; "prosperity" (*al-rafah*), which should be achieved by state control of the means of production; and "progress" (*al-taqaddum*), which should be brought about by free, universal education, free health care, a comprehensive insurance program, and women's emancipation. *Al-sha'biyya* emphasized the need for a representative parliamentary form of government in order to achieve these goals. The people would elect representatives from their own ranks; peasants would elect peasants to represent them, and workers would elect workers. This method was considered to be "real" (*haqiqi*) representation that would lead to genuine popular democracy. Those elected would be required to be "intelligent and honest men," not "professional politicians," if a truly democratic system was to succeed.[63] According to Ibrahim:

> Democracy was to achieve independence as well as social-ism. It would give the opportunity to every Iraqi to improve the quality of his life and his material standard of living. Peasants and workers would seek to improve their conditions, educate their children, organize themselves in trade unions, and demand higher wages and better working conditions. The Iraqi people wanted a sovereign state, free from foreign influence and interference.[64]

The founders of the Ahali group believed that backwardness resulted from the corrupt and stagnant political system, itself due to subordination to foreign powers. But they basically left unanswered the question of how their objectives could be achieved so long as the British were the ultimate authority and most of the public remained backward and uneducated. Ibrahim, probably the

---

62. *Mutala'at fi'l-Sha'biyya*, vol. 2, pp. 1–14.
63. *Ibid.*
64. Interview with Ibrahim.

161

most suggestive writer, opposed what he called "capitalist nationalism," which he compared to imperialism, and endorsed
"popular nationalism," which he associated with India. He dis-
approved of "superficial" dictatorship as typified by Turkey, Iran,
and South American countries whose regimes depended on the
military. After an early period of fascination with Italy's fascism,
he and the others turned against Mussolini because the Italian
fascists disregarded individual liberties; and while approving
much of its ideology, they rejected Russian communism because
it did not give proper emphasis to religion or the family.[65]

CONCLUSION

The Ahali group remained aloof from participation in the
practical side of Iraqi political life until it attracted the attention
of prominent political personalities such as Kamil al-Chadirchi.
Under his direction and influence, the group gained greater
cohesion and a new sense of direction. It also attracted other
well-known political leaders such as Abu'l-Timman and Hikmat
Sulayman, who, having become disillusioned with the policies of
the ruling elite, joined the group. However, the growing prominence of al-Chadirchi and his increasing influence over the group
led to a split with one of the group's outstanding founders, the
more radical 'Abd al-Fattah Ibrahim.[66] In 1933, the group inau-
gurated a wide campaign to eradicate illiteracy throughout Iraq by
establishing a cultural and political club named Nadi Baghdad,
and coordinated activities to boycott the foreign-owned electric
company in Baghdad. Finally, it formed a secret political organization called al-Jam'iyya al-Sha'biyya (al-Sha'biyya Society).

The success of these activities, which created a wide following in different parts of the country, combined with the wide-
ranging political connections and ambitions of al-Chadirchi,
Abu'l-Timman, and especially Sulayman, led the group to em-
bark on far greater participation in day-to-day Iraqi political
affairs. Beginning in 1935, it cooperated with other politicians in
intrigues with a number of tribal leaders that ultimately brought

65. See *al-Ahali*, March 29, 1932.
66. Khadduri, *Independent Iraq*, p. 73.

down the governments of 'Ali Jawdat and Jamil al-Madfa'i.[67] However, when Yasin al-Hashimi came to power in March 1935, his government was particularly vigorous in suppressing opposition parties and especially Jama'at al-Ahali. This drove it into an uneasy but vital alliance with General Bakr Sidqi, who led a strong faction in the army and was a friend of Hikmat Sulayman. The quick expansion of the Ahali group unexpectedly encouraged some army officers to give it support and to promise to implement its ideas by ousting the government. Consequently, the Ahali group and its leaders played a key, if hesitant, role in the preparation of Sidqi's military *coup d'état* of 1936, the first of its kind in Iraq or the Arab world.[68]

But despite its support of the coup and the fact that it held a majority in the Cabinet, its members were quickly relegated to the role of spectators. In general, two factions emerged: the Arab nationalists and the conservative groups, who were not in favor of major social and economic change; and the Ahali group, which wanted extensive social reform. Sulayman, with one foot in each camp, left the Ahali group and sided with Bakr Sidqi when the rift between the two groups could not be healed, and soon after the reformists were forced to resign. The experience proved disastrous for Ahali members. Their program of reform, which had been announced upon formation of the new government, was virtually ignored and their influence non-existent. They even feared for their lives because of an assassination plan apparently ordered by Sidqi himself. Furthermore, what association they had with Sidqi and the coup condemned them to the political wilderness for a long time to come; they were not acceptable to the other political factions, especially the pan-Arab faction that dominated the political stage until 1941.

By 1942, the local and international political situation became more favorable to the group's ideas and encouraged it to

67. Al-Hasani, *Tarikh al-Wizarat al-'Iraqiyya;* and Khadduri, *Independent Iraq*, pp. 50–52.

68. On the Ahali group's participation in the coup, see Edith and E.F. Penrose, *Iraq: International Relations and National Development* (London: Ernest Benn, 1978), pp. 88; and Phebe Marr, *The Modern History of Iraq* (Boulder: Westview, 1985), p. 71.

regroup, resuming publication of its newspaper but now calling it *Sawt al-Ahali (Voice of the People).* Its appearance in September 1942 signaled the resumption of Jama'at al-Ahali's political activities and a new stage in Iraqi political life. But ideological and personal factors soon reappeared and eventually divided the group into three main political parties: al-Hizb al-Watani al-Dimuqrati (National Democratic Party), which was led by Kamal al-Chadirchi and resembled the original social democratic Jama'at al-Ahali before the coup of October 1936; Hizb al-Ittihad al-Watani (National Union Party), which was headed by 'Abd al-Fattah Ibrahim and was to the left; and Hizb al-Sha'b (the People's Party), which was headed by 'Aziz Sharif, who had strong Marxist leanings, and was even further to the left of Jama'at al-Ahali. After the Second World War, *Sawt al-Ahali* became the party newspaper of the National Democratic Party. (It survived until October 1961 when al-Chadirchi, protesting the lack of freedom under the military government of the time, shut down the presses.)

The groupings that originated from al-Ahali remained active in Iraqi politics for some time and created the core of opposition to the monarchy. The result was two distinct and essentially conflicting camps in Iraq, with the monarchical government and its supporters in one, and the opposition, supported by the mass of the population, in the other. This polarization led to the increasing alienation of the government and the ruling class from the people and contributed significantly to the ease with which the *ancient régime* was overthrown in July 1958.

The significance of the newspaper and its influence on Iraqi political life, indeed, can hardly be exaggerated. It signalled the emergence of a new political trend, directed by a group of young men with fresh ideas and approaches to politics, society, and the economy. In addition to being "a thorn in the side of the government,"[69] *al-Ahali* established itself as "the spokesman of all revolutionary, patriotic, and progressive forces in Iraq."[70] It

69. Paul Knabenshue to Department of State, July 16, 1932, U.S. National Archives, Washington, D.C., 890g.00/209.

70. F. Vitol, "The Coup D'Etat Government in Iraq," *The Revolutionary East* [Moscow] (1937), translated into Arabic in *al-Thaqafa*

became the most prominent daily paper in the country.[71] This did not come about because of a shortage of other newspapers or simply because it was an opposition paper, but rather because it consistently maintained high standards in editorials, reporting, and investigation.

Ideologically, Jama'at al-Ahali has generally been described as leftist. It is important to note, however, that this description must be seen in the context of the period in which it emerged. What was considered leftist or radical in the 1920s and 1930s cannot be so described today. Yet it is true that the group was to the left of most political groups in Iraq at the time and advocated "welfare for all the people" without distinctions of wealth, birth, religion, or sect.[72] Reflecting popular demands, it called for sweeping social reforms and for limitations on land ownership, and stressed the need to protect the interest of the workers and peasants. These views were radical in the context of Iraqi politics in the 1930s[73] and, in this sense, the Ahali group may be seen as having encouraged the thinking of the next generation of political activists who founded the Ba'th Party.

al-Jadida (June 1971), p. 58.

71. Khadduri, *Independent Iraq*, pp. 69–70.

72. Khadduri, *Political Trends in the Arab World*, p. 106.

73. Salah al-Aqqad, "Tatawwur al-Yasar fi'l-'Iraq," *al-Katib* [Cairo], No. 72 (March 1967), p. 98.

PART IV

Politics and Diplomacy in the Middle East

CHAPTER NINE

The Communist Movements in the Arab World

TAREQ Y. ISMAEL

Although the specific experience of communist parties in the Arab world has varied from country to country, a certain common evolution underlies their individual histories. The key to this commonality lies in the two powerful, and often contradictory, forces which have shaped a distinctly "Arab" communism: the Soviet-dominated world communist movement, and cultural, economic, and political conditions in the Arab world.

With the exception of the Sudanese Communist Party, all the major communist parties in the Arab world were founded under the aegis of the Comintern. All looked to a world communist movement dominated by the Communist Party of the Soviet Union (CPSU) for political and ideological leadership and material support. With this acceptance of the Soviet orthodoxy came an uncritical acceptance of the canons of Soviet Marxism-Leninism-Stalinism and a concomitant failure to formulate independent social analyses of the specific conditions within the Arab world.

However, as Soviet support for, and control over, Arab communist parties began to weaken after the death of Stalin, Arab communism was forced to attune itself to local circumstances and sensitivities. It was through this process, through the interaction of forces of conformity and adaptation, that a distinctive Arab communism was born.[1]

FOUNDATION OF THE ARAB COMMUNIST PARTIES

In contrast to Europe where socialist ideas had been generated and acted upon amid the immediate social pressures of rapid industrialization, the Arab world first encountered Marxism at the end of the nineteenth century on a purely intellectual level, as a result of study in or of the West or through contact with European socialists in the Middle East. Early Arab Marxists were mesmerized by the works of Marx and Engels. However, they failed to adapt Marxism to the conditions of the Middle East where capitalism was only incipient; where the national bourgeoisie was weak (too weak to accumulate capital), merely acting as a comprador for Western imperialist interests; where semifeudal production relations still prevailed; and where a class-conscious proletariat was almost nonexistent and had very limited ties with the peasantry. Marx and Engels had written very little about the unique problems of the Arab territories under Turkish rule. Indeed, despite the "Arab awakening" of the time and the growing importance of Arab nationalist resistance to Turkish (and later, European) control of the Middle East, the early Arab Marxists also acquired and transmitted to their successors Marx and Engels' devaluation of nationalism per se as an effective and progressive social force. Thus, there was an enormous gulf between the primary object of Marxian analysis—the evolution of European capitalism—and the conditions of Arab society. The early Arab Marxists did very little to bridge this gap in their own analyses. Instead, their distaste for foreign capitalist domination and desire for a socialist society seemed sufficient reason for them to embrace Marxism. Confined to very limited intellectual circles and politically unorganized, early Arab Marxism was insignificant other than as a precursor.

1. The author wishes to acknowledge gratefully the research assistance of Rex Brynen, and financial assistance from a University of Calgary Research Grant. A more detailed examination of the themes discussed in this essay can be found in my *Arab Communist Parties* (forthcoming).

This situation changed with the Bolshevik Revolution. The success of Leninism as a political and organizational strategy attracted the attention of Arab Marxists and others. The power of the new Soviet government sparked hopes that a new ally might be found in the struggle against European imperialism. This latter perception was soon confirmed when, within a month of the October 1917 revolution, the Council of People's Commissars issued an "Appeal to the Muslims of Russia and the East" in which it denounced all European and Czarist partition plans in the Middle East.[2]

On January 19, 1918, the Soviet government established a Commissariat for Muslim Affairs. A Central Bureau of Muslim Communist Organizations was set up in November 1918 by a regional Muslim congress meeting in Moscow. In November 1919, a meeting of Muslim communists passed a resolution calling for the establishment of communist parties throughout the Muslim world. Subsequently, the Third International issued a call to the Muslim people to attend a congress devoted to a discussion of the Muslim peoples to be convened at Baku.[3] Only three Arab nationalists, none of them communists, attended the Baku congress, which met in September 1920. As a result of this conference, the Communist International issued a Manifesto to the Peoples of the East stressing:

> Peoples of the East! What has England done to Mesopotamia and Arabia? Without any ado, she declared these independent Muslim countries to be her own colonies, drove from the land the former owners, the Arabs, deprived them of the best fertile valleys of the Tigris and Euphrates, deprived them of the best pastures indispensable to subsistence, took away the richest oil resources of Mosul and Basra, and thus depriving the Arabs of all means of subsistence, counted on starvation to make them her slaves.

> What has England done to Palestine, where, at first, to please the Anglo-Jewish capitalists, she drove the Arabs from their

2. I. V. Kluchnikov and A. Sabanin (eds.), *Mezhdunarodnaia Politika noveishego vremeni v dogovorakh, notakh i deklaratsiakh* (Moscow, 1925–1928), vol. 2, pp. 94–96.

3. *Izvestiia* [Moscow], July 3, 1920.

lands in order to transfer these lands to the Jewish settlers, and then in order to provide an outlet for the discontent of the Arabs, she turned them against the very Jewish settlements she had established, sowing discord, hostility, and resentment among the various tribes, weakening both sides, in order to rule and govern herself?

What has England done to Egypt, where the entire native population already for the eighth decade is sighing under the heavy yoke of the English capitalists, a yoke even heavier and more ruinous for the people than the past yoke of the Egyptian pharaohs, who with the labour of their slaves built the huge pyramids?[4]

Following its establishment in March 1919, the Comintern first directed its attention toward Palestine, where its representatives attempted to establish a communist party among Jewish immigrants (many of them Russian) there. Within a year, according to official British sources, Bolshevik propanganda and ideas began to appear in Palestine,[5] and in September 1920 a communist group, the Jewish Socialist Workers' Party (Mifleget Poalim Sozialistim Ivrin or MOPSI), was formally established by Jewish immigrants associated with the left wing of the Poale Zion (Workers of Zion) movement. Although the group subsequently collapsed in 1921 amid disputes over its attitude to Zionism and under the strain of suppression by the British authorities, its cadres played a major role as midwives to the birth of later communist parties.

A new communist organization—the Palestine Communist Party—soon emerged from the wreckage of MOPSI, and by 1922 it had assumed a distinct identity and an anti-Zionist stance. The Palestine Communist Party was admitted into the Comintern in 1924, receiving at that time instructions to increase its Arab membership.[6] In the Maghreb, the Tunisian and Algerian Com-

4. *Kommunisticheskii Internatsional* [Petrograd], December 20, 1920, p. 3147.

5. Bols to Foreign Office, June 1, 1920, FO 371/5114, p. 2.

6. Walter Laqueur, *Communism and Nationalism in the Middle East* (New York: Praeger, 1956), p. 81.

munist Parties began as extensions of the French Communist Party soon after the First World War, and continued as such until the 1930s. They gained autonomy in 1934 and 1936 respectively. In Egypt, the Socialist Party of Egypt, established in 1921, transformed itself into the Egyptian Communist Party and was admitted to the Comintern in 1923. In Lebanon and Syria a Beirut-based Marxist study circle created in 1920 (the "Spartacus Group") later formed the core of the communist party. The Communist Party of Syria and Lebanon was formally established in 1925, and joined the Comintern in 1928. The party subsequently divided into separate Syrian and Lebanese branches during the Second World War.

The origins of the Communist Party of Iraq are less clear. Some historians[7] contend that Comintern representative "Abboud" undertook correspondence with Yusuf Salman Yusuf in 1929, leading to the creation of the al-Nasiriyya Marxist circle. Soon afterwards, Yusuf Salman Yusuf and others formed the shortlived Jam'iyyat al-Ahrar al-la-Diniyya (Non-Religious Freemen's Society) on Marxist principles. The group kept in touch with Abboud, who sent them the Beirut Marxist periodical *al-Shams*. Others[8] suggest that Comintern agent Butrus 'Ali Nasir (also known as Comrade Petroff), posing as a tailor, arrived in al-Nasiriyya in 1929. He converted Yusuf Salman Yusuf to Marxism and enabled him to travel to Moscow to study Marxism-Leninism-Stalinism. Yusuf returned home in 1939 to lead the Iraqi Communist Party, adopting the pseudonym "Fahd," while Comrade Petroff, his mission accomplished, returned to Moscow. Still others assert that Iraqi Marxists tried to establish a communist organization in the 1920s, even before the creation of trade unions. This account also acknowledges Fahd's conversion to Marxism in al-Nasiriyya in 1929.[9] A fourth view glosses over

---

7. 'Abd Allah Amin, *Shuyu'iyya 'ala al-Safud* (Beirut, 1974), p. 81; and 'Abd al-Jabbar al-Jubburi, *al-Ahzab wa'l-Jam'iyyat al-Siyasiyya fi'l-Qutr al-'Iraqi, 1908–1958.* (Baghdad: Dar al-Hurriyya, 1977), pp. 108–109.

8. Qadri Qalaji, *Tayrubat 'Arabi fi'l-Hizb al-Shuyu'i* (Beirut: Dar al-Katib al-'Arabi, 1959), p. 23.

9. Su'ad Khayri, *Min Tarikh al-Haraka al-Thawriyya fi'l-'Iraq,*

these early tentative attempts at communist organization in Iraq. Instead, it emphasizes the importance of a meeting of Iraqi communists held on March 31, 1934, at which those present agreed to organize a Committee for Combatting Imperialism and Exploitation (Lajnat Mukafahat al-Isti'mar wa'l-Istithmar), led by 'Asim Flayah.[10] At the end of 1935, the Committee decided to adopt the name of the Communist Party of Iraq (CPI) and issued its periodical, *Kifah al-Sha'b* (The People's Struggle) with hammer and sickle emblazoned on its masthead.

The Fourth Congress of the Comintern (Moscow, 1924) urged the creation of politically conscious cadre in the East—including the Arab world—able to lead the progressive national movement against the colonial powers. Accordingly, further representatives were dispatched to Palestine, Iraq, Syria, Lebanon, and Egypt during the 1920s and 1930s to propagate Marxist-Leninist ideas, recruit members, and send the most promising to Moscow for further training in the University of the Toilers of the East, which had been established in Moscow in 1921. Among those who graduated from this institution were 'Asim Flayah, member (and unofficially first General Secretary) of the Iraqi Communist Party; Yusuf Salman Yusuf, official founder and General Secretary of the Iraqi Communist Party; Khalid Bakdash, General Secretary of the Syrian Communist Party; and Nikola Shawi, General Secretary of the Lebanese Communist Party.

CONSOLIDATION OF ARAB COMMUNISM

By the 1930s, communist organizations had been established in all the most important Arab countries. Yet despite the pervasiveness of the sort of social exploitation and imperialist domination that the communist movement opposed, recruitment and expansion were slow. At no time during this period did the membership of any one party exceed a few hundred; in some cases it could be numbered in the tens.

1920–1958 (Baghdad: Matba'at al-Adib, 1973), vol. 1, p. 55.

10. Author's interview with 'Asim Flayah, Baghdad, February 18, 1959.

A number of factors contributed to this weakness. The level of industrialization remained so low that the proletariat accounted for only a small fraction of the total population, and was characterized by a low degree of class consciousness. The labor movement was only beginning to organize, and was encountering stiff opposition from mandate governments when it attempted to enter the political sphere (as it inevitably did). Thus Arab communism lacked access to the organized proletarian base which had been the theoretical and political underpinning of European socialism. The ideological appeal of Marxism-Leninism was too narrow and too complex to attract the masses, and this was often compounded by direct attacks on religious beliefs which only further alienated popular opinion. Furthermore, because of their social exclusion or greater level of education, the memberships of many of the parties consisted of a disproportionate number of minorities—Jews in Palestine, Jews and Christians in Egypt, Christians in Syria and Lebanon, Jews and Kurds in Iraq. Many European immigrants also played an important role in the Egyptian and Palestinian parties. This further diminished their appeal to Muslim Arabs. Finally, the governments of the area—whether colonial, mandatory, or Arab—opposed the expansion of communist influence and actively suppressed the nascent parties. While this suppression often added to the appeal of communism—the local population generally assuming that anything so disliked by colonial or mandate governors could not be all bad—it kept the parties small, fugitive, and underground.

Much changed, however, with the outbreak of the Second World War and especially with the entrance of the Soviet Union into the war on the allied side in 1941. In many areas, the authorities began turning a blind eye to communist activities, many of which were directed at building anti-fascist alliances or otherwise supporting the allied war effort. For their part the communist parties muted their revolutionary rhetoric. In Syria, for example, Khalid Bakdash set forth an exceedingly moderate social program during the election campaign of May 1943:

The issue for us in our opinion is not the establishment of a socialist system in Lebanon or Syria. All that we demand and struggle for with our few members of Parliament of both Syria and Lebanon is the introduction of some democratic

175

reforms accepted by all as necessary. . . . we have not demanded, do not demand now, and not even contemplate
socializing national capital and industry. On the contrary, we
wish that both national capital and industry should make
progress. We only want the improvement of the living
conditions of the national workers and democratic labor
legislation to regulate labor relations between employers and
employees. We promise the land owners that we shall not
demand in Parliament the nationalization of their land or
property. On the contrary, all we want is to help them by
demanding irrigation, the mechanization of agriculture, and
the importation of fertilizer. All we want of them is that they
should pity the peasant, and that an effort should be made to
help get the peasant out of his present state of poverty,
illiteracy, and disease. We promise the big merchants that we
shall not demand the confiscation of their trade no matter
how large it is, and we only want to put an end to specula-
tion. We shall support the small merchants and demand a
lightening of their big burden of taxes.[11]

The Arab communist parties benefited from the wartime
prestige and popularity of the Soviet Union and its preeminent
military role in the war in Europe. The war also stimulated a
rapid expansion of the level of industrialization in the Arab world
and a corresponding growth in Arab trade unionism. In Palestine,
for example, Arab trade union membership rose from 5,000 (1936)
to 20,000 (1945).[12] Here and elsewhere in the Middle East, the
communist parties forged close ties to many of the emergent
trade unions—indeed, played a significant role in their formation—and benefited accordingly. Because of such factors,
1941–1945 was a period of considerable communist expansion.
According to Arab communist sources, the membership of the
combined Syrian and Lebanese Communist Party alone increased
from 3,000 in 1941 to 23,000 in 1946.[13]

11. *Sawt al-Sha'b* [Beirut], May 9, 1943.
12. J. C. Hurewitz, *The Struggle for Palestine* (New York: Green-
wood Press, 1968), pp. 123, 189. This still only represented about 20
percent of Palestinian Arab workers.
13. Laqueur, *Communism and Nationalism in the Middle East*, p.
151.

Conditions deteriorated for the various Arab communist parties once more after the war, when state repression reappeared or intensified (Iraq and Egypt, 1946; Syria and Lebanon, 1948) in the context of the emerging cold war. Nevertheless, the increased visibility of the communist movement during the Second World War had helped in the dissemination of communist propaganda and the establishment of ties to the trade union movement. Moreover, the communist parties had utilized the opportunity of wartime semi-legality to centralize their organizations. Because of this, and because of its discipline compared to other oppositional parties (an organizational model that was to be copied by many), the communist movement was generally more resilient in the face of government repression, and found itself able to produce clandestine publications regularly. Although unable to penetrate the rural population, the communist parties had modest success in recruiting members of the better-organized and developed sections of the urban proletariat, and had significant success in gaining sympathizers among the small but influential ranks of teachers, civil servants, university students, and even in police and army circles.[14]

Throughout this period, the relationship of Arab communists with nationalist and other parties had varied. From their foundation in the 1920s until the Sixth Congress of the Comintern in 1928, these communists had in theory favored tactical alliances with bourgeois nationalist and democratic parties in the framework of a common front. In practice, however, the tiny size of the communist movement and the fact that nationalist parties had much more appeal to the general population undermined such an approach. Many Arab communist parties thus adopted a hostile

14. Hanna Batatu, in his seminal examination of the Communist Party and others in Iraq, has calculated that in the late 1940s 27.6 percent of the members of the Iraqi Communist Party were students; 9.7 percent, professionals; 9.1 percent, "white collar" (of whom 5.2 percent were civil servants); 6.7 percent, petty bourgeoisie; 2.6 percent, peasants; 25.7 percent, workers and semi-proletarians; and 15.6 percent, armed forces and police. See: Hanna Batatu, *The Old Social Classes and the Revolutionary Movements of Iraq; A Study of Iraq's Old Landed and Commercial Classes and of its Communists, Ba'thists, and Free Officers* (Princeton: Princeton University Press, 1978), pp. 1168–1171.

attitude toward potential allies in the struggle against Western imperialism. Yet this restiveness with the Comintern line indicated a degree of autonomy on the part of local parties.

With Stalin's ascendancy in the mid-1920s the Middle East became a slightly more important area of Comintern activity, and Arab communist parties gradually became subservient to Soviet foreign and domestic policy interests. This was manifest in more rigorous Arab communist adherence to Comintern policy. Indeed, there can be little doubt that Stalin conceived of the Arab communist parties primarily as an appendage of Soviet foreign policy and only incidentally as native groups seeking to bring about a socialist revolution in their countries. He was highly suspicious of genuinely popular and successful revolutionary groups, since such groups were correspondingly less reliant on Soviet assistance and hence less amenable to Soviet control. Instead, Stalin insisted on rigid discipline and tight Soviet control of foreign communist parties.

Thus, in 1928, when the bitter experience of the Chinese communists at the hands of the Kuomintang led the Sixth Congress to alter the Comintern position regarding "common front" tactics, the Arab communist parties were directed to follow suit. Henceforth, any cooperation with bourgeois groups against imperialism in the colonial and semi-colonial countries was to be carried out with the utmost caution: "bourgeois nationalism" was to be opposed, and the communist parties were to maintain the autonomy and pursuit of revolutionary goals at all times. The Sixth Congress also called on communist parties in the colonial world to work to obviate the need for a bourgeois-democratic stage of development and try to establish socialism directly.

Subsequently, in 1935, at the Seventh Congress of the Comintern, the colonial question receded into the background as Europe drew nearer to war and attention focused on the rise of Germany and Italy. At that congress, the Comintern reemphasized the utility of the United Front. European communist parties were directed to enter into alliances with social democratic forces against fascism and Nazism. In the colonial and semi-colonial areas, communist parties were once more called to ally with the reformist bourgeoisie in the struggle against imperialism, in accordance with a new slogan that stressed that "the work for the creation of an anti-imperialist front is the main task of the Communists."[15] Arab communist parties faithfully followed the new line by forging tactical alliances with many of the same parties that they had reviled since 1928. In Iraq, this was manifest in communist support for the military coup which overthrew the government in 1936. The eruption of war between the Soviet Union and Germany in 1941 and the wartime alliance with the West led the Soviet Union to dissolve the Communist International and suspend its support of Arab communist parties, which were generally left to their own resources and thus forced to make concessions to local conditions.

With the end of the Second World War, however, the dissolution of the wartime alliances and the onset of the cold war saw the reassertion of Soviet control over the Arab communist parties. In a series of speeches and addresses in 1947, Stalin and Andrei Zhdanov outlined the doctrine of rigid bipolarity. Arab communist parties were enjoined to sever Popular Front alliances with bourgeois national groups that had flourished during the war, and to reassert their independence and commitment to orthodox communist doctrines. In the international sphere, the decisive criterion distinguishing between the national progressive movement and reactionary national bourgeoisie was to be the respective attitude of each group toward the Soviet Union and the West. Only wholehearted acceptance of the Soviet Union as leader of the world proletarian movement could qualify a group for Moscow's approval and enable it to cooperate with the communists within the framework of a "Progressive Front." Neutralism was, in Stalin's eyes, tantamount to support for imperialism.

The most influential leader of the communist parties in the Arab world and Secretary General of the Syrian-Lebanese Communist Party, Khalid Bakdash, in his report to the plenary session of the Central Command of the Communist Party in Syria and Lebanon held in January 1951, adopted the orthodox Stalinist line fully:

The principal orientation of our effort and activity must be [directed] toward isolating the [Arab] nationalist bourgeoisie

15. Laqueur, *Communism and Nationalism in the Middle East*, p. 294.

and putting an end to its influence among the people. For this bourgeoisie, no matter how much the names of its parties may vary, uses its influence to deceive the people and turn it away from the revolutionary struggle; it works also for an understanding with imperialism.

We must work constantly also to unmask groups and parties claiming to be "socialist," such as the Arab Socialist Party, the Islamic Socialist Front, the Ba'th [Renaissance] Party in Syria; and the Socialist Progressive Party of Jumblat, etc. in Lebanon . . . , for through their seductive propaganda they constitute a danger to the growing democratic national movement against war and imperalism, feudalism, and exploitation. They try to exploit the increasing popular orientation toward socialism . . . they especially destroy [the effectiveness of our] slogans of "distribution of the lands of the feudalists and big landowners to the peasants," and they call for the buying-out of foreign companies . . . and the putting of these companies under the control of the reactionary, feudalistic government which serves imperialism. This they call "nationalization," etc. They also try to prevent the growth of popular sympathy for the world camp of peace and socialism led by the Soviet Union by calling for a so-called "third force" or "neutrality" between the two camps.[16]

The exertion of control over Arab communist parties by the Soviet Union had severe implications for their development. Arab communists followed a Soviet ideological line which often paid scant regard to objective conditions in the Arab world and which was subject to occasional shifts or even reversals as demanded by Soviet *realpolitik*. This was evident in the Arab communists attitude toward bourgeois democratic and nationalist movements, with the constant revision of position preventing them from ever building a truly effective anti-imperialist front, and permanently damaging relations with many nationalist forces. Moreover, in order to maintain ideological purity and political

16. "For the Successful Struggle for Peace, National Independence and Democracy We Must Resolutely Turn Towards the Workers and Peasants," abr. trans. from Arabic by Harold W. Glidden, *Middle East Journal*, 7, No. 2 (Spring 1953), pp. 206–221.

loyalty in the face of a constantly changing political line, the parties were forced to suppress deviant opinions. This served both to fragment the communist movement—by encouraging the formation of dissident groups—and to ensure its Stalinization at the core.

Palestine and Arab Communist Parties

The problems of rigorous Arab communist adherence to the Soviet position on issues of both revolutionary strategy and developments in the Arab world is nowhere more clearly illustrated than in the context of the Palestine question. For Palestinian Arabs, the inter-war influx of Jewish immigrants into Palestine and the declared aim of the Zionist movement and British government to transform the area into a Jewish national home represented a fundamental threat to their right of self-determination and national survival. The issue was also important in the broader Arab world, as Palestine had long held a special place in the Arab consciousness. It was a country at the crossroads of the Arab world, a land bridge between the Arab East and the Arab West, and it had figured prominently in centuries of Arab history, in part because of Jerusalem, a site holy to Muslim and Christian Arabs alike. Finally, events in Palestine seemed to encapsulate the injustices of European colonialism, and the cause of the Palestinian people became a symbol for the struggle of the Arab people as a whole.

For the most part, Soviet theorists and political leaders had also maintained a hostile attitude toward Zionism. Lenin, for example, condemned Zionism as "absolutely false and essentially reactionary."[17] Later, the Executive Committee of the Comintern described it as "the exponent of the exploiting, big power, imperialist oppressive strivings of the Hebrew bourgeoisie" which, through the Balfour Declaration and the Palestine Mandate, had been "converted into a weapon of British imperialism."[18] Following the rise of Stalin, however, theoretical posi-

17. V. I. Lenin, "The Position of the Bund in the Party" in *Collected Works* 7 (1903), pp. 92–103.
18. Executive Committee of the Comintern, November 20, 1930. Cited in Alden H. Voth, *Moscow Abandons Israel for the Arabs: Ten*

tions on the subject were increasingly subordinated to Soviet foreign and domestic policy interests, with little regard for Arab sensibilities. The Comintern and the CPSU issued directives on the matter; local communist parties were expected to follow these directives, regardless of local consequences.[19]

Before the Second World War, the Soviet Union's major link with the Palestine question had been through the Palestine Communist Party (PCP). The PCP had made little political progress during the 1920s: its "Jewish" character inhibited Arab recruitment, while its anti-Zionism was unpopular among many Jews. This dilemma was apparent in the party's publications, which (in Hebrew and Yiddish) stressed Arab-Jewish solidarity, and (in Arabic) militant anti-Zionism.[20]

At this time, the Palestine Communist Party (like other Arab communist parties) faithfully followed Moscow's instructions. Accordingly, early in 1929 the party initiated implementation of the Comintern Sixth Congress resolutions with their warnings against cooperation with national bourgeoisies. A campaign against the traditional, nationalist, Palestinian Arab leadership was launched, and joint class struggle by the Jewish and Arab proletariats emphasized. A few months later, the Jerusalem riots and Arab-Jewish fighting erupted, throwing the PCP into confusion, and provoking an acrimonious debate among Moscow's Middle East specialists.[21]

By September 1929, the Comintern had decided on a new course of action for the PCP. Henceforth, the party was to assume a vanguard role in revolutionary activity in Palestine. The party was also directed to increase its recruitment of Arab members and to purge its ranks of those who refused to accept the PCP's

Crucial Years in the Middle East (Lanham, MD: University Press of America, 1980), pp. 23–24.

19. For a discussion of the Soviet Union's changing attitude to Zionism see Walid Sharif, "Soviet Marxism and Zionism," *Journal of Palestine Studies*, 6, No. 3 (Spring 1977), pp. 77–97.

20. Laqueur, *Communism and Nationalism in the Middle East*, p. 81.

21. For details of this debate, see Walter Laqueur, *The Soviet Union in the Middle East* (New York: Praeger, 1959), p. 94.

new position. By 1934, the PCP Politburo did have a majority of Arab members. Despite this, the party generally failed in its efforts to achieve mass support from Palestinian Arabs. By the mid-1930s, many of the Palestine party's Arab cadres had turned to Palestine's pan-Arab Istiqlal (Independence) Party in pursuance of the struggle against Zionism and the British.

When the Palestine revolt of 1936–1939 broke out, the Soviet Union and the PCP largely supported it, thus causing the latter to lose many Jewish members. By the end of 1938, however, the Soviet Union's fight against fascism, combined with the pro-German sympathies of many Palestinian nationalist leaders, had led it to condemn the revolt's leader, Haj Amin al-Husayni, as a fascist agent. Subsequently, the PCP also expressed some concern about "Fascist infiltration" of the revolt.[22] The Mufti was partially rehabilitated in Soviet statements after August 1939 (and the Soviet-German Pact), only once more to be condemned following the German invasion of the Soviet Union in June 1941.[23]

By this time, the polarization in Palestine, the PCP's vacillation, and schisms within the party, effectively sounded its death-knell. Separate Jewish and Arab organizations thereafter arose in its place. In any event, the intensity and focus of the Soviet Union's Palestine policy changed with the war and its aftermath. After 1941 Moscow, anxious to secure Jewish support for the Soviet war effort, effectively suspended its criticism of Zionism. Indeed, a few statements and actions by Soviet spokesmen during this period even seemed to be supportive of Zionist aspirations in Palestine.[24] Nevertheless, such a suspension of Soviet anti-Zionism appeared tactical rather than ideological in nature, and with the war's end Soviet condemnation of Zionist aspirations returned.

22. Laqueur, *Communism and Nationalism in the Middle East*, p. 99.

23. Laqueur, *The Soviet Union and the Middle East*, pp. 118, 126–127.

24. J. B. Schectman, "The USSR, Zionism, and Israel," in Lionel Kochan (ed.), *The Jews in Soviet Russia since 1917*, 2nd ed. (London: Oxford University Press, 1972), pp. 114–115.

When, in 1947, Britain referred the Palestine issue to the United Nations, however, the Soviet Union supported Zionist demands for Jewish statehood and voted for the UN Partition Plan. This did not indicate sympathy for Zionism; rather, it was the result of several political considerations. First, the conservative pro-Western Arab governments were all staunchly anti-Soviet in their international relations and anti-communist in their domestic policies, vigorously suppressing communist parties and groups after the Second World War. Second, the Zionists were anti-British and frequently left-wing; the Soviet Union may have looked forward to a weakening of the British position in the Middle East and the establishment of a progressive Jewish state in Palestine. Third, the Soviet Union may have sought to aggravate differences between Britain and the United States over the Palestine issue.[25] Walter Laqueur has suggested a fourth, rather novel, reason: the Palestine issue might have had so little relevance to the geopolitical preoccupations of the Soviet leadership that the pro-partition policy was proposed and accepted at a relatively junior level.[26]

Regardless of the reason, Moscow supported the establishment of the Jewish state. *De jure* recognition was granted to Israel within two days of the unilateral Zionist proclamation of the creation of Israel on May 14, 1948. The subsequent Arab armed mobilization and declaration of war in defense of Arab Palestine was condemned by Moscow as "an aggressive war against the legally constituted state of Israel,"[27] and it can safely be assumed that Czech arms deliveries to Israel during the 1948 war received Moscow's approval.[28]

The reversal of the Soviet position in 1947–1948, needless to say, threw the Arab communist parties into confusion. In Palestine the PCP, which had heretofore opposed partition, withdrew

---

25. Arnold Krammer, "Soviet Motives in the Partition of Palestine 1947–48," *Journal of Palestine Studies,* 2, No. 2 (Winter 1973), pp. 117–118.

26. *The Soviet Union and the Middle East,* pp. 146–147.

27. *Pravda* [Moscow], August 28, 1948.

28. Arnold Krammer, "Arms for Independence: When the Soviet Bloc Supported Israel," in Walid Khalidi (ed.), *From Haven to Conquest* (Beirut: Institute for Palestine Studies, 1971), pp. 745–754.

from the fight. Other parties, many of which had expended considerable effort in establishing popular anti-Zionist organizations in support of the Palestinians, fell into disarray. Deep divisions appeared in all parties as their respective leaderships sought to bring dismayed and angry members into line behind the new Soviet position. Many cadres quit, or formed splinter groups.

Eventually all Arab communist parties lent some degree of formal support to the Soviet plan. But the costs were high. Much public sympathy for the communist movement disappeared, or was redirected into other radical movements. Government repression intensified. The communists further widened the division between themselves and the nationalist left. Arab communist recognition of the foundation of the State of Israel continued for two decades thereafter, despite popular opinion. Indeed, when the Palestinian resistance emerged in the 1960s to take up the struggle for Palestinian liberation, Arab communists condemned it as a "reckless trend."[29] Only toward the end of the 1960s did Arab communist parties begin to criticize their earlier uncritical support of the Soviet position on Palestine, a position which had been and continued to be dictated by great power considerations. By then, however, it was too late: most of the damage to their position had already been done.

ARAB COMMUNIST PARTIES AFTER STALIN

Stalin's death in 1953 ended an era for the Arab communist parties. In the years that followed, the communist movements in the Arab world underwent a slow and subtle change, emerging from the shadow of rigid Soviet control and assuming a revised ideological orientation which has essentially continued into the 1980s. This transformation can, in turn, be attributed to at least two major developments in the post-Stalin period: the nationalist

29. G. Batal, A. Rashal, and M. Harmel, "Vital Tasks of the Arab National-Liberation Movement," World Marxist Review, 11, No. 9 (September 1968), p. 53. A similar appraisal can be found in the statement issued by the Arab communist parties after their August 1968 conference. See al-Hayat [Beirut], August 21, 1968.

challenge in the Arab world, and the changing nature of the world communist movement.

The Nationalist Challenge

The death of Stalin coincided with the intensification of the decolonization process and the concomitant growth of leftist, nationalist movements and governments in the emerging Third World. In the Middle East, this process was manifest in the toppling of the Western-oriented regimes in Egypt (1952), Syria (1954–1956), and Iraq (1958), and the launching of armed struggle against colonial occupation in Algeria (1954). The social, political and strategic character of the region thus began a fundamental transformation.

In the forefront of this struggle against colonialism and neo-colonialism stood a number of broadly socialist Arab nationalist parties and forces, notably Nasirism, the Arab Ba'th Socialist Party, the Arab Nationalist Movement, and the Algerian Front de Liberation Nationale (FLN).[30] In their socialism, such groups threatened to co-opt the Arab communists' political programs and potential popular constituency—even though their socialism was, in many ways, a response to the communist parties and to the socio-economic issues that they had raised. In their nationalism and commitment to pan-Arabism, these groups stood in stark contrast to the anti-nationalist Arab communists—and more in line with grass-roots Arab opinion.

Because of their ideological rejection of Arab nationalism as a bourgeois ideology and the perception of nationalist politics as a threat to the communist movement, the Arab communist parties set themselves in opposition to the nationalist tide. In Syria, Khalid Bakdash and his party opposed the formation of the United Arab Republic (UAR) with Egypt in 1958, and went into exile rather than accept dissolution. In Iraq, the CPI willingly allowed itself to be used by President Qasim as a counterweight to his Arab nationalist opponents, who favored unity with the UAR in the aftermath of Iraq's 1958 revolution. It continued to

30. On the emergence of this Arab "new left" in the 1950s and 1960s, see Tareq Ismael, *The Arab Left* (Syracuse: Syracuse University Press, 1976).

cooperate with Qasim until 1959–1960 when he grew alarmed at its strength—perhaps 20,000 members, and tens (or hundreds) of thousands in communist-dominated women, youth, or trade union organizations[31]—and moved to limit its power. In Algeria during the 1940s and early 1950s—indeed, until the very eve of the revolt in 1954—the Algerian Communist Party favored the gradual integration of the broad Algerian masses into the mainstream of French metropolitan life, i.e., the policy of the French Communist Party with which it was affiliated. The outbreak of the armed revolution took Algerian communists by surprise. They clung to their original theses for years afterward, gradually losing contact with the Arab nationalist sentiments of the people. It was not until much later, after Algerian independence in 1962, that the party admitted its decisive error in not casting its lot at the outset with the FLN and the national liberation movement.

The Arab communist parties' anti-nationalist stance and their continued support for the partition of Palestine earned them the hostility of Arab nationalists. 'Abd al-Nasir, faced with communist opposition to Arab unity in Syria and Iraq, labeled the Arab communists as "[foreign] agents who neither believe in the liberty of their land nor their nation, but only do the bidding of outsiders"[32] and severely suppressed them. In a similar vein, Michel 'Aflaq, a founder of the Ba'th, stated:

> We consider the communist party to be destructive for two reasons. One, in its deceptive socialism, it promises the Arab nation the achievement of its basic needs, while its basic aim is to tie the destiny of the Arab people to another state—namely Russia. Two, [it is destructive] in its anti-nationalist stance.[33]

In Algeria the communists were suppressed and forcibly integrated into the FLN. In Iraq, despite past repression at the hands

31. Batatu, *The Old Social Classes and Revolutionary Movements of Iraq*, pp. 896–897.

32. President 'Abd al-Nasir's speech in Damascus (March 11, 1959), in *President Gamal Abdel-Nasser's Speeches and Press-Interviews* (Cairo: UAR Information Department, n.d.), p. 123.

33. *Fi Sabil al-Ba'th*, 2nd ed. (Beirut: Dar al-Tali'a, 1963), p. 210.

of Qasim, the CPI mobilized its supporters to defend the government in the face of the Ba'th-led coup of February 1963. After
fierce fighting, however, Qasim's regime collapsed. Scores of
important communists (including First Secretary Salam 'Adil)
were killed, and thousands more imprisoned by the victorious
nationalists.[34]

Moreover, and more importantly, the Arab communists'
anti-nationalist stance cost them considerable public sympathy.
As the Lebanese Communist Party report of July 1968 later noted,
through communist opposition to Arab nationalism and to Arab
unity and especially communist condemnation of the UAR, "the
party's popularity in 1959 as well as all the alliances it succeeded
in building during the period 1954–1959 were again destroyed
because of the immature leftist [i.e. anti-nationalist] line."[35]

The Changing World Communist Movement

After Stalin's death the nature of the world communist
movement changed in at least three major ways. The first of these
was related to the restructuring of Soviet foreign policy. After
1953, Soviet foreign policy became increasingly concerned with
fostering good relations with the emergent Third World. The
"rigid bipolarity" of the late Stalin era was replaced by pragmatism as the basis of Soviet diplomacy. The Soviet Union now
pursued a course of active cooperation with moderately progressive regimes whose main redeeming feature was opposition to
Western imperialism. With this change in policy also came a shift
in the Soviet Union's theoretical position: the nature and role of
national liberation movements, national democracy, and the
transition to socialism were all reassessed.[36]

34. "In Memory of Hussein Ahmed Al-Radhawi (Salem Adil)," and
"The February Events in Iraq," *World Marxist Review*, 6, No. 4 (April
1963), pp. 36–39.

35. Communist Party of Lebanon, *Khamsa wa 'Ushrun 'aman min
Nidhal al-Hizb al-Shuyu'i al-Lubnani* (Beirut: Matba 'at al-Amal, 1968),
p. 126.

36. As Walter Laqueur has noted, such changes in the USSR's
theoretical position on these issues followed (rather than preceded) the
reorientation of Soviet foreign policy: *The Soviet Union and the Middle
East*, p. 156.

Nowhere in the Arab world was this transformation more evident than with regard to Soviet-Egyptian relations. In 1952, the Egyptian revolution had been described in Soviet analyses as the work of a "reactionary officers' group linked with the USA" who, after seizing power, had set in motion the "savage repression of the workers' movement."[37] By 1955, however, opposition to the Baghdad Pact and Egypt's obvious importance within both the Arab world and the growing non-aligned movement had spurred Moscow to forge close and friendly links with President 'Abd al-Nasir. The extent of this relationship was manifest in the signing of numerous trade agreements, cultural exchanges, and Soviet approval of the momentous Czech-Egyptian arms deal. Furthermore, the Egyptian government—which had been described as "madly reactionary, terrorist, anti-democratic, [and] demogogic" only a year earlier—was recognized in Soviet statements as playing a progressive role in the Egyptian national liberation movement and the Arab struggle against imperialism.[38]

These shifts were accompanied by a second development—a change in the relationship between the Arab communist parties and the Soviet Union. With Stalin's death, the Soviet Union's grip over the Arab communist parties relaxed significantly. Equally important, however, was the communists' declining importance as mechanisms of Soviet foreign policy. Until the Twentieth Congress of the CPSU, the Arab communist parties could usually count on the support of the Soviet government and Communist Party for their activities, which were after all primarily directed against colonialist or anti-Soviet neo-colonialist regimes. After the Twentieth Congress, however, Moscow often paid little attention to the needs and conditions of the Arab communists. Instead, pragmatic considerations were allowed to determine the

37. *Bol'shaya Sovetskaya Entsiklopediya*, vol. 15, p. 460 in *Mizan Newsletter*, 2, No. 11 (December 1960), p. 2.

38. L. N. Vatolina, *Imperialistacheskaya Borba sa Afriku i Osvoboditelnoye dvishenie narodov* (Moscow, 1954), pp. 97ff, cited in: Laqueur, *Communism and Nationalism in the Middle East*, p. 262. On the changing Soviet view of Egypt, see *Mizan Newsletter*, 2, No. 11 (December 1960), pp. 2–5.

cordiality of Soviet relations with Arab regimes—relations to which Arab communist activities could be as much hinderance as help. This in turn often placed the Arab communist parties in an awkward position: on the one hand, the Soviet Union maintained cordial relations with the government in question, while on the other hand the government was often actively engaged in suppressing the local communist party. The new pragmatism apparent in Soviet policy also made it difficult for Arab communists to provide justification for sudden shifts in Soviet policy dictated by tactical considerations, a situation which often proved highly embarrassing.

The fate of the Egyptian Communist Party illustrates this dilemma well. The Egyptian communists were often suppressed by 'Abd al-Nasir, who saw in them a domestic political threat, opposition to the United Arab Republic, and an obstacle to Arab unity. After 1955, however, the Soviet Union enjoyed excellent relations with Egypt. It thus made little effort to assist the Egyptian communists, and although Khrushchev did denounce 'Abd al-Nasir's suppression of communist activity before the CPSU Twenty-first Congress in 1959, he also stressed that "differences in ideological views must not interfere with the development of friendly relations [between the Soviet Union and Egypt] and the business of a joint struggle against imperialism."[39] Khrushchev also denied that Moscow had any responsibility for, or control over, communist parties outside the Soviet Union. Six years later, it looked on as the Egyptian Communist Party dissolved itself and entered 'Abd al-Nasir's Arab Socialist Union (ASU). Indeed, some Soviet analysts seemed willing at that time to ascribe to the ASU the role of Egypt's revolutionary "vanguard"—a title and task normally reserved for *bona fide* communist parties.[40]

A third change in the nature of the post-Stalin communist movement was a tendency towards greater ideological pluralism.

39. Khrushchev's statement on the Middle East before the Twenty-first CPSU Congress, translated and excerpted in *Mizan Newsletter*, 1, No. 2 (February 1959), Appendix A.

40. See for example: G. Mirsky, "United Arab Republic: New Stage," *New Times*, 48 (December 1, 1965).

Although "monolithic communism" had always been a myth, the emergence of the Sino-Soviet split in the late 1950s made it even more so, and offered Arab and other communists a somewhat greater range of ideology and support from which to choose.

The success of the Chinese revolution in 1949 had made little impact on Arab communist parties at the time, and despite the insight that might have been gained regarding the processes of revolution and socialist transformation in underdeveloped and agrarian nations, the Arab communists had paid little attention to the Chinese experience. The only exception was a small faction of the Egyptian communist movement, which adopted the Maoist version of Marxism-Leninism in 1949, and continued to expound it thereafter. When the dispute between Moscow and Peking became more apparent after the Twentieth Party Congress, and particularly in the 1960s, the vast majority of Arab communists supported Moscow. This occurred despite the fact that the Chinese position on issues such as Palestine and Arab nationalism was, particularly after the 1967 Arab-Israeli war, far closer to the general Arab view than was the ambiguous Soviet position. Admittedly, there were some minor exceptions to this general pattern: the Egyptian faction mentioned above continued to expound Maoism, while the Party of Socialist Revolution (Hizb al-Thawra al-Ishtirakiyya) and the Arab Communist Party (al-Hizb al-Shuyu'i al-'Arabi) were formed in August 1964 and February 1968 by pro-Chinese elements of the Lebanese and Syrian Communist Parties respectively. There was also a split within the Sudanese Communist Party in late 1964 and early 1965, culminating in the formation of the pro-Chinese al-Hizb al-Shuyu'i al-Sudani al-Thawri (the Revolutionary Sudanese Communist Party). In addition, some observers reported a significant decline in recruitment by the established communist parties among students and workers as a result of dissatisfaction with their pro-Moscow orthodoxy.[41] Yet none of the pro-Chinese splinter groups ever managed to attract a significant following. The Egyptian group was disbanded in 1956, while the Lebanese,

41. Ibrahim Salama, "al-Shuyu'iyyun al-'Arab," *Malaf al-Nahar* [Beirut], No. 15, June 21, 1968.

Syrian, and Sudanese splinters withered away within a few years of their foundation.

Reflecting this support for the CPSU, the communist parties of the Arab world passed a strongly pro-Soviet and anti-Maoist "Resolution on the Situation in the World Communist Movement" at their May 1967 general meeting. In this they stated:

> The Mao group is making feverish attempts to poison the relations of friendship, cooperation and solidarity between the new Arab states and the Soviet Union and other socialist countries, to undermine the relations between the Arab countries themselves. It concentrates on combatting the Communist parties of the Arab countries as it continues its fruitless attempts to split their ranks. It tries to foil efforts toward cooperation between revolutionary and progressive forces throughout the Arab world and in each particular Arab country, and makes futile attempts to strengthen adventurist trends in the Middle East, playing into the hands of the imperialists and of Israel.[42]

In the same statement the Arab communists also reaffirmed their adherence to "the principles of Marxism-Leninism and the general line of the world Communist movement," and vowed to "continue the fight against the splitting and subversive activity of the Mao Tse-tung group."

At the same time, the Sino-Soviet split did provide Arab communist parties with somewhat greater leverage over the Soviet Union in the event of ideological or policy disputes. Arab communists could seek to pressure Moscow by subtly hinting at a move closer to Peking; for its part, the People's Republic was almost always willing to support potential dissidents from the Soviet line. This approach was adopted by Khalid Bakdash of the Syrian Communist Party in 1958–1961, when he made overtures to China in order to indicate his displeasure with Soviet support of the UAR. Similarly, in Iraq the radical "Central Leadership" faction of the CPI, which rejected accommodation with the governments of Presidents 'Abd al-Salam and 'Abd al-Rahman 'Arif and which criticized Soviet support of the Iraqi regime,

42. *Information Bulletin* [Prague], 100 (1967).

192

accepted Chinese support in its fight with the CPSU-supported "Central Committee" group for control of the party.

Transformation of the Arab Communist Parties

The beginning of the Arab communist parties' post-Stalin ideological transformation came, as it did for many communist parties, with the Twentieth Congress of the Soviet Communist Party in February 1956, when Khrushchev's denunciation of Stalinism knocked many of the Arab communists' ideological underpinnings from underneath them. At that time, a number of Soviet analysts called for a fundamental reappraisal of communist theoretical formulations regarding the national liberation question in general and the Middle East in particular.[43]

Thereafter, major changes in the Soviet Union's theoretical position on Third World liberation were manifest at the CPSU Twenty-first (1959) and Twenty-second (1961) Congresses, and at the 1960 Conference of Communist and Workers' Parties in Moscow. The theoretical pronouncements of the 1960 conference, attended by no less than 81 communist parties including party representatives from Algeria, Iraq, Jordan, Lebanon, Morocco, Syria, Sudan, and Tunisia, can be summarized as follows:[44]

1. The doctrine of peaceful coexistence between the socialist and capitalist states was advanced, with the struggle between the two systems to be pursued through competitive rather than combative means.

2. Neutralism, and the peaceful roads to national liberation and socialism, were recognized as legitimate options for Third World nations.

3. The progressive role of a "broad national front" in the struggle for national liberation was emphasized. Such an alliance would include elements from all classes (including the national

43. Wayne Vucinich, "Soviet Studies on the Middle East," in Ivo Lederer and Wayne Vucinich (eds.), *The Soviet Union and the Middle East: The Post World War II Era* (Stanford: Hoover Institution Press, 1974), p. 182.

44. *Pravda*, December 2, 1960. "Statement of Conference of Representatives of Communist and Workers' Parties," *Ibid.*, December 7, 1960.

bourgeoisie): "all elements of the nation that are ready to fight for national independence and against imperialism."

4. Stress was placed upon the "formation and consolidation of national-democratic states" in the Third World, i.e., independent states antagonistic to Western imperialism. Such states could progress to socialism without passing through a capitalist stage, along the "non-capitalist road to socialism."

Over the next few years, these theoretical formulations underwent further elaboration and development at numerous Communist Party conferences and seminars. Some changes were made: for example, the concepts of "revolutionary democracy" and later "socialist orientation" were formulated to deal with the theoretical dilemma caused by the adoption of socialist programs by non-communist governments such as those of the UAR and Algeria. In essence, however, the revised doctrine enunciated in the first decade following Stalin's death became the ideological basis of Soviet policy towards the Third World for the next quarter century.

This ideological revision was largely accepted by Arab communist parties, partly because of Soviet influence, but also because it resulted in theoretical formulations more in line with conditions in the Arab world. Hence, when in September 1964 the various Arab communist parties held their first general conference, their statements reflected recognition of the "non-capitalist road to development" and acceptance of the need for "an exchange of experience and the establishment of the closest relations of co-operation between progressive parties, organizations, and movements in the Arab world."[45] Similarly, a seminar on "Africa—National and Social Revolution," which was held in Cairo in October 1966 under the auspices of the Egyptian journal *al-Tali'a* and the Czech journal *World Marxist Review*, saw Arab communist representatives discussing the problems encountered in African national liberation struggles within the theoretical framework set forth at the 1960 Moscow conference and at the Twentieth, Twenty-first, and Twenty-second Congresses of the CPSU.[46] At their 1968 general conference, the Arab communist

45. *Ibid.*, December 11, 1964.
46. For a summary of the Cairo seminar, see: *World Marxist*

parties produced significant praise for non-communist Arab regimes:

> . . . countries like Egypt and Syria are marching toward a new path of development, a path characterized by great blows to the remnants of feudalism and capitalism. They have achieved great social and economic transformation, which could develop (with the right subjective and objective conditions) into the foundation of these countries' transformation to socialism according to Marxist-Leninist principles.[47]

What was more significant, however, was the degree to which the Arab communist movements began to engage in independent theoretical analyses, either rejecting elements of the Soviet orthodoxy or adding new elements of their own. With the relaxation of Soviet dominance over (and concern with) the Arab communist parties, they had been forced to stand on their own feet. One effect of this was greater inter-party cooperation in the Arab world, manifest in the holding of annual Arab communist general conferences after 1964. A second effect was an increased willingness on the part of Arab communists to undertake theoretical criticism and to attempt innovation. Such innovation should not be overstressed since the Arab communist parties continued to adhere generally to Moscow's position. Nevertheless, given their slavish behavior during the Stalin era, the situation after his death represented a significant change.

The advantages of independent communist action in accordance with local conditions were perhaps most evident in the Sudan. From 1944 until Sudanese independence in 1956, the communist movement operated under the rubric of the Sudanese Movement for National Liberation, and fought for liberation of the country from British colonial rule. The Sudanese Communist Party itself was not formally established until a month after independence, and thus crystallized at a time when Moscow was preoccupied with 'Abd al-Nasir's Egypt and when Soviet control

Review, 9, No. 12; 10, No. 3 (December 1966–March 1967).

47. "Pronouncements of the Communist and Workers' Parties Concerning Conditions in their Countries," *al-Nida'* [Beirut], August 4, 1968.

over local communist parties was in decline. As a result, the Sudanese party was able successfully to resolve the dilemmas which had so damaged other Arab parties: it maintained total independence from Moscow, and could synthesize Marxism-Leninism and communist internationalism with Islam, on the one hand, and with Arab nationalism on the other. As a result the Sudanese Communist Party was, by the late 1960s, the largest and best organized in the Arab world, boasting some 50,000–80,000 members and supporters.[48] 'Abd al-Khaliq Mahjüb, founder and Secretary-General of the party until his execution in 1971, was highly respected by Arab nationalists and was a close friend of 'Abd al-Nasir. The party had a reputation for honesty and commitment to the Arab national liberation struggle, and it was strengthened as a result.

Theoretical divergence from the Soviet line among the Arab communists was particularly evident with regard to two key issues: the role of the communist party, and the communists' relationship with Arab nationalism. Examination of these two issues shows how, in the 1950s and 1960s, the Arab communists' loss of Soviet support and concomitant self-reliance forced them to formulate theoretical positions more in tune with their status and potentialities in the Arab world.

Role of the Communist Party

As has already been noted, Soviet theoreticians in the post-Stalin era placed an increased emphasis on united fronts and the progressive role of non-communist movements and governments, to the extent of occasionally honoring non-communist groups (the ASU in Egypt, the FLN in Algeria) with the title of "vanguard" parties. At the same time, Soviet foreign policy placed a decreasing value on the use of foreign communist parties and communist ideology, relying instead on inter-governmental links and pragmatic calculations. No longer could the Arab communists count on automatic or extensive Soviet support. The USSR took little or no real action to protest anti-communist actions by

48. *Financial Times* [London], July 26, 1971; *al-Nahar*, July 28, 1971.

friendly Arab regimes, and it provided approval through silence for the Egyptian Communist Party's dissolution in 1965.

All of this spelled a considerable threat to the Arab communist parties, and it forced them to define their role within the Arab world and assert the continued necessity of Arab communist activity. Thus, in an address before an international seminar on national liberation sponsored by the *World Marxist Review* in December 1962, 'Aziz al-Hajj of the Iraqi Communist Party expressed his concern that the role of the communists was being diminished in contemporary theoretical pronouncements:

> There are, in my opinion ... some wrong evaluations in the studies of several Marxists concerning the state of national democracy and the non-capitalist way of development. These could be summed up as an exaggeration of the progressive role of some national governments. There are views that regimes led by progressive intellectuals can carry out general democratic transformations in the independent countries where capitalist relations exist but are not dominant, or where such relations have only recently become dominant and where, as a result, the national bourgeoisie is relatively weak. In my opinion, however, radical democratic reforms cannot be attained under the sole leadership of either the national bourgeoisie (even its left wing) or the progressive intellectuals from among the petty bourgeoisie. For these transformations to be realized, *the working class and its Marxist-Leninist party must play an active and influential role in the political development of the country.* (emphasis added)[49]

Similarly, Khalid Bakdash (writing in the aftermath of the Egyptian Communist Party's self-dissolution and the FLN's suppression of the Algerian Communist Party) warned that while the unity of progressive forces in the national liberation struggle was desirable, he did not "consider it permissible to go so far as to deny the role of the communist parties and to call for their

---

49. "Exchange of Views: The Socialist World System and the National-Liberation Movement," *World Marxist Review*, 6, No. 3 (March 1963), p. 66.

dissolution."[50] In a statement issued by the Arab communist parties at their May 1967 joint conference, it was strongly emphasized that "[the] Communists have been and will remain an indispensible and effective force in the fight against imperialism . . . [and for] . . . the provision of the prerequisites of the transition to the socialist stage of development." Thus:

> . . . every attempt to split the progressive forces, to bring confusion into their ranks, to ignore or attack the Communist parties, serves, as the sad experience of the past has shown, none but the interests of the imperialists and reactionaries; it injures the national liberation movement and progress—that is, the cause of the whole Arab people.[51]

By the 1970s, a balance between support for non-communist progressive movements and regimes and continued communist activity had been struck. The important role of progressive parties in the Arab national liberation struggle was recognized, and communist willingness to enter into united fronts with such groups in the struggle against imperialism emphasized. It was also stressed, however, that such cooperation would not come at the expense of communist autonomy: the "organizational, political, and ideological independence" of the Arab communist parties and their right to engage in political activity were all to be upheld.[52]

Arab Nationalism

A second issue which the Arab communist parties were forced to address in the late 1950s and early 1960s was that of Arab nationalism. As already noted, up to 1956 they maintained an anti-nationalist stance, which cost them heavily among the Arab masses. Partial change came in 1956, when Soviet theorists began placing somewhat greater emphasis on nationalism's anti-imperialist aspects and the Arab communists began paying lip-service to the ideals of Arab unity. The change was very limited,

---

50. *World Marxist Review*, 8, No. 12 (December 1965), p. 17.
51. *Information Bulletin*, 100 (1967), p. 1052.
52. "Important Statement by Arab Communist Parties," *al-Nida'*, October 5, 1973.

however: Soviet analysts still classified nationalism as a bourgeois ideology (albeit one with some progressive features), while
the Arab communists opposed the formation of the UAR and
pursued an anti-nationalist policy in Qasim's Iraq.

Nevertheless, it gradually became clear to many Arab communists that anti-nationalist parties had little future in the Arab
world. As a result, divisions appeared within the ranks of most
parties as those cadres more amenable to Arab nationalism
asserted their views and sought to alter party policy. Gradually,
and often only after bitter infighting and the formation of myriad
splinter groups, party after party began assuming a more nationalist stance: the Iraqi Communist Party after 1964, the Lebanese
Communist Party after 1968, and the Syrian Communist Party
after 1969. At their May 1967 conference the Arab communist
parties called for unity—but the "unity of progressive forces in
the Arab world" against imperialism, rather than an indiscriminate Arab unity.[53] At their 1968 joint conference the Arab
communists, although laudatory of the achievements of the Arab
national liberation movement and the nationalist regimes,
avoided any explicit endorsement of Arab nationalism, criticized
Palestinian armed struggle against Israel, and continued to em-
phasize "progressive," rather than "Arab," unity.[54] By the time of
their September 1973 joint conference, however, all of the Arab
communist parties had accepted Arab unity, the Palestinian
resistance, and other nationalist issues as major tasks to be
addressed.[55] This accommodation with and acceptance of Arab
nationalism was also manifest in the formation in 1970 of a
communist guerrilla organization, al-Ansar (The Companions),
within the framework of the Palestine Liberation Organization,
in improved communist-Ba'th relations in Syria and Iraq, and in

53. "Statement on the Situation in the Arab Countries," *Information Bulletin*, 100 (1967), p. 1052.

54. "Pronouncements of Communist and Workers' Parties in the
Arab World Concerning Conditions in their Countries," *Al-Nida'*, August 4, 1968; *al-Hayat*, August 21, 1968.

55. "Important Statement by the Arab Communist Parties," *al-
Nida'*, October 5, 1973.

the close ties forged after 1969 between the Lebanese Communist Party and various Arab nationalist groups in Lebanon.

CONTEMPORARY ARAB COMMUNISM

The Arab communists' adaptation to local circumstances has done much to enhance their viability in the Arab world, particularly now that they cannot count upon Soviet support and assistance to insulate them from local developments. Nonetheless, the Arab communist parties have neither individually nor collectively prospered in the past decade. In most Arab countries they are very small and vigorously suppressed by the government.

In Syria the Communist Party has enjoyed semi-legality since 1972 as a member of the National Progressive Front, a broad-based alliance of pro-government political parties formed by Syrian President Hafiz al-Asad, and it is represented in the Syrian cabinet. Its activities, however, are tightly controlled by President Asad and the Ba'th; and its identification with an unpopular regime has stripped it of any significant popular support. Many Syrian Communist Party cadres have formed splinter groups, or have left to join other political organizations. Indeed, since December 1973 there have been, in effect, two Syrian Communist Parties. One, led by Bakdash, has favored accommodation with the Ba'th and close relations with the Soviet Union. The other, led by a dissident majority of members of the party Politburo, is suspicious of the government and favors a more independent party policy.

In Lebanon, the Lebanese Communist Party and its various splinter groups have suffered as religious polarization has undermined it and boosted the fortunes of sectarian militias and parties. Similarly in the Palestinian diaspora al-Ansar has faded away, and the Palestine Communist Party continues to be overshadowed by the Popular Front for the Liberation of Palestine and other leftist Palestinian guerrilla organizations.

Only in Israel, and possibly in the Sudan, are local Arab communist parties enjoying any significant degree of popular support. In the former case this is because the "Arab" communist party splinter, Rakah, has become one of the few legal avenues of protest open to Palestinians in the Zionist state. In the latter case, the Sudanese Communist Party managed to retain some of its organization and support despite years of suppression by President al-Numayri, and in the wake of his overthrow in April 1985 it appeared to be a significant political force. The party's previously noted reputation for flexibility on local issues has played a major role in this.

Ideologically and politically, Arab communist party policy in the 1970s and 1980s represents a continuation of doctrines developed in the 1950s and 1960s. A typical example of this policy can be found in the statement issued by a meeting of the Communist and Workers' Parties of the Persian Gulf and Arabian Peninsula in December 1980.[56] In this document, the Arab communist parties define their "general national-democratic tasks" in the following terms:

1. [The] achievement and strengthening of national independence in the countries of the region . . .

2. [The maintenance of] democratic freedoms for the peoples of the region . . .

3. [The development of] the national economy without its subordination to the world imperialist market; the creation of industry . . . [the] elimination of multinational imperialist monopolies; the use of the natural resources of the region . . . for the benefit of its peoples; [the creation of] a national oil policy meeting the requirements of national economic development, and resolute economic measures . . . against the United States, arch-enemy of our people.

4. [The] pursuit . . . of an independent peaceful foreign policy, . . . non-participation in the schemes of imperialism, . . . and extension of spheres of cooperation with [the socialist countries].

5. [The strengthening] of ties with the national-liberation movements in the countries of the region, and cohesion with

56. "Statement by Communist and Workers' Parties of the Persian Gulf and Arabian Peninsula" [December 1980], in *Communist Affairs*, 1, No. 1 (1981), pp. 69–82.

the revolutionary forces in the world, especially the socialist community headed by the USSR.

6. [The] struggle against all conceptions and ideas imposed by imperialism and reaction, against right and "left" opportunism, national chauvinism, anti-communism and anti-Sovietism, Trotskyism and Maoism . . .

According to this statement the primary method for achieving such goals and advancing the Arab national liberation movement is the formation of united fronts:

The advance . . . of the national liberation struggle in the region calls for the unification of the social anti-imperialist, anti-reactionary forces in each individual country, . . . and also the cohesion of the ranks of the democratic parties, organizations and forces in these countries within the framework of a national alliance, *with each of the participants remaining ideologically and organizationally independent* as the basic condition for its success. (emphasis added)

The Arab communists' continued concern with defining a leading role for communist activity is reflected in the statement's emphasis on communist autonomy within the framework of the "national alliance."[57]

Somewhat less attention to Arab nationalist themes can be detected in the statements of the Arab communist parties in the 1980s. This, however, should not be construed as a return to an anti-nationalist position, but rather as the result of two developments. First, the power of Arab nationalism as a political force has been declining. This decline has manifested itself in the political fragmentation of the Arab world, and in the partial replacement of radical Arab nationalism by Islamic fundamentalism as the major challenger to imperialism and the social *status*

---

57. A more detailed explanation of the need for the "political, organizational and ideological independence of each participant" within the national alliance can be found in: "Statement by the Communist and Workers' Parties of Arab Countries" [1981], in *Information Bulletin*, No. 16 (1981), pp. 12–13.

quo in the region. Second, East-West tensions have risen, and this explains the tendency of the Arab communists to stress internationalist themes in support of the Soviet Union over Arab nationalist themes.

As this suggests, the Arab communist parties' recognition of the CPSU as the "chief force" and leader of the "world Communist and working-class movement" continues.[58] Laudatory references to the Soviet Union, calls for closer Arab-Soviet relations, and condemnation of the Soviet Union's political and ideological opponents are still routine features of Arab communist party statements. Although Soviet control over the Arab communist parties has been relaxed since the death of Stalin, and despite greater innovation and independence, Soviet influence remains very significant indeed.

CONCLUSION

It is clear that communism has survived rather than flourished in the Arab world. Ideological rigidity, tactical and strategic mistakes, competition with the nationalist left, and past domination by the CPSU have all taken their toll. Despite the establishment of a Marxist regime in South Yemen and, at one time or another, the participation of prominent communists in the cabinets of Jordan (1956–1957), Syria (1971–present), Iraq (1959–1960, 1972–1978), and the Sudan (1969–1970), no Arab communist party has yet gained sufficient political power to put its program into effect. It must be pointed out that, although the National Liberation Front of South Yemen (later the Yemeni Socialist Party) embraced "scientific socialism" in 1969, it has neither evolved from nor claimed to be a communist party. Instead, the roots of its ideology lie in the Arab Nationalist Movement and the Arab new leftism of the 1960s. As a hybrid distinct from the strands of Arab communism, it has been excluded from analysis here.[59]

58. "Statement by the Communist and Workers' Parties of the Persian Gulf and Arabian Peninsula," p. 78.

59. For further information on the Yemeni Socialist Party and its evolution, see T. Y. Ismael and J. S. Ismael, *The People's Democratic*

In general terms, no surge in Arab communism seems likely in the near future. Indeed, the rise of radical Islamic ideologies in opposition to social exploitation and foreign domination does not augur well for Arab communist parties, since such ideologies are commonly directed at the Arab communists' own prime potential constituency. Nonetheless, it is important not to underestimate the indirect contribution of Arab communism to the social, political, and economic development of the Middle East. Leninism, as a political and organizational strategy, has been used—often to considerable effect—by political parties across the ideological spectrum. The Arab communists played a significant role in pointing out the potential role of the Soviet Union as an ally against Western imperialism, and hence paved the way for Arab neutralism and non-alignment. The Arab trade union movement owes much to early communist organizers, and in many countries it was communist-led political campaigns that led to the first progressive labor legislation.

Perhaps most importantly, the Arab communist movement has had a fundamental impact on the political discourse of the Arab world. The non-communist Arab left, represented by Nasirism, the Ba'th, the Arab Nationalist Movement, the FLN of Algeria, and the Palestinian resistance have all borrowed from the communist movement or have been forced to formulate their own responses to the issues which the communists have raised. The same might also be said of other groups elsewhere on the ideological spectrum. While this may not have been a major goal of the Arab communist movement—it has only served to inhibit their expansion by strengthening rivals on the left—it nonetheless remains their most important continuing legacy in the Arab world.

Republic of Yemen: The Politics of Socialist Transformation (London: Frances Pinter, 1986).

CHAPTER TEN

The Gilan Soviet Revolution, 1920–1921

GEORGE S. HARRIS

In June 1920, Moscow newspapers hailed the birth of a new communist state. A Soviet republic had been proclaimed in Gilan, carved from Iran's Caspian Sea province of the same name. The Kremlin hoped it would be the forerunner of an irresistible wave of communist revolutions in the East. But soon Soviet hopes were dashed. By December 1921, Reza Khan had destroyed the new entity and reincorporated its territory into the Iranian state. For a time thereafter, communist apologetics filled the air. Then the Kremlin's interest flagged; the Gilan episode sank into near oblivion until a new Soviet experiment in Iranian Azerbaijan in 1946 demonstrated that Moscow's designs on northern Iran had not disappeared.

Gilan's Soviet experience, however, is instructive in shedding light on the difficulties of exporting communist revolution to neighboring Muslim states. Even with the passage of time and the enunciation of the "Brezhnev doctrine" rejecting the possibility of a demise of a Soviet regime, it is worth a closer look at how and why northern Iran passed through the first of its two flirtations with communist power. The story of the birth and death of this Soviet entity makes clear the obstacles facing the Soviets in making inroads into this troubled part of Iran and may even help explain Moscow's inability to take advantage of the expulsion of the Americans after the overthrow of the Iranian monarchy many decades later.

The revolutionary process in Gilan was one of considerable complexity. In it, the communists were neither the initiators nor were they passive spectators. Theirs was a continuing bid for supremacy. Although they never managed to achieve uncontested control of the revolutionary movement in Gilan, the ebb and flow of their effort strongly affected the outcome of this experiment.

A major problem for the communist camp throughout the period was the deep intramural dispute over tactics, doctrine, and personality. Those whom the Soviets called "leftists" continually pressed for radical social reform, thereby offending the sensitivities of the traditionally-oriented workers and peasants to whom the party hoped to appeal. More conservative elements among the communists argued that revolutionary social engineering should be left until after victory over the party's external opponents had been won.

The mainstay of revolution in Gilan was a native movement which had begun by 1915 in Azerbaijan. This rebellion had come about largely in response to the decline of central power in Tehran and in reaction to the excesses of the Qajar dynasty. It was encouraged and abetted by the Germans and Turks, who wanted to confound the British and Tsarist Russians who were then dominant in Iran. Although initiated by Azeris and all along tinged with localism, the Gilan revolution did not start as a frankly separatist move, and its inception owed nothing to communism or to the Russian revolution, which took place years after the Gilan insurrection was well under way. To be sure, sheer opportunism and the view that the communist upheaval in Russia might sweep over the East produced an alliance of convenience between the Gilanis and the communists. But this combination was always fragile and imperfect.

Even more important was the Soviet military occupation of points of Gilan during the life of the Soviet republic. In fact, foreign intervention played at times a determining role on the fate of the movement. Ironically, although decisions made in London, Moscow, Istanbul, and Berlin were of key significance, the moves by the foreign players were often taken without immediate reference to what was going on in the field in Gilan.

Finally, the rise of Reza Khan's central government in Tehran was to prove the ultimate factor in ending this experiment in Soviet government beyond the borders of the former Tsarist domains. Needless to say, the Gilanis had no control over this development. Thus it was the interplay of communism and rival native nationalisms on the stage of international diplomacy that ultimately dictated the fate of Soviet power in Gilan.

PROLOGUE TO GILAN

The First World War ended with the British as the major foreign power in Iran. At the end of 1918, British forces were extending their occupation into nearby regions abandoned by the Russians and Turks. In part, London sought to support the White Russian armies fighting the Bolsheviks around the Caspian Sea and, in part, wished to create a belt of friendly states in the Caucasus to preserve influence in this strategically important area. These British moves, which necessarily involved dominating the Tehran government, outraged nascent Iranian national feeling.

The government of Ahmad Shah was in chaos. A small class of semifeudal powerbrokers defied central authority at every turn. The Shah had no effective national army with which to reassert his power. British officers commanded the South Persian Rifles. While the Cossack Brigade under White Russian officers comprised the only other military unit worthy of the name, the British controlled it too through large subsidies. This British monopoly of effective military power, emphasized by the continuing presence of Dunsterforce, the expeditionary unit of British troops under General Dunsterville, further focused dissatisfaction against the British and inflamed Iranian nationalists.

Economic crisis only added to popular unhappiness. The disruption of trade with Russia, trade essential for the economic stability and prosperity of the Caspian provinces in particular, inflicted hardships on the country. Guerrilla warfare, a legacy of the First World War, aggravated an already difficult situation. In addition, the exorbitant exactions of the traditional system of control by landlords and tribal leaders had serious economic consequences. In 1918 and the succeeding year, famine ravaged the country, leaving in its wake widespread unrest. British

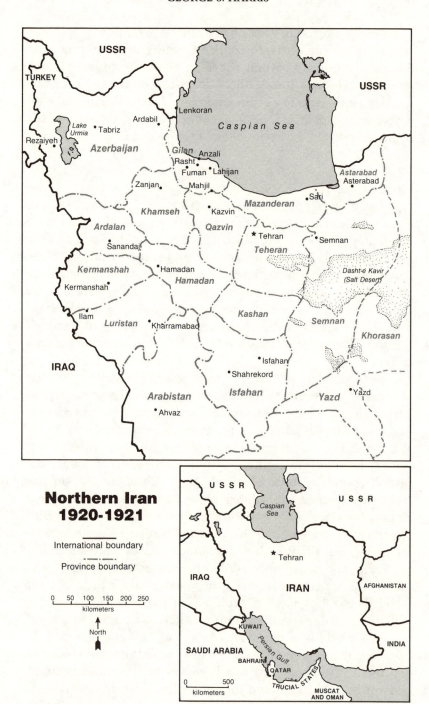

**Northern Iran
1920-1921**

International boundary

Province boundary

0   50   100   150   200   250
kilometers

North

occupation and the incompetence of the Shah's regime received much of the blame for these problems in Iranian eyes.

Growing anti-British sentiment peaked with the signing of the Anglo-Iranian Treaty of August 1919. By this treaty, Lord Curzon hoped to guarantee a stable Iran as a buffer to safeguard British India. Its provisions would have given London virtually complete control of the Iranian army, finances, civil administration, and future economic development. Not surprisingly, the Iranian press strongly opposed ratification of the document, whereas the cabinet headed by Vosugh ed Douleh urged its approval. Coming at the moment of British withdrawal from the Caucasus, popular pressure prevailed; the accord was never ratified.

In addition to arousing antipathy toward the British, this treaty also fostered a swing toward Russian orientation in Iran. No mass conversions to communism took place, but the semi-official paper *Iran* printed editorials claiming that "the doctrines of Bolshevism closely resemble the pure Gospel of Islam." Iranian tactics were more an attempt to play off the Soviets against the British, however, than an expression of new-found love for their northern neighbor. In Iran, suspicion of the Russians ran deep.[1]

By 1920, opposition to the Anglo-Iranian Treaty and the Shah's government took more concrete form. In March of that year, Premier Vosugh ed Douleh issued a manifesto defending the treaty and challenging his opponents to justify their objections to it. In answer, the Tabriz Democratic Party under Shaykh Muhammad Khiyabani rose in rebellion, soon gaining control of the whole of Iranian Azerbaijan. The Democrats, one of the older political groups in Iran, proclaimed their opposition to the Shah's government. They called for its replacement by a new free

---

1. Sir Percy Sykes, *A History of Persia* (London: Macmillan & Co., 1930), p. 526. Both Nasrollah S. Fatemi, *Diplomatic History of Persia, 1917–1923* (New York: Russell F. Morse Co., 1952) and Sephr Zabih, *The Communist Movement in Iran* (Berkeley & Los Angeles: University of California Press, 1966) cover this period in some detail, drawing on Iranian as well as Soviet and other sources. Since they wrote, other materials have become available to clarify some of the perplexities of this revolutionary movement.

society, with no ties to foreign powers. Their demands expressed the interests of the petty bourgeoisie; but the Democrats took an intermediate position between defending the traditional social order and espousing the radicalism of the communists. In fact, Khiyabani's supporters directly attacked the communists, who were spreading propaganda in Iranian Azerbaijan. This uprising added to the prevailing tension in Iran and put further pressure on the British to withdraw Dunsterforce from the country.[2]

Soviet Intervention

At this point, with the central government shaken and tottering, a Soviet force, pursuing the White Russian Caspian fleet which had sought refuge in the Iranian port of Anzali, took that city on May 18, 1920. Repercussions were immediate. For the first time, serious doubts were voiced about British will and ability to defend the country. As a result, British prestige fell to a new low.

A few weeks later, on June 4, 1920, a mixed Gilani and Soviet Russian group in Rasht proclaimed the formation of the Soviet Socialist Republic of Iran. This act caused the fall of Vosugh ed Douleh's pro-British cabinet and its replacement by one more nationalistically inclined. In addition, the British troops that had been stationed in the Caspian provinces were forced to retire to Tehran. Following orders, they did so without engaging the Bolsheviks in action.

At the same time, demands for the British to quit Iran entirely grew in intensity, in part because of eventual clashes between the British and Soviets on Iranian soil. The position of the British had deteriorated to such an extent that it was clearly impossible to revive the disruptive Anglo-Iranian Treaty. The undisputed British monopoly of power over Iran was over.

2. A. Vishnegradova, "Revoliutsionnoe dvizhenie v Persidskom Azerbaidzhane," *Novyi Vostok*, vol. 2, provides a general view of Khiyabani's movement, but deemphasizes the resistance to communism among the populace. For the view of an Azeri participant, see G. Mammedli, *Khiabani (Azerbai'an Halgynyn milli azadlyg muberizesi tarikhindan)* (Baku, 1949).

However, the new Soviet republic in Gilan claimed more than it could deliver. It was not a purely communist creation, but represented rather a Bolshevik facade plastered over what remained essentially a native revolutionary movement. To appreciate the continuity with the past, it is necessary to review the course of events in Gilan prior to the Soviet landing at Anzali.

Rise of the Jangali Brothers

Gilan, which borders the Caspian Sea on the southwest, is a region of narrow coastal plain backed by rugged mountains covered with dense forest (called "Jangal"). These mountains effectively cut the Caspian region, including Gilan, from the main body of Iran, focusing this region's orientation toward the north and weakening central government control. Gilan was one of the richer provinces, its warm humid climate and fertile soil producing large quantities of grain and rice. Industry was lacking, but the coastal towns of Anzali and Rasht were commercial and artisan centers. A depressed peasantry, numbering some half million under its feudal landlords, formed the backbone of Gilan's agricultural economy. The whole region was economically linked to Russia in the north, and this tie created opportunities for the Soviets to fish in troubled waters.[3]

As part of the Russian sphere of influence under the Anglo-Russian Agreement of 1907, Gilan had developed in ways different from those of the southern provinces, particularly in the far more pronounced growth of political consciousness. Gilanis, for example, were highly active in the famous march on Tehran in 1909 during the struggle for a constitution. Since that time, Gilan had never long been free of partisan bands, which found a certain immunity in its forests. Such agitation contributed in turn to the disruption of normal commerce and social life, creating an atmosphere hospitable to revolution.[4]

With the advent of the First World War, two outstanding local leaders, Mirza Kuchuk Khan and Ehsanollah Khan, took

3. I. M. Reisner and N. M. Gol'dberg (eds.), *Ocherki po novoi istorii stran Srednego Vostoka* (Moscow: Izdatel'stvo Moskovskogo universiteta, 1951), p. 212.

4. Sykes, p. 407.

advantage of the opportunity to defy Tehran's control. Kuchuk Khan was born in 1880 in Gilan to an Azeri middle-class family. As a theological student, he took an active role in the 1906 constitutional struggle. His stance against the monarchy gained him great popularity in his home province. He hated the British and developed some interest in mild social reform, although he remained to the end a traditionalist, interested principally in political change. Pragmatic in his willingness to make deals with groups of various persuasions, he showed himself at the same time somewhat naive and credulous. He was steadfast in his determination to be recognized as a leader.[5]

Ehsanollah Khan was a personality of a very different stripe. A largely detribalized revolutionary who opposed the existing social order, he became a member of the *Komite-i Mojazat* (Committee of Retribution) set up by terrorists in Tehran in April 1917 to murder Anglophiles. He had little patience with religion and appeared dedicated to revolutionary activity for its own sake. These differences in view with Kuchuk Khan contributed to tension between the two, as Ehsanollah Khan persistently pushed for more radical stands.[6]

After the outbreak of war in 1914, these two figures decided to organize a military movement to free Iran from Russian and British domination and to overthrow the Qajar dynasty. In this, they were encouraged by the Germans and the Turks, who wanted to face the British and Russians with new problems. Although preliminary plans were laid in Tehran in 1915, both leaders realized that they must base their activities in the provinces, and especially Gilan, where they would be out of central government control and in easier contact with their German and Turkish supporters. Moreover, they hoped to exploit

5. A. Vinogradova, "Natsional'no-osvoboditel'noe dvizhenie v Persii," *Mezhdunarodnaia Zhizn'*, no. 5 [123] (1922), p. 15; M. N. Ivanova, *Natsional'no-osvoboditel'noe dvizhenie v Irane v 1918–1922 gg.* (Moscow: Izdatel'stvo vostochnoi literatury, 1961), p. 17.

6. See the memoirs of Ehsanollah Khan in R. Abikh, "Natsional'noe i revoliutsionnoe dvizhenie v Persii," *Novyi Vostok*, vol. 23–24, p. 236; Ervand Abrahamian, *Iran Between Two Revolutions* (Princeton: Princeton University Press, 1982), p. 21.

Kuchuk Khan's great popularity in Gilan. Thus Kuchuk Khan went directly to that province, where he and several aides founded the "Jangali (Forest) Brothers." Ehsanollah Khan followed a more circuitous route and only moved definitively to Gilan after the government managed to suppress the *Komite-i Mojazat* in May 1917.[7]

By 1917, their movement had become an armed revolt which swept over Gilan. Kuchuk Khan turned his Jangali Brothers into the *Ittihad-i Islam* (Union of Islam) Committee in order to broaden the movement. It embraced a number of local leaders, including Ehsanollah Khan, who joined despite its religious flavor. The new organization was dedicated to "a war of independence against foreigners under the flag of Islam." At this time, however, its program did not define the nature of relations with the Shah; nevertheless, the committee's official organ, the paper *Jangal*, which began to appear on May 23, 1917, took a position sharply hostile to the Tehran regime. The committee was mainly supported by Rasht and Anzali merchants who sought to weaken Tehran's grip over them. As usual, the peasantry remained passive in political affairs, and the rebels met little local opposition.[8]

From the fall of 1917 to the summer of 1918, no military action took place in Gilan. The Shah's troops did not attack and Kuchuk Khan was preoccupied with consolidating his power. During this lull, however, Gaffar Zadeh Asadollah, the founder and leader of the Adalat (Justice) Party, was murdered while attempting to make contact with Kuchuk Khan.

Adalat on the Scene

The Adalat Party, organized by Bolsheviks in Baku as a mechanism to subvert Iran by attracting Iranian dissidents, was founded in 1916. Its aims and platform closely resembled those of the communists; in fact, after the February Revolution in Russia, it merged with the Iranian Communist Party. The Adalat branch

---

7. Abikh, "Natsional'noe i revoliutsionnoe" p. 238; Ivanova, *Natsional'no-osvoboditel'noe dvizhenie*, pp. 21, 24.

8. Abikh, "Natsional'noe i revoliutsionnoe," *Novyi Vostok*, vol. 26–27, pp. 127–130.

of the Communist Party, although weak, sent workers to Iran to carry on propaganda, especially in the north. These agents advocated too extreme a course to suit the *Ittihad-i Islam* Committee. Communist radicalism would alienate the merchants and landlords on whom Kuchuk Khan relied. In addition, Asadollah's followers tried to set up a branch of the Communist Party in Gilan, thereby threatening Kuchuk Khan's hegemony. As a result, relations between the Jangalis and the Adalat Party leadership were strained. And political as well as personal considerations were undoubtedly reflected in Asadollah's assassination.[9]

While the main body of Jangalis was showing hostility to the communists, Ehsanollah Khan moved to Anzali, where he became closely connected with the short-lived Anzali Revolutionary Committee. This committee was set up by Soviet Russian agitators on orders from communist leaders in Baku. Its members were drawn from the ranks of Russian soldiers retreating from Iran, and its authority depended directly on the presence of these Russian troops. Consequently, from its high point early in 1918, the Anzali committee progressively declined in power as the Russians continued their evacuation. Its leaders were power-hungry leftists, whose views coincided well with Ehsanollah Khan's interests. It is especially significant that Ehsanollah Khan undertook liaison with these Bolsheviks while Kuchuk Khan remained aloof in the forest. Such a pattern was to become a major theme of the Gilan revolution.[10]

In the summer of 1918, after this interval without fighting, the British Caspian expedition of General Dunsterville engaged the Gilanis in action. Dunsterforce, showing great superiority in combat, quickly routed Kuchuk Khan's men. This defeat produced far-reaching effects on the whole Jangali movement. The partisan bands became demoralized and many deserted. The *Ittihad-i Islam* Committee was disposed to disband entirely and to cease activity permanently. However, before the Jangalis took such a radical step, Dunsterville offered peace in August 1918.

9. Irandust, "Klassy i partii sovremennoi Persii," *Mirovoe khoziaistvo i mirovaia politika*, no. 2 (1926), pp. 84–85.

10. Abikh, "Natsional'noe i revoliutsionnoe," *Novyi Vostok*, vol. 26–27, p. 130.

The committee eagerly accepted his terms which permitted it to name the governor of Rasht in exchange for British freedom of movement in Gilan and permission to buy provisions there. In effect, the British now guaranteed the Jangalis freedom from outside interference.[11]

Despite this guarantee, the revolution in Gilan now entered difficult times. Dissension broke out inside the committee on the issue of the accord with the British, as the left wing refused to abide by the agreement. Military defeat and the inaction required by the accord seriously weakened the Gilan revolutionary movement; it ceased to be a match for the Shah's own forces. In the spring of 1919, the Tehran government, whose attention had previously been occupied by internal affairs, put pressure on the British to withdraw protection from the Gilanis. The British agreed. They annulled their accord with Kuchuk Khan on the pretext that he had violated its terms by refusing to negotiate with the Shah. Profiting from this turn of events, the Cossack Brigade easily took Rasht in March 1919, forcing the Gilani leaders to flee to the mountains. The Gilan revolutionary movement was temporarily in eclipse.[12]

The Adalat Party had been almost completely destroyed in September 1918 by the Turkish conquest of Baku. It was only after the Musavat government was established in Soviet Azerbaijan that the party was able to be reconstituted there in March 1919. The Adalat central committee in Baku thereupon began to print Azeri and Persian newspapers for distribution both in Baku and in Iran itself. Having only a small membership, the party worked mainly in the commercial centers of Tabriz, Rasht, and Ardabil.[13]

11. *Ibid.*

12. *Ibid.*, pp. 134, 141.

13. Fatemi, *Diplomatic History*, p. 218. The editor of the new journal *Horiyet* (Freedom) was Ja'far Jevad Zadeh, the Ja'far Pishevari who was subsequently premier of the Autonomous Republic of Azerbaijan in 1945. The Adalat Party also published *Eldash* (Comrade). See Irandust, "Klassy i partii," pp. 84–85; Ivanova, *Natsional'no-osvobodi-tel'noe dvizhenie*, pp. 69–71.

The reverses of the Gilani movement and the commonality in Adalat's opposition to the Shah's regime made an alliance of convenience more attractive to Kuchuk Khan. For the first time, he began to show interest in cooperating with the Communist Party, even apparently asking the Adalat leaders in Baku for Soviet support, but the withdrawal of Soviet forces from Russian Azerbaijan in 1918 prevented such assistance. Kuchuk Khan, however, remained wary of the communists. In a letter to *Izvestiia* in December 1918, he demanded a renunciation of Soviet influence in Iran as the basis of Russo-Iranian friendship.[14]

Yet by June 1919, the need to assure the survival of the Gilan revolutionary movement and Ehsanollah Khan's prodding had led Kuchuk Khan to step up his efforts to seek Soviet aid. To this end, he prepared to go to Lenkoran in Soviet Azerbaijan to contact Kolomyitsev, the communist envoy to Iran. But the Musavat government's destruction of the Bolshevik center around Lenkoran frustrated this plan.[15]

In the fall of 1919, the British decided to evacuate the Caucasus under pressure from the Bolshevik drive southward. At the same time, the Shah withdrew most of his forces from Gilan, evidently considering the partisans there to have been crushed. Thus encouraged, Kuchuk Khan returned to Gilan in the winter of 1919 and set up a new Revolutionary Committee. While he carried on some sort of opportunistic collaboration with the Bolsheviks, he was also careful not to antagonize either the British or the Shah unnecessarily. Therefore, after initial military action which regained for him most of Gilan, Kuchuk Khan accepted Tehran's offer of limited sovereignty in the forests of Gilan. The Shah and the British evidently felt compelled to negotiate with the Jangalis in order to head off more effective Jangali-Bolshevik cooperation. They also hoped that removing opposition would cause the unity of the Jangali Brothers to evaporate. The British went so far as to make overtures to the partisans, assuring them support even against Tehran, if they would oppose the communists. Kuchuk Khan refused, fearing

14. Irandust, "Klassy i partii," pp. 84–85.

15. Abikh, "Natsional'noe i revoliutsionnoe," *Novyi Vostok*, vol. 29, p. 92.

that he would antagonize both sides, and remained inactive until the spring of 1920.[16]

A few weeks before the Bolshevik landing at Anzali in May 1920, Adalat Party leader Sultan Zadeh (pseudonym of Avetis Mikaelian) sent an open letter from Baku to Iranian communists and radicals urging them "to rise on the day of the Russian invasion of Iran and seize all the government offices and military establishments and arrest all the members of the government, the aristocrats, merchants, landlords, and any others who had collaborated with the British." This manifesto was followed on May 17, the night before the Anzali landing, by a message from the Soviets announcing their imminent arrival and requesting Gilani cooperation. The Kremlin had ordered the Soviet force to "unite the Kuchuk Khan forces and the Persian Communist and Democratic groups against the British." These appeals were heeded by Ehsanollah Khan's wing, which put pressure on Kuchuk to welcome the Bolsheviks with open arms. Kuchuk Khan remained wary of committing himself to the communist cause, however, and reserved judgment until he had conferred with them in person.[17]

PROCLAMATION OF THE SOVIET REPUBLIC

Several days after the Soviet landing, Kuchuk Khan went to Anzali to negotiate. The Soviets promised not to interfere in Gilani internal affairs and not to implement communist demands for radical social change, such as abolishing private property. They claimed that their sole aim was to liquidate the White Russian refugees. Throughout the negotiations, Kuchuk Khan insisted on his autonomy. Although he desired Soviet aid, he was

---

16. *Ibid.*, pp. 94, 96–99; Fatemi, *Diplomatic History*, pp. 219–220.

17. Fatemi, *Diplomatic History*, pp. 192–193; Abikh, "Natsional'noe i revoliutsionnoe," *Novyi Vostok*, vol. 29, pp. 100, 102; Zabih, *Communist Movement*, p. 18. The text of a letter sent by the Lenkoran branch of the Communist Party of Russia to Kuchuk Khan on April 30, 1920, praising his service to the liberation of "the oppressed people" of Iran, is in Schapour Ravasani, *Sowjetrepublik Gilan: Die Sozialistische Bewegung in Iran seit End des 19. Jhdt bis 1922* (Berlin: Basis-Verlag, 1973), pp. 581–583.

unwilling to accept orders from Moscow as the price. To forestall possible Soviet control over Gilan, he secured a Soviet promise that the Red Army would not advance further without his permission. As proof of his independence, he granted asylum to fifteen White Russian officers who sought refuge. Against this anti-Bolshevik gesture, Ehsanollah Khan protested in vain.[18]

When Soviet forces took Rasht on June 3, 1920, Kuchuk Khan was on hand to proclaim the Soviet Socialist Republic of Iran. Thus far the Gilan revolution had in essence consisted of guerrilla attacks by the revolutionaries against the Tsarist and British presence as well as against the Shah's regime. With the fall of the Tsars, Britain and the Shah remained the main focus of these partisan forays. Although communists and radicals participated, they had up to now played a quite secondary role in the Gilan movement. Indeed, rather than a communist design, the insurrection had followed a program of local autonomy tinged with mild social reform rooted in respect for Islam. In future, the situation would be complicated by the presence of foreign communists on Iranian soil and by the spread of the Gilan revolution over a larger area.[19]

Although many elements joined under the banner of the Soviet Socialist Republic of Iran, important contradictions lay just below the surface. The very choice of such a grandiose title for a movement based on the periphery and composed largely of Azeris and Kurds reflected the common aim of overthrowing the Shah. But to the communists, this framework also offered scope to expand their foothold, taking advantage of the call for "close cooperation" which Kuchuk Khan sent to Lenin from the proclamation ceremony. As for Kuchuk Khan, his impeccably phrased appeal to the Third International to help in liberating all of Iran did not signify willingness to countenance radical social reform or abandon his long-standing religious orientation. Indeed, it was

18. Abikh, "Natsional'noe i revoliutsionnoe," *Novyi Vostok,* vol. 29, p. 103. Ravasani, *Sowjetrepublik Gilan,* pp. 286–287, reports that Kuchuk Khan and Grigorii Ordzhonikidze reached a nine-point agreement regulating Soviet-Gilani relations.

19. Irandust, "Voprosy Gilianskoi revoliutsii," *Istorik-Marksist,* no.5 (1927), p. 132.

his moderate face that seemed responsible for the warm reception that the people of Gilan gave the Soviet regime. Ehsanollah Khan represented a still different strain. At one with the more extreme communists in desire for far-reaching agrarian reform to change the social structure, he appeared less willing to bind himself to the discipline of subservience to foreign direction. Thus sooner or later conflict within the Gilan movement was inevitable.[20]

The first order of business after proclaiming the Soviet Socialist Republic of Iran was to form a united front government. This unstable coalition was dominated initially by Kuchuk Khan as president and commissar of war. His moderate faction of former Jangali leaders, including at least one German renegade, Kauk, who under the alias of Hushang was to share Kuchuk Khan's lot to the end, occupied posts of secondary power in the new regime. The radicals were also well represented, and they were extremely powerful. Ehsanollah Khan played a major role in close collaboration with the Bolsheviks. Also important were Soviet commanders and the civilian governor of Rasht. With their fingers on positions of power, Adalat Party members held a great advantage in efforts to control the new regime. From the start, the strong position of the Bolsheviks and their inclination to use it to further their radical program endangered the united front.[21]

The arrival of the Red Army from the Soviet Union naturally influenced the future course of the Gilani movement. In the first place, it provided a prop for the communist elements in the coalition government, securing them a base of power outside Kuchuk Khan's partisan bands. Such support permitted the communists to act freely regardless of whether Kuchuk Khan agreed with them. In addition, the Red Army's conquests increased the area under the new government's control. As a result, Soviet agitation and propaganda could be carried on in the open in some regions where up to now it had been underground.

20. *Ibid.*, p. 132; Abikh, "Natsional'noe i revoliutsionnoe," *Novyi Vostok*, vol. 29, pp. 106–107.

21. Fatemi, *Diplomatic History*, pp. 221–222, 229–230; Alexandre Barmine, *One Who Survived* (New York: G. P. Putnam's Sons, 1945), p. 110.

Bolshevik aims in Iran were no doubt large. One cannot credit Chicherin, the Soviet Foreign Minister, who disavowed any official connection with the Red Army forces in Iran, insisting that they were operating on "their own initiative." The Comintern had made no secret that Iran was considered ripe for revolution. And various Soviet figures had signaled their belief that it had the potential to be a "revolutionary beacon" for the whole East. Thus there seems no question that the Soviet troops aimed to stimulate revolution over all the country by putting pressure on the Tehran regime, even if they were ready as a first step to settle for fostering Caspian separatism.[22]

As a result, after the Anzali landing, forces composed of Jangalis, Azerbaijanis, and Soviets advanced east through Mazanderan to Asterabad, and west through Gilan as far as Ardabil where Khiyabani's partisans blocked their path. The British, retreating before the Soviet advance, blew up the Manjil bridge on the main route to Tehran, but did not confront the Red Army. By July 1920, Tehran was threatened from three sides: from the west along the Manjil-Kazvin road, over the mountains from Mazanderan in the north, and from Asterabad in the east. For its defense, the central government had at its disposal only 6,000 Cossacks. The British no longer had sufficient military forces in Iran to help.

Breaking Ranks

At this critical point, the Iranian communists called their first congress in Anzali on June 23, 1920. The ostensible purpose of this congress was to decide proper agrarian policy, to work out the party program, and to change the party name from "Adalat" to the Iranian Communist Party. The congress was also intended as a demonstration of communist "democracy," as in theory the rank and file members would decide policy and elect their own superiors. However, inspection of the abridged record of the proceedings leaves no doubt that the Kremlin intended to use the congress to exert Comintern control. Party leaders of whatever stripe had to defer to decisions from Moscow. Even the very

---

22. *Pravda*, May 23, 1920; S. Iranskii, "Russko-Persidskiye otnosheniia za piat' let," *Novyi Vostok*, vol. 3 (1926), p. 105.

convocation of the congress took place on the initiative of the Turkistan wing of the party at Soviet instigation.[23]

The opening speech of Viktor, the Azerbaijani Central Committee representative, set the tone of the congress. He outlined the special significance which Iran held for communist activity and for the establishment of Soviet power. Viktor emphasized the flexibility of communist tactics in their adaptation to the Iranian scene. He was followed by the leader of the "Iranian Red Army," who cautioned the assembly that success in war could come only through united military action by all revolutionary elements. This advice ran counter to many of the ideas espoused by the local communist leaders.

The second session of the congress was devoted to reports and speeches by Iranians. They uniformly praised the Red Army for its role in stimulating communist activity. However, the striking feature of the reports was the evident weakness of the communist movement in Iran at this time. In all of Anzali, for example, the Bolsheviks claimed only 100 members, blaming this low figure on mistakes of the Russian communists who misjudged local exigencies. After the reports, Sultan Zadeh, the party's main theoretician, took the floor to propound the Iranian view of party policy. He advocated radical agrarian reform as the only means of winning the people to communism. This striking cleavage between native and Russian communists was to plague the Iranian Bolshevik movement until the end of the Gilan Soviet experiment.

At the final session of the congress, Moscow's line prevailed. Sultan Zadeh's theses were rejected outright. Stressing the harmony of revolutionary interests, Comrade D. Neinashvili flatly stated that "the time has not come for a communist revolution in Iran." In his dispassionate approach, he noted the exodus of landlords from Gilan, declaring it necessary "to convince hesitating forces that in fact Soviet power does not threaten either

23. "Pervyi S'ezd Persidskoi Kommunisticheskoi Partii "Adalat," *Kommunisticheskii Internatsional* (henceforth *KI*), no. 14 (1920), pp. 2889–2892; Sultan-Zade, "Ob Iranskoi Kompartii," *KI*, no. 13 (1920), p. 2549.

landlords or the bourgeoisie. Then they would support the national-liberation movement." The congress passed resolutions
proclaiming the party slogans to be "Away with the British!" and
"Down with the Shah!". Land reform was rejected at this stage.[24]

The extremist wing, headed by Sultan Zadeh and Ehsanollah
Khan, was roundly defeated at the congress, but only on paper.
Despite the fact that at the congress the Communist Party issued
an appeal "to support the government of Kuchuk Khan in every
way," the Central Committee of the Iranian Communist Party on
July 10, 1920, ordered Kuchuk Khan removed from power. This
split came over the issue of social reform. Kuchuk Khan refused
to agree to the confiscation of all large estates without compensation to their former owners. He maintained the sanctity of
private property as expressed in the Qur'an and opposed Sultan
Zadeh's cherished program of land reform.[25]

On July 19, 1920, therefore, Kuchuk Khan severed his connections with the Soviet Republic of Iran and left Rasht for the
Jangal forests. His departure was accompanied by an exodus of
landowners from Gilan. These developments ruined Soviet hopes
of further conquest by removing his partisans from the expeditionary force moving on Tehran. Without his troops, the Red
Army and Ehsanollah Khan's partisans were no longer strong
enough to take on the central government forces. Moreover, the
rapidly widening rift between moderates and extremists in the
party weakened the whole Gilan movement.[26]

Kuchuk Khan's departure formalized the division of the
movement into two major camps, a division that underlay the
future course of the Gilan revolution until its final destruction.
Kuchuk Khan was repelled by the anti-Islamic orientation of the
radicals, an approach that directly conflicted with his insistence
on the "protection of Islam." Moreover, he would not allow the
communists to usurp his power without a struggle. He saw that
he was losing control of the Gilani movement by participating in
the united front. Therefore, he quit the Soviet regime in an effort
to keep his moderate faction free of communist infiltration. He

24. "Pervyi S'ezd," *KI*, pp. 2890–2891.
25. Irandust, "Voprosy," p. 140.
26. *Ibid.*, p. 132; Sultan-Zade, "Ob Iranskoi Kompartii," p. 77.

moved to the forest, which was his base of power, leaving Ehsanollah Khan and the communists in control of the urban areas.[27]

Realignment of Forces

By the end of July 1920, the Gilan Soviet revolution had entered its second stage. For roughly nine months, the revolutionary front would remain shattered, until the radicals saw the need to reunite to survive. During this time of fragmentation, several realignments of forces took place, without affecting the essential dichotomy of Kuchuk Khan on the one hand and the Iranian communists on the other.

Kuchuk Khan's Jangalis were isolated in the forest, where they resisted attempts at interference in their affairs by the communist radicals. Kuchuk Khan based his faction on an alliance with the merchant class and the petty bourgeoisie. These elements opposed land reform because they were for the most part landlords themselves. As a sop to the peasantry, however, Kuchuk Khan did institute such mild social reform as the restoration of the Muslim *zakat* tithe as the principal tax. This step eased the lot of the peasants by fixing the total tax level at 10 percent. Kuchuk Khan sought to keep his movement from attacking the traditional social order out of concern to retain his popularity among the people. He did not try to expand the area under his control, recognizing that his troops would not be effective against Tehran. At the same time, he valued the Soviets at Rasht as a buffer to keep the central government forces at bay.[28]

The new Bolshevik government established at Rasht on July 31, 1920, also represented a coalition, although its parts appeared somewhat more compatible than those of the earlier regime. Ehsanollah Khan had the top spot. He had won over the Kurdish leader, Halu Qurban, whose traditionalist troops formed a major

27. Irandust, "Voprosy," p. 140. Ravasani, *Sowjetrepublik Gilan,* pp. 585–587, gives the 34-article "Program of the Jangal Movement 1920," which illustrates the amalgam of Islam and mild social reform espoused by Kuchuk Khan.

28. Irandust, "Voprosy," pp. 135, 140–142; Fatemi, *Diplomatic History,* p. 242.

portion of the indigenous fighting forces behind the regime. Communist loyalists formed the main political arm of the government; they were heavily influenced by Sultan Zadeh and Ja'far Pishevari. The new government, however, depended directly on assistance by the Red Army and a predominantly Kurdish militia "supervised by Red Army officers, armed with Red Army guns, and decorated with Red Army insignia."[29]

Although the new communist government in Rasht took office almost simultaneously with the Anzali party congress, the regime leaders declined to follow the dictates of that assembly. Hewing instead to the theses recently elaborated at the Second Congress of the Comintern, they favored the possibility of skipping the bourgeois stage of revolution and of passing directly to the socialist phase. To establish a communist regime in Iran, they advocated the use of terror. As Sultan Zadeh himself said: " 'Give the masses the opportunity to show their authority and their prestige. Let them give free course to their passions and take revenge for their misery on their masters." The eventual goal of such action was the expropriation of all land to create a class of agricultural sharecroppers. These were indeed radical concepts and efforts to apply them seriously affected the course of the revolution.[30]

As their first step, the communists confiscated the land of all medium and large landlords in the area where their writ ran. At the same time, they ordered the tax system changed to put the burden on artisans and the peasantry. They also purged the civil service of non-communists and killed or exiled many of the bourgeoisie and feudal elements. In this reign of terror, Rasht was partially looted and mosques were defiled in a gesture of contempt for the Islamic beliefs of the populace. The middle classes, which were the hardest hit, fled from Gilan to Tehran, where they became spearheads of opposition to the Soviet regime. These refugees warned the rest of Iran against the communist experiment in the north and effectively countered Bolshevik propaganda in the country. The defection of these merchants also

29. Aurelio Palmieri, *La Politica Asiatica dei Bolscevichi* (Bologne: N. Zanichelli, 1924), pp. 209, 212.

30. Fatemi, *Diplomatic History*, pp. 233–234.

greatly weakened the Soviet cause inside Gilan itself. The disruption of economic and social life in the urban centers of Gilan which followed produced a lasting crisis.[31]

After Kuchuk Khan's departure, the communists ordered a general mobilization of peasants from 18 to 45 years of age to lead an attack on his forces. He was accused of maladministration and misappropriation of revolutionary funds. But the Jangalis proved too strong a match. To make matters worse, the Tehran government launched its own counterattack. In a series of meteoric marches, Staroselsky, at the head of the Cossack Brigade, retook Rasht on August 22, 1920. The communist leaders retreated in confusion after only desultory resistance.[32]

Although temporary, this defeat had important effects. Moscow evidently concluded that the Soviet state in Iran had little prospect of surviving. The Kremlin thus offered to begin negotiations for a treaty to regulate future Russo-Iranian relations. The Shah's government promptly accepted his offer and sent a representative to Moscow.

At the same time, in September 1920, the Comintern convened the Baku Congress of the Peoples of the East in an effort to harness the masses of the underdeveloped world against the Western industrial powers. The Iranian contingent included Sultan Zadeh, future Iranian party leader Ja'far Pishevari, Ehsanollah Khan, and the rising star of the nationalist wing of the organization, Haydar Khan. Their speeches reflected unanimity on the need for social reforms and "the dictatorship of the proletariat." But Haydar Khan's second address reflected such a bourgeois nationalist tinge that it evoked loud boos from part of the audience. Zinoviev, who played a leading part at the congress, repudiated Iranian radicals Sultan Zadeh and Ehsanollah Khan. He directed the Iranian party to cooperate with the national-liberation movement. The prominent expert on the Islamic world, Pavlovich, seconded this recommendation, but urged the creation of "peasant Soviets" and "Soviets of the toilers." As

31. Irandust, "Voprosy," pp. 140–142; Fatemi, *Diplomatic History*, pp. 231–232.
32. Iranskii, "Russko-Persidskiye otnosheniia," pp. 105–106; Ravasani, *Sowjetrepublik Gilan*, pp. 298–300.

befitting a gathering that sought to combine communist and non-communist revolutionaries, the Baku Congress broke up without clearly ruling on the question of the indispensibility of radical social reform.[33]

The Shah's forces had succeeded by this time in suppressing Khiyabani's revolt in Azerbaijan. However, fortune soon turned against Tehran, as the communists rallied and regained Rasht on October 21. Yet the Bolsheviks failed to restore rule over Mazanderan, which had fallen to the Cossacks, even though Staroselsky was pushed back to Manjil. At this point, the British withdrew their subsidy from the Cossack Brigade, considering the White Russian officers incompetent. Staroselsky's influence at court vanished, and the Cossack Brigade foundered. As a result, military action against the Soviet regime in Rasht ceased for several months.

In prevailing over the Cossacks, the Bolsheviks in Rasht had been aided by tribal leaders. These "representatives of reaction" had taken over to some extent the place in the revolutionary movement vacated by the flight of Kuchuk Khan's middle class supporters. However, the cooperation of feudalistic elements in a movement which aimed in theory to destroy their power was merely a tactical maneuver. They wished only to turn the revolution to their own ends. In fact, they secretly organized anti-communist agitation. Faced with mounting opposition, the central committee of the Iranian Communist Party was forced to abandon part of its radical program. The traditionalist elements steadily gained in strength in the party, while the Ehsanollah Khan government became increasingly unpopular.[34]

Return to a United Front

On October 22, 1920, the central committee of the Iranian Communist Party took a step toward reconciliation with Kuchuk Khan. Under the aegis of Haydar Khan, who had insinuated

---

33. For the record of the Baku Congress, see Brian Pearce (tr.), *Congress of the Peoples of the East, Baku, September 1920: Stenographic Report* (London: New Park Publications Ltd., 1977).
34. Irandust, "Voprosy," pp. 140–141.

himself into the position of party chairman following the Congress of the Peoples of the East, the central committee declared that "revolution in Iran was possible only after bourgeois evolution had been accomplished." This declaration also marked the end of attempts to create a proletariat in Gilan by importing Red Army elements from Baku and Russia. However, despite a proposal in an exchange of letters with Kuchuk Khan to restore the united front in November 1920, the communist radical wing did not cease to oppose the Jangalis.[35]

A major reason for Moscow's willingness to go along with Haydar Khan's theses on the need for bourgeois revolution evidently was the start of negotiations between the USSR and Iran looking toward a treaty to regulate their mutual relations. The Kremlin had clearly become convinced that the Gilan movement could not spread over all of Iran. Hence, the Soviets sought to open relations with the central authorities in Tehran to encourage the Iranians to move against the British.

That prospect accorded well with the intentions of the Iranian government, which sought through diplomacy to persuade the Soviets to withdraw from Gilan. The Tehran rulers were encouraged when in January 1921, the government of the Soviet Republic of Azerbaijan announced that it would recall the Red Army troops in Iran as soon as the British had evacuated. A month later, on February 26, 1921, Moscow signed a Treaty of Friendship with Tehran. It permitted Soviet occupation of Iranian territory solely if Iran were to be used as a base for foreign attack on the Soviet Union. In effect, this treaty legalized the presence of Soviet troops in Gilan, but only as long as the British remained in southern Iran. It thus applied pressure on London to withdraw its forces from Iran in order to secure recall of the Red Army.[36]

In Tehran meanwhile a major regime change was taking place. On February 21, 1921, Zia ed Din Tabatabai and Reza Khan

35. *Izvestiia*, November 6, 1921; Irandust, "Voprosy," p. 135; Ravasani, *Sowjetrepublik Gilan*, p. 314.

36. *Soviet Russia*, March 1921, p. 295. For the text of the Soviet-Persian Treaty, see J. C. Hurewitz, *Diplomacy in the Near and Middle East: A Documentary Record* (Princeton: Van Nostrand, 1956), vol. 2, pp. 90–94.

took power in a *coup d'état*. The Cossack Brigade, of which Reza Khan was a ranking officer, provided the base of power for this nationalist move. The new rulers faced the urgent tasks of restoring internal harmony, regaining popular confidence, and reasserting national sovereignty. To solve these problems, Zia ed Din hoped to win over the people by a program of reforms, including a far-reaching land reform. Reza Khan had less confidence in this tactic, believing that in Iran power could be based effectively only on a strong and loyal army. Thus his first care was to rebuild the Cossack Brigade into a well-disciplined striking force, committed to the new regime. He dismissed the British advisers and took steps to restore morale. Thus began the making of a strong Iranian central government.

These events in Tehran soon affected the balance of forces in Gilan. In this region of Iranian Azerbaijan, the communist radicals first reacted by seeking alliance with the traditionalist leader of Talysh (north-west Gilan) against both Reza Khan and Kuchuk Khan's Jangalis. The Talysh chief wanted guns in exchange for his store of supplies; the Bolsheviks had arms but needed provisions. This marriage of convenience showed the lengths to which the communist radicals would go in seeking to preserve their hegemony over the movement.[37]

This tactic, however, must have added to concern in the Kremlin leadership that the hard-line faction was violating the Treaty of Friendship with Iran. The Soviets clearly had decided that their interests demanded the repudiation of the policies of the radicals in order to make up with the new regime in Tehran. To this end, Haydar Khan, who was identified with the line that the national bourgeoisie was a legitimate revolutionary force which could be turned against the West, returned to Iran in April 1921 from Soviet Azerbaijan. Following Moscow's new approach, he adjusted the composition of the Revolutionary Committee on May 6, 1921, dropping some of the radicals from membership.[38]

37. Irandust, "Voprosy," pp. 140–141.
38. A. P. Pouyan and M. Mani, *Iran, Three Essays on Imperialism, The Revolutionary Left and the Guerilla Movement* (Florence, Italy: Edition MAZDAK, n.d.), p. 56.

The new leadership of the Iranian Communist Party broke off the Talysh connection and sought to compose differences with the Jangalis, probably with a view to toning down Kuchuk Khan's conflict with Tehran. The attempt of the Bolsheviks to carry out a purely communist revolution had generated such resistance that it was clear that extreme social reform could no longer be pursued. While the left faction of the Iranian Communist Party never gave up its dreams of more extensive social engineering, with this recognition of the failure of "militant communism" came a change to a new economic policy, similar in some respects to that adopted in Soviet Russia at that time. In the political sphere, this new policy demanded reconciliation with Kuchuk Khan.[39] The shift in reform emphasis paved the way for the Jangalis to agree to paper over their differences with the communists. In this situation, a united front of revolutionaries was revived in Gilan in May 1921.

Cooperation between the factions, however, was tenuous at best. For the next three months, until August 1921, the various groupings inside the revolutionary front worked at cross purposes. The basic dichotomy of the Jangalis and the communists provided a thread of continuity with the past. But inside each of the two main camps new shades of internal conflict arose. This period also marked the start of concerted efforts by the communists to infiltrate Kuchuk Khan's own forces in an effort to subvert his movement from within.

Each of the five members of the new Revolutionary Committee (Kuchuk Khan, Mohammadi, Halu Qurban, Ehsanollah Khan, and Haydar Khan) headed a separate faction. Kuchuk Khan's supporters, as usual most numerous in Jangal's forests, centered their activity around Fumen. From this vantage point, Kuchuk Khan could wield maximum power without leaving his natural base of support. Nearby at Rasht was another band of his close allies under this long-time collaborator, Mohammadi. This group of urban bourgeoisie represented the moderate faction of city dwellers backing the Gilan revolution.[40]

---

39. Irandust, "Voprosy," pp. 135, 140.
40. *Ibid.*, pp. 134, 143.

Rasht also served as the base of a Kurdish military organization led by Halu Qurban. These Kurds had initially furnished Kuchuk Khan much of his fighting strength; yet after they had refused to accompany Kuchuk Khan into the forest in mid-1920 and had supported Ehsanollah Khan, their position in Rasht had become tenuous. The Kurds were an alien group that lived off the population and with time came increasingly into friction with Mohammadi's followers. Even these three groups, which generally comprised the more traditionalist wing, were not harmonious.[41]

The radical camp was likewise divided. In Lahijan, Ehsanollah Khan now headed a Kurdish group whose military prowess had been important to communist strength. Unlike Halu Qurban's followers, Ehsanollah Khan's band favored extreme social reform. On the other hand, Haydar Khan based his faction in Anzali, where it was in easy communication with the party central committee in Baku. His supporters were said to consist mainly of artisans, many of whom came from Baku, as well as the few native stevedores and longshoremen in Anzali. Iranian workers from the Caucasus were evidently also an important component of his forces.[42]

As leader of the Iranian Communist Party, Haydar Khan sought to conquer Gilan through armistice with Kuchuk Khan and internal subversion. For this purpose he persuaded Kuchuk Khan to permit certain changes. First Haydar Khan secured his own election as chairman of the unified Revolutionary Committee, which functioned as the government of Gilan. Using the power of his new office, he then reorganized the administration to facilitate communist infiltration of the top posts. At the same time, he increased the number of communist cells. He issued instructions to the local committees of the Communist Party outlining the goals of the party and the tactics to be followed. In effect, these instructions called for large-scale agitation and propaganda along with the establishment of a spy system.[43]

41. *Ibid.*

42. *Ibid.;* see also Abikh, "Natsional'noe i revoliutsionnoe," *Novyi Vostok,* vol. 29, pp. 88–107.

43. G. Ducroiq, "La Politique du gouvernement des Soviets en

Haydar Khan's hopes of achieving undisputed communist supremacy were seriously undermined, however, by a badly calculated step by Ehsanollah Khan. In June 1921, Ehsanollah Khan raised a force of Iranians and Red Army troops from Soviet Georgia to march on Tehran. This military move immediately divided the united front. Both Kuchuk Khan's men and his allies as well as Haydar Khan's group abstained from this venture, judging it unwise to provoke the nationalist regime of Reza Khan so directly.[44]

Since the British had withdrawn their last units in May, Reza Khan's forces were left alone to meet the attack. The Soviets had not yet evacuated Iran as the treaty with Moscow stipulated. In fact, more troops landed in Anzali as late as July 1921. Nevertheless, the combined Red Army expeditionary force itself was too weak and disorganized to present a serious threat to Tehran, despite the fact that Reza Khan had not yet had time to whip his army into shape. Ehsanollah Khan's attack was easily parried; he was obliged to retreat in disorder. His defeat paved the way for the future reconquest of Gilan by the central government.[45]

The Soviet Republic of Gilan

As part of his new program, Haydar Khan proclaimed a "Soviet Republic of Gilan" on August 4, 1921. This newly-minted entity formally replaced the earlier "Soviet Socialist Republic of Iran," which had become a casualty of the internal factional struggle. With proclamation of the Soviet Republic of Gilan, Haydar Khan's influence appeared to have reached a peak. Nevertheless, the Communist Party did not enjoy sufficient popular appeal to provide a base for consolidating its gains. Ehsanollah Khan's defeat had greatly weakened Bolshevik military prestige. In consequence, Haydar Khan's position was not secure.[46]

Perse," *Revue du monde musulman*, 52 (December 1922), pp. 144–145.

44. Reisner and Gol'dberg (eds.), *Ocherki*, p. 220.

45. *Ibid.*

46. Irandust, "Voprosy," pp. 133, 143.

During the months before the formation of the Soviet Republic of Gilan, Kuchuk Khan's movement had increasingly emphasized its separatist rather than its Iranian nationalist nature. Perhaps this course was inevitable, inasmuch as its leaders were either Azeris or Kurds and the revolutionary movement had been so long confined to one isolated northern province, distant from the broader nationalism that had arisen in Tehran. In this final stage of the movement, Kuchuk Khan also seemed to have been more willing to compromise with the communists than before, although he did insist that reforms be moderate. Nevertheless, it is hard to explain why he permitted Haydar Khan to consolidate so much authority. Perhaps Kuchuk Khan genuinely wanted to prove his loyalty to the united front, or perhaps he intended to test communist good intentions. Undoubtedly he hoped to strengthen the revolutionary movement by encouraging its unity.

Beginning of the End

Between the proclamation of the Soviet Republic of Gilan in August and the end of September 1921, the final breakup of the united front took place. The internal factions continued to work against each other, but ever more openly as time passed. In fact, the Soviet Republic of Gilan was stillborn.

Haydar Khan continued his program of subversion, growing more bold with every new success. When Kuchuk Khan refused to publish the proposed Communist Party program, Haydar Khan had it issued himself in the name of the Commissar of Foreign Affairs, one of his posts in the government. This defiance opened an ever-widening breach between these two leaders. In September 1921, Haydar Khan formed a special communist detachment of picked men, although Halu Qurban, the Commissar of Military Affairs, was the only one empowered to organize new forces. This last act evoked quick retaliation by Kuchuk Khan and precipitated the downfall of communist hopes in Iran for years to come.[47]

Haydar Khan's actions even provoked disapproval in the Comintern. At the Third Congress of the Comintern in the summer of 1921, Sultan Zadeh's supporters, especially Ja'far

---

47. *Ibid.*, p. 143.

Pishevari, had strongly attacked nationalist opportunists who created their own "pseudo-communist parties." It was clear that without naming names these radicals were calling Haydar Khan's approach into question. These arguments won support in the Third International, which saw need to tighten organizational control in order to prepare for a world revolution which no longer seemed just around the corner. The implication of these organizational decisions was that only one communist party could be legitimate in any country. That in turn signalled strongly that Haydar Khan and his opponents would have to resolve their differences under the Kremlin's guidance. Under this impetus, the Baku headquarters of the Iranian Communist Party apparently convened a gathering of 169 delegates on August 19, 1921, at which Sultan Zadeh's line and that of Haydar Khan's group were both rejected. Significantly, this Soviet-controlled assembly condemned the declaration of the Soviet Republic of Gilan as contradicting Comintern policy toward Iran. Clearly Haydar Khan's course was bitterly divisive within the larger communist context.[48]

The effects of Moscow's disapproval were soon visible in Gilan. In September 1921, Soviet troops finally withdrew from Iran, thus removing a major support of the Gilan regime. Moscow had decided to prove its sincerity in accepting the treaty with Iran by observing its terms. Moreover, the Soviets must have recognized the futility of continuing their Gilan adventure, which was by now obviously headed toward destruction. Although many of the local communists in the field might be loath to abandon the struggle, the Kremlin then, as on many other occasions, was ready to sacrifice indigenous communists in the interests of Moscow's larger plans.[49]

48. Ravasani, *Sowjetrepublik Gilan*, pp. 335–337; Communist International, *Bulletin des III. Kongress der Kommunistischen Internationale*, no. 23 (July 19, 1921), pp. 521–522 (speech of Agha Zadeh); Communist International, *Protokoll des III. Kongresses der Kommunistischen Internationale, Moskau, 22. Juni bis 12. Juli 1921* (Hamburg: C. Hoym, 1921), pp. 326–328 (speech of Javad Zadeh, later known as Ja'far Pishevari).

49. Zabih, *Communist Movement*, pp. 40–42.

To make this meaning unmistakable, Soviet Ambassador Andrew Rothstein followed up with a letter to Kuchuk Khan disavowing "the situation of last year"—a clear reference to the radical policies of social revolution that had bothered the Jangalis. The ambassador warned that inasmuch as revolution at this time "is not only useless, but also harmful," the Soviet government is "obliged to remove our support from the revolutionaries and their operations." And he explained Soviet hopes to see Kuchuk Khan either "disarmed" or "withdraw to some corner" to wait for a more propitious moment.[50]

Under these circumstances, Kuchuk Khan began to denounce the Bolsheviks as traitors to the revolution. His attacks increased progressively in ferocity, and soon he joined the traditionalist elements in direct opposition to the radicals. Kuchuk Khan even tried to negotiate with Reza Khan to see if a *modus vivendi* could be arranged. Reza Khan, however, would not share power, so that no agreement could be reached. Despite this rebuff, Kuchuk Khan's faction decided to move against the communists in Gilan. Thus toward the end of September 1921, Kuchuk Khan arrested Haydar Khan and his associates. In the internecine struggle between the factions, Kuchuk Khan's forces rapidly prevailed. On September 29, 1921, many of the communist leaders, including Haydar Khan, were killed. The communist threat to Gilan was over.[51]

In liquidating communist control in Gilan, Kuchuk Khan showed himself in his true colors. He was not willing to surrender leadership of the movement to communists controlled from abroad. Moreover, he could not countenance Bolshevik efforts to sabotage his movement through infiltration and the introduction of radical social change that alienated the population. Kuchuk Khan did not share their beliefs in agrarian reform or in the violent rearrangement of classes. Much less could he agree to accept Moscow as the source of policy guidance. Finally, the communists had both estranged those around him and weakened

50. Pouyan and Mani, *Iran*, pp. 56–57, quoting E. Mir Fakhraii, *Sardar Djangal, Mirza Kuchik-khan* (Tehran, 1344/1965), pp. 307–312.

51. Vinogradova, "Natsional'no-osvoboditel'noe dvizhenie," p. 18; Ivanova, "Natsional'no-osvoboditel'noe dvizhenie," pp. 124–127.

the whole revolutionary movement. Thus Kuchuk Khan's final assault against the Communist Party in Gilan came as a logical step, even though this move also reduced total Gilani strength against the central government.

Meanwhile, the constellation of forces in Iran was moving rapidly against the Gilanis. Reza Khan had proceeded with the army reorganization. Zia ed Din Tabatabai had been forced to flee when his policies conflicted with those of Reza Khan, who as Minister of War then became master in Tehran.

One of the most immediate tasks facing Reza Khan was the restoration of order. Just after the *coup d'état* in February 1921, Mohammad Taqi, the governor of Khorasan, refused to recognize the new regime and led his followers in revolt. This rebellion was a purely military uprising, a protest against Reza Khan rather than a social movement. It had no deep roots or popular support, and Reza Khan's new army suppressed it easily by bribing the tribes to desert. By early fall of 1921, Khorasan province had been pacified, and Reza Khan was free to concentrate on Gilan.[52] Following the evacuation of Soviet troops, there was no outside force to prevent Reza Khan from advancing. Moreover, he could now do so without fear of triggering an international incident. Thus the Tehran regime had little reason to agree to Kuchuk Khan's effort at negotiations.

Toward the start of October 1921, Reza Khan's troops marched on Gilan. Halu Qurban and his Kurds, who were the largest military force in Gilan, were bought off by the central government and deserted. In fact, using his intimate knowledge of the Jangali forest, Halu Qurban led Reza Khan's troops against the remnants of the Jangali band. Kuchuk Khan's units could not withstand the superior forces flung at them and were easily defeated. Ehsanollah Khan, who had managed to escape Kuchuk Khan's wrath, succeeded in finding a refuge in Baku. Kuchuk Khan himself fled to the mountains where he either froze to death or was captured and killed. In any event, his head was severed to be displayed to the Iranian populace as proof of his demise.[53]

52. Ivanova, "Natsional'no-osvoboditel'noe dvizhenie," pp. 128–141.
53. *Ibid.*, pp. 124–127.

In this way, by December 1921, the province was pacified and Tehran's sovereignty was restored. The Soviet experiment in Gilan was over, a victim of the emerging tendency in Moscow to value relations with established central governments, however, reactionary, over support to communist parties. But memories of this revolutionary effort lingered among both the communists and the native Gilanis. Thus the Soviet republic in Gilan formed a precedent for a successor break-away movement in the wake of the Second World War under Ja'far Pishevari, whose revolutionary eye teeth had been cut in the earlier experiment.

SUMMING UP

In retrospect, it seems clear that the Gilan revolution failed not, as various Soviet commentators sought to claim, because of dissension within the Communist Party or even because of inappropriate tactics by ultra-leftists seeking to carry out a distorted version of communism. To be sure, these were contributing factors. But when all was said and done, the main problem for the Soviets was the lack of appeal of their basic message to a traditional Muslim society. Communism as a doctrine was not well known in the Islamic world in 1920. Thus, at first, the incompatibility of Islam and Marxism was not clear to many, whose assumption that the communalism of communism might equate to the feeling of solidarity of the *umma* (Islamic community) was soon exploded as excessively naive. In the end, therefore, it was only professional revolutionaries or the handful of intellectuals who, rejecting tradition, proved reliable proponents of Soviet revolution.

The others involved in the Gilan movement behaved as though it was a traditional-style rebellion played according to long-hallowed rules of tribal engagement. While the leaders might mouth revolutionary slogans, most were not inclined to fight to the finish when faced with frontal assault by superior forces. Many were thus quite willing to make accommodation with a more powerful central government, a tactic not seen by them as a sacrifice of honor. As traditionalists, they did not by any means owe total allegiance to the revolution. Indeed, their proclivity to switch sides when pressed doomed the movement.

Such an understanding of the character of the Gilan experience would, no doubt, have prepared the leaders in the Kremlin for the collapse of Soviet regimes in northern Iran whenever Moscow's forces were withdrawn. Indeed, in the twentieth century, tribal revolts required outside support to withstand increasingly powerful central governments. That was the case in Gilan in 1921 and even more so in Azerbaijan in 1946. On both occasions, the communists were unable to change the nature of the contest by generating supporters whose ideological commitment would match the fervor of proponents of the traditional system. The aspiration to liberation from Tehran's control represented the time-honored desire of the provinces to be left alone; hence, it could not be translated into passion for class warfare in alliance with Moscow in order to overturn the tribal order.

What the Gilan experiment proved above all was that clan and family bonds were stronger than ideology, especially where religious values were intertwined as supports for the soial structure. Thus, for all its outward Soviet trappings, the Gilan revolution never passed beyond its traditionalist mold. Rather than a harbinger of the new, it was a testimony to the persistence and power of old patterns and old ways.

CHAPTER ELEVEN

The 1820 Expedition to the Gulf and the Decline of British Commercial Shipping: The Paradox of the Cost of Security

STEPHEN R. GRUMMON

In his study *Oman Since 1856*, Robert Landen has noted that in the 1860s Western-controlled economic enterprises (and the modern technology which accompanied them) began to establish themselves in the Persian Gulf region. For example, regular steamer service between India and the Gulf began in 1862; the British trading firm of Paul, Gray, and Company (later to become Gray, Mackenzie, and Company) opened an office in Bushire in the mid-1860s; and the telegraph was introduced in the region in the mid-1870s. These developments profoundly altered the economic environment of the Gulf region, undermining its traditional economy and its shipping and commercial communities. Landen believes that the introduction of the steamship was particularly disruptive, dealing a major blow to the prosperity of Arab and Persian shipowners who at that time almost totally dominated shipping between the Gulf and India.[1]

Persian and Arab shipowners, however, had not always dominated shipping in the region. In fact, during much of the

---

1. *Oman Since 1856* (Princeton: Princeton University Press, 1967), pp. 79–80.

eighteenth and early nineteenth centuries, British-owned shipping competed successfully for the opportunity to carry cargo between India and the Gulf. Ironically, it was the 1819–1820 British expedition to eliminate "piracy" in the Gulf which set the stage for the decline of British-owned commercial shipping in the region.

The expedition laid the groundwork for what became a British-imposed maritime peace in the Gulf and assured that British political interests there would be paramount. While overall British economic interests generally benefited from the emerging maritime order, there was an unanticipated development: British shippers increasingly were unable to compete successfully with their Persian and Arab counterparts. The relationship between the *pax Britannica* and the economic cost of security lay at the heart of this peculiar development problem. More specifically, because the British did not charge fees or tolls in return for the maritime peace which they imposed in the Gulf, Arab and Persian shipowners could easily undercut their British competitors. This was so because they generally had lower operating costs, which in turn meant they could offer merchants contracting for cargo space lower freight rates on the run between India and the Gulf. The key point is that the cost of security was a significant factor in determining the competitiveness of the two groups.

THE RELATIONSHIP BETWEEN TRADE AND SECURITY

Modern commercial trade generally is conducted within a secure political environment. That is to say, there is a widely accepted code of international commercial law and numerous multinational and bilateral commercial treaties which, taken together, have defined and established a generally accepted legal framework within which trade is carried out. Contracts are honored, international payments made, and disputes settled according to the recognized legal procedures. In today's world, security costs generally are synonymous with insurance costs, which focus primarily on risks ranging from loss of cargo to failure to deliver goods according to a specified contractual date. Moreover, piracy is virtually unknown. While overseas commerce today does face risk, this risk is basically related to market costs—i.e., is there sufficient demand for a product? is the price too high or too low? will exchange or short-term interest rates move against the buyer or seller?

The merchant living in previous ages faced many of the same market risks, particularly those related to market supply and demand. He also confronted two other major security problems which generally do not plague his modern counterpart: how could goods be safely transported over vast distances that were largely unpoliced, subject to arbitrary action by numerous, often antagonistic, political entities; and how could trade be protected from capricious and illegal seizure after it arrived at its destination?

The historian Fredrick Lane believes that in the pre-modern world a very substantial portion of the costs which a merchant faced was related to paying for protection—that is, making payments to political entities in order to carry on business. He argues that these security costs were a critical factor in determining which trade routes would be used. In the trade between India and the Mediterranean world, for example, the question was whether the Persian Gulf/Levant or the Red Sea/Egyptian route would be used. Such costs significantly influenced a merchant's rate of profit.

Lane's concept of "protection," or what he calls "the economic consequences of organized violence," starts with the observation that governments (termed "violence producing/violence controlling organizations") provide the community with an economic service in furnishing "protection" or security.[2] This service directly affects the amount and distribution of material wealth in a society through the costs which the government incurs in providing security and the prices it charges those who benefit from the service.

Protection is of two types: one is security from third parties, i.e., a national government protecting its population from another state or entity; and second is protection from the so-called protector, i.e., the population is forced to pay to keep the

2. "The Economic Consequences of Organized Violence," *Journal of Economic History*, 18 (1958), pp. 401–417. The same article also appears in Lane's collected papers, *Venice and History* (Baltimore: The Johns Hopkins Press, 1966).

protector away.[3] In essence, the price (taxation or at least that part of it used for security services) is what members of a society have to pay in order to avoid more severe losses, or outright confiscation, of their material wealth.

Lane believes that a monopoly is the most rational economic form which can be employed in the "production" of security. Protection can be provided more cheaply by a monopoly because absence of internal challengers lowers operating costs (i.e., defense and police expenditures in modern vocabulary). Germany during the Thirty Years' War and much of Iran in the eighteenth century are examples of countries in which a monopoly on the production of "legalized violence" did not exist. In both, rival "violence producing" organizations competed for protection payments over much of the same territory. Since operating costs were high, payments of a corresponding nature were demanded from the population by all "protection producing" enterprises involved.

By establishing a monopoly on violence production, the single, violence-generating entity is theoretically in a position to lower its operating costs. However, as Lane points out, lowered operating costs have not necessarily resulted in lower taxes. Because of its monopoly, the violence producing entity can keep up the " 'sales price' or even raise (prices) to the point at which it encountered a kind of sales resistance."[4] This resistance could take the form of riots, smuggling, or population flight, including the migration of a merchant community from port cities.[5]

---

3. Lane notes that this last situation is not unlike "the racketeer who collects payments for 'protection' against a violence which he himself threatens. . ." *Ibid.*, p. 414.

4. *Ibid.*, p. 416.

5. There are numerous examples in Gulf history of merchants moving from one port to another in search of more favorable conditions under which to trade. To cite only one illustration of many, in the 1750s the ruler of Bandar Rig, the notorious Mir Muhanna, drove much of the merchant community from the port because of his arbitrary and repressive commercial policies. The port of Bushire benefited as an East India Company official noted: "The Shik [of Bushire] having found it worth his while to deal fairly by everybody, many rich merchants have resorted to it from Bunder Rig. . .". *The Gambroon Diary*, Factory Records, G/29/7,

According to Lane, the concept of protection costs is crucial for understanding the nature and sources of profits derived from international trade in the late Middle Ages and the first centuries of Europe's oceanic expansion. In his view, merchants were compelled to make numerous security payments, which could include convoy fees, tribute to local freebooters (the equivalent of the nineteenth century Barbary pirates), higher insurance for voyages, and bribes or gifts to customs or other government officials. Lane calls these types of payments "protection rent" and clearly differentiates these costs from traditional economic costs, such as those for labor and materials. These "protection" expenditures constituted a substantial component of the total costs confronting the overseas trader. More importantly, Lane asserts that "lower payments for protection [were] often the decisive factor in competition between merchants of different cities and kingdoms."[6]

Niels Steengaard has built on Lane's ideas in his masterful study of Asian trade in the early seventeenth century.[7] He poses the question of how it was that the European East Indian companies (British, Dutch, and French) were able to seize control of the Asiatic trade at that time and thereby eventually triumph over the carracks (a sailing ship which the Portuguese used) and the caravans of the Asians, particularly the Moguls. Steengaard concludes that the companies were able to "internalize the production of security" so significantly that they were able to make major reductions in the marginal cost of a "unit" of protection.

Lane's and Steengaard's works provide a framework for explaining why the expedition of 1819–1820 against piracy in the Gulf had the ironic impact of benefiting Arab and Persian shipowners at the expense of their British counterparts. Their ideas

April 9, 1755. Here and throughout the notes, all documents listed are found in the India Office Library and Records, London.

6. Lane, "Economic Consequences," pp. 420–421.

7. *Carracks, Caravans, and Companies: The Structural Crisis in the European-Asian Trade in the Early Seventeenth Century* (Lund: Studentlitteratur, 1973). See Chapter 1 in particular.

are also useful for analyzing the broad trends of Persian Gulf politics in the period preceding the British attack.

COMMERCIAL RIVALRY BETWEEN OMAN AND BUSHIRE

In the late eighteenth and early nineteenth centuries, southern Persian Gulf politics were dominated by Oman's attempt to establish political and economic hegemony in the region.[8] The Omanis, however, did not act in a political vacuum. Karim Khan Zand, the founder of the dynasty which ruled much of Iran in the 1760s and 1770s, had equally ambitious designs in the Gulf. Thus he served as a significant check to the Omanis until his death in 1779. With the disappearance of a Persian counterweight, the Arab shaykhdoms on the southern shore of the Gulf were the only possible block to Omani amibitions. By the 1780s, leaders of several Arab city-states had established themselves successfully on the southern shore (for example, the Al Khalifa of Bahrain and the Qawasim in what is now much of the United Arab Emirates) and, as Landen notes, "were ready to challenge Oman's domination over Gulf trade and maritime activity."[9] It was this trade war into which the British stumbled and which set off a spiral of attacks on British shipping, particularly in the decade before the expedition. The eventual result of these developments, of course, was the decision to send an expedition to the Gulf in 1820.

From a slightly different perspective, Omani expansion can be viewed as an effort to impose a maritime peace over the Gulf region and then to charge for this "service" (i.e., the collection of protection payments). This policy led to a partially successful effort to seize strategic land in the region as a means of controlling trade lanes. For example in 1794, Sayyid Sultan ibn Ahmad, who ruled Muscat from 1793 to 1804, succeeded in "renting" Bandar Abbas from Muhammad Qajar, who had just established

8. For a detailed account of this effort, see J. G. Lorimer, *Gazetteer of the Persian Gulf* (London: Government Printing, 1908, 1915); Samuel Miles, *the Countries and Tribes of the Persian Gulf*, 2nd ed. (London: Frank Cass, 1966); J. B. Kelly, *Britain and the Persian Gulf* (Oxford: Clarendon Press, 1968); and Landen, *Oman Since 1856.*

9. Landen, *Oman Since 1856*, p. 25.

himself in Iran after defeating his principal rivals, the declining Zand family. Toward the end of the eighteenth century, Sayyid Sultan turned his attention to the central Gulf, making an unsuccessful attempt to seize Kharg Island in 1798 and Bahrain in 1800. These forays were resisted not only by the ruling family of Bahrain, the Al Khalifa, but also by the al-Muzkur family who had ruled Bushire, the most important port on the Gulf's northern littoral, since the early 1750s.[10]

Bushire and its merchant community had been sparring intermittently with Sultan over the increasingly contentious issue of direct shipping between India and Bushire. This issue—which provides an important perspective for understanding why the 1820 expedition had the impact that it did—was relatively simple. Shipowners from Bushire were sailing directly between that port and India. In doing so, they were bypassing Muscat and avoiding a custom duty to which the Imam of Muscat claimed he was entitled. The practice of "non-stop" sailing probably began in the late 1790s with the rise of several Bushire-based merchant princes, including Hajji Khalil and Muhammad Nabih Khan, who was Iran's ambassador to India from 1805 to 1807.[11] By 1800 Sayyid Sultan ibn Ahmad had determined that the practice had to be stopped or he would suffer financially. In a memorandum to the East India Company's (EIC) Bombay Council in the spring of 1800, the British agent in Muscat clearly delineated Sayyid Sultan's predicament:

> From some private hints I have lately had, I think it is probable Seyd Sultan will soon address the Hon'ble Board on a subject in which he is nearly concerned; namely, the prospect there is of his revenues suffering a considerable diminution from the establishment of Persian agents at

10. "The Imam [of Muscat] is now at war with Abushire [Bushire] on account of Bahareen [Bahrain]." David Seton, East India Company agent at Muscat to Jonathan Duncan, Governor in Council, Bombay, *Home Miscellaneous Series*, vol. 474, pp. 108–109, December 29, 1800.

11. For more details about Bushire's merchant community, see Stephen R. Grummon, "The Rise and Fall of the Arab Shayhkdom of Bushire: 1750–1850" (unpublished doctoral dissertation, The Johns Hopkins University School of Advanced International Studies, 1985).

Bombay, who purchase goods there for their principals and freight them on vessels directly for Bushire by which practice it is evident they save the duties that have hitherto been levied at this port [Muscat][12]

The duty in question was a 2.5 percent custom charge which, according to the EIC agent in Muscat, David Seton, "the Imams of Muscat have thrust down the throat of the natives of the Gulf."[13] Seton went on to explain:

The Imam of Muscat having cleared the Gulf of pirates established a duty to be paid by those who benefited by the protection thus afforded to their trade . . . I believe he will endeavor to make this a general rule throughout the Gulf.[14]

News of Sayyid Sultan's disquiet apparently reached Bushire and its leading *shaykh*, Shaykh Nasir, some time in the spring or summer of 1800. Later in the year, Nasir dispatched a diplomatic emissary to Muscat with orders to resolve differences over the issue of direct trade between India and Bushire as well as Bahrain. The negotiations, however, were inconclusive.[15]

Hostilities between the two parties continued to flare up intermittently. For example, in 1801 a vassal of Sayyid Sultan, who lived on Qishm Island, seized a boat belonging to Muhammad Nabih Khan. When informed of the development, East India

12. Dr. A. Bogle, EIC agent at Muscat to Duncan, *Home Miscellaneous Series*, pp. 125–126, April 2, 1800.

13. David Seton to Duncan, *Home Miscellaneous Series*, vol. 474, pp. 108–109, December 29, 1800.

14. *Ibid.*, vol. 474, pp. 108–109, December 29, 1800.

15. According to Seton, Sayyid Sultan ibn Ahmad made three demands: Commercial agents from Bushire should not be permitted to reside in Bombay; the *malik-i-tujjar* (chief or leader of the merchants), who at the time was Hajji Khalil, should be turned over to Sultan; and Kharg Island should be "delivered up" to Oman. The demands suggest Sayyid Sultan had no interest in negotiating with Nasir. Capitulation by Nasir on the first two demands would have effectively stopped the practice of direct shipping, while the third would have given to Sayyid Sultan through diplomacy what he was unable to achieve through military means—a base in the central Gulf.

Company officials in Bombay interpreted the Omani action as an attempt "to discourage direct communication between ports of the Persian Gulf and India." Jonathan Duncan, the EIC's governor general in Bombay, was reported to have termed the Omani policy "unjust."[16] In a foreshadowing of events to come, he instructed the Resident at Muscat to inform Sayyid Sultan ibn Ahmad that he should not encourage or protect "pirates who make their prey on unprotected trade passing between this port and Bushire or Bussorah [Basra] to which it is equally the duty and determination of this government to extend the upmost possible security."[17]

BRITISH SHIPPING INTERESTS

David Seton in Muscat was not as perturbed as Duncan about the "immorality" of Sayyid Sultan's actions. To the contrary, he shrewdly noted that British shipping interests benefited because of the piracy and maritime instability in the Gulf. In fact in a letter to Harford Jones, the Resident at Basra, Seton baldly asserted:

> It cannot be well for the interest of the English to remove the trammels the natives lay on the trade of one another as it secures their [the English] vessels a preference.

Seton then explained that the "preference" for English vessels would not exist in a more stable environment because "the Arab from the cheapness with which he sails his vessels would deprive them [English shippers] of freight was he not burdened with extra duties and a tedious voyage."[18]

16. Robert Richards, Secretary to Duncan, writing to David Seton, *Home Miscellaneous Series*, vol. 477, p. 323, August 13, 1801.

17. *Ibid.* It was several years later (1809 and then again in 1820) before the British finally reacted with military force to the attacks, and, when they did, it was against the Qawasim Arabs rather than the Omanis.

18. Seton to Harford Jones, *Home Miscellaneous Series*, vol. 475, pp. 450–451, February 28, 1801.

Seton had hit upon an important point. The competitive position of British shippers was linked to security costs. As long as security costs were high, the British could expect to compete successfully with their Arab and Persian counterparts. And compete they did, as numerous examples drawn from the East India Company records show. For example, in 1796 the EIC Resident in Bushire prepared a report for the Bombay Council on Persian merchants living in Musulipatam, which is located on the Coramandel coast of eastern India. He commented that many of these merchants owned several chintz weaving factories in the town and that they sent their chintzs to Bushire "primarily on English bottoms."[19]

Six years later the EIC Resident in Bushire wrote:

The political situation [in the Bushire area] is very serious. At present, by sea no traffic is carried on but in English ships as the country vessels dare not venture out these ports for fear of the Bani Utuba Arabs.[20]

In 1817 William Bruce, the EIC Resident in Bushire, estimated that British owned vessels made up about two-thirds of the shipping entering and leaving Bushire. (At that time the full impact of the Qawasim raids was being felt throughout the central and southern Gulf.) In the same report he indicated that the principal merchants of Bushire specifically had asked that a British vessel preparing to sail to Bombay be delayed so that treasure which was momentarily expected to arrive from Isfahan and Shiraz could be consigned to it.[21]

British ships offered their customers two types of security. First, the ships were generally better armed and hence better able to protect themselves from predators. Security of this nature was especially attractive during periods of serious instability, particularly when a merchant might be shipping treasure to India, as in the example just cited.

19. *Secret and Political Proceedings*, range E, vol. 11, p. 1766, August 30, 1796.
20. *Bushire Residency Records*, R/15/1/5, August 14, 1802.
21. *Ibid.*, R/15/1/20, June 9, 1817.

Second, shipping with the British held out the possibility that if some misfortune did befall the vessel, the merchant's cargo might be recovered or compensation extracted from the offending party. The experience of two British ships, the *Alert* and the *Hector*, provides a graphic example of this last point. In 1803 the two ships ran aground near the port city of Nakhilu and were promptly plundered by the local *shaykh*.

The British Resident—on behalf of the merchants who had shipped cargo on the vessel, most of whom were Persian—demanded that the Prince of Shiraz, whose jurisdiction included the Gulf littoral, recover the plundered goods or pay compensation for them. The Prince, who had little interest in the affair and who certainly had no intention of paying compensation to the merchants, claimed that Shaykh Nasir of Bushire was responsible for the actions of the *shaykh* of Nakhilu. Accordingly, Nasir was ordered to proceed against Nakhilu. For two years, Nasir procrastinated,[22] but finally under constant pressure from the British and threats from Shiraz, he organized an expedition which sailed to Nakhilu in 1805. In a meat-axe approach to the problem, Nasir plundered the port, and eventually the merchants, who had cargo on the two ships, received some compensation for their losses.

Despite such security advantages, British shippers still faced stiff competition from Arab and Persian counterparts. The Persian and Arabs generally had much lower operating costs. In his *Report on the Trade of Persia*, Sir John Malcolm noted that "the natives could freight goods for a third of the sum that they are on European and well-founded vessels."[23] Two years later a trade report issued by the Bombay Residency noted that the Imam of Muscat's operating costs were one-third the costs of the British.

22. In late 1803, Samuel Manesty, the EIC Resident at Basra wrote, "I have received such information from persons recently arrived from Bushire as persuades me that Shaik Nassir decidedly means to decline obedience to the orders received by him at Sheras [Shiraz] to proceed to Nukheloo and that he has already formed rather plausible excuses for his intended conduct." *Bushire Residency Records*, R/15/1/6, November 26, 1803.

23. Persian Gulf Factory Records, G/29/22, February 26, 1800.

The report claimed that the reason the Imam could operate so cheaply was that he used slave labor and did not buy insurance.[24]

In the two or three decades preceding the 1820 expedition, British shipowners, with their comparative advantage in security, were able to compete with Arabs and Persians, with their comparative advantage in lower operating costs. In times of intense maritime security, British shipowners tended to have the upper hand, while in intervening periods the advantage shifted toward the Arabs and Persians. The 1820 expedition, however, tipped the scales decisively against the Europeans, primarily because the cost of security became much less critical as a component in a merchant's calculation of his total expenses and liabilities. This was so because the British made no effort to "charge" for the protection service that they imposed on the Gulf.

The impact of the British action became discernible within a few years. As already noted, in 1817 British ships accounted for an estimated two-thirds of the shipping entering and leaving Bushire. Seven years later (and four years after the expedition), the EIC Resident in Bushire estimated that British shippers carried about 50 percent of cargoes bound to and from Bushire. However, he warned that

> ... the security with which small vessels now navigate the Gulf ... has caused a considerable part of the carrying trade to pass from the hands of Europeans to those natives who can do it cheaper. It is probable that the same cause will continue to operate and diminish the share which the European shipowners still have in this trade.[25]

As it turns out, that prediction proved devastatingly correct. "Native" shippers maintained and indeed strengthened their hold on the carrying trade between India and the Gulf as the British maritime peace took hold. In fact, the extent of this development formed the backdrop of an EIC bureaucratic dispute which occurred in the mid-1830s. At that time a proposal was floated with EIC councils to increase significantly the duty levied on

24. *Bombay Commercial Reports*, R 419, vol. 40, 1802–1803.
25. *Secret Letters and Enclosures from Persia*, L/P and S/9, vol. 37, July 14, 1824.

Arab and Persian vessels entering British controlled Indian ports. In a long minute on the subject, Samuel Hennell, the EIC Resident in Bushire, strongly opposed that idea. Hennell argued that the effect "of the proposed change in the duties will be eventually to transfer the commerce of this Gulf to vessels under British colors and passes."[26] He felt that this advantage to British shippers had to be weighed very carefully against "the prospective evils which may arise to our political views [policy] for the permanent suppression of piracy should the proposed change be made in the rates of duties. . ."[27] Essentially, he feared that if the "natives" could no longer participate in the "carrying trade," they would return to their old predatory habits.[28]

Hennell's arguments are grounded in considerations of politics and strategy. Generally, he skirts the issue of the negative economic impact which the maritime peace was having on British shipping. In his concluding paragraph on the subject, however, Hennell quoted from an October 1830 minute prepared by the venerable Sir John Malcolm, who was wrestling with the question of whether to reduce the presence of the EIC navy in the Gulf. His minute directly linked economic and political considerations and is worth quoting extensively:

> We cannot have a better proof of the happy progress of the change we desire [i.e., maritime peace in the Gulf] than the fact of the trade with the Gulf being now carried on much more than it was before by the Arabs in Dowes and small craft from India—but this while it has been a great means of reclaiming men from predatory habits has diminished the number of English vessels engaged in this commerce . . . Agreeably [presumably, Malcolm meant "according"] to the

---

26. *Bushire Residency Records*, R/15/1/72.
27. *Ibid.*
28. *Ibid.* According to Hennell, the trade which India afforded "engages several hundreds of restless Arabs . . . and were it not for the occupation thus afforded by commercial pursuits, [they] would be driven by poverty not less than by inclination to a recurrence to their former habits of piracy and rapine." Hennell estimated that on the southern shore of the Gulf (including Oman) some 300 boats and 8000 men were engaged in the India trade.

statement lately received from the Resident in the Persian Gulf, it appears that about three-fourths of the trade from India to Bushire is carried on by natives and Arab craft. This is certainly a large proportion but as tending to encourage and keep up a commercial spirit it ought rather to be a matter of congratulation to us than otherwise.[29]

The pattern was set for the next several decades. Arab and Persian shippers would dominate Gulf shipping until the advent of the steamship, which, in turn, would alter forever the structure and organization of Gulf shipping.

BRITISH TRADING INTERESTS

Overall British trading interests in the Gulf did not suffer as a result of the 1819–1820 expedition. Following a world-wide trend, the quantity of British goods—especially cheap cotton cloth—entering Gulf markets via native shipping increased dramatically, particularly in the 1830s and 1840s. The port of Bushire is a case in point, for it can be postulated that trends there generally paralleled the experience of most other ports on the Gulf.

India was by far southern Iran's most important trading partner during the period under consideration, and Indian manufactured goods made up the bulk of the imports passing through Bushire. For example, in 1789, Charles Watkins, the EIC Resident at Bushire, prepared an extensive trade report for EIC officials in which he estimated that at least 68 percent of all imports coming into Bushire were of Indian origin. In contrast, European manufactures made up about 3.5 percent of Bushire's imports.[30]

Surprisingly, later in the eighteenth century, the western coast of India (including Bombay) was not Bushire's most impor-

29. *Ibid.*

30. "The Charles Watkins Trade Report," *Bushire Residency Records*, R/15/1/microfilm, November 20, 1789. In 1801, Malcolm figured that European manufactured goods accounted for approximately 13 percent of Bushire's total imports. Malcolm, *Report on the Trade of Persia.*

tant trading partner.[31] That position was reserved for Musulipatam. However, its rise was a relatively late development, as Watkins noted:

> With regard to the trade of this place [Bushire] from India it is from the best information that I can obtain increased of late years which is owing chiefly to the much greater consumption of [Musulipatam] goods than formerly. The articles bought from [Musulipatam], consisting chiefly of chintzes, form the principal branch of commerce of Bushire.[32]

Watkins estimated that chintzes made up almost 65 percent of Bushire's total cloth imports or approximately 33 percent of all imports.

Musulipatam retained its commanding position in the Bushire market for at least the next two decades. For example, in 1796, Nicholas H. Smith, then the EIC Resident in Bushire, wrote that "the greatest individual custom collected in Persia is on the Musulipatam chintz, which is annually imported at Bushire."[33] Scott Waring, who visited Bushire at the turn of the nineteenth century, calculated that over 60 percent of Bushire's treasure exports (primarily gold and silver) were bound for Musulipatam.[34] In 1816, imports from Musulipatam made up almost 40 percent of total imports on British flag vessels and in 1820 they accounted for an incredible 75 percent of British flag vessel imports.[35] However, within the next decade or so Musulipatam chintzes had ceased to figure as an important import item.

Like so many other native weaving industries all over Asia, Musulipatam chintzes were falling victim to the increasing flood of cheap English cotton cloth. This process is vividly reflected in the changing source of Bushire's cloth imports. In 1789 Charles Watkins estimated that Iranian imports of EIC woolens averaged

31. "The Charles Watkins Trade Report."

32. *Ibid.*

33. *Bombay Secret and Political Proceedings*, August 30, 1796, page 1766.

34. Edward Scott Waring, *A Tour to Sheeraz* (London: T. Cadell and W. Davies, 1807), footnote on page 8.

35. "The Stannus Trade Report," L/P and S/9, vol. 37.

about 3 percent of Bushire's total cloth imports, while imports of Indian cloth had well over 50 percent of the market.[36] By 1829 English piece goods made up approximately 34 percent of cloth imports, with Indian piece goods capturing only about 13 percent of the market. During the rest of the century, a pattern of English goods dominating the market emerged.[37]

CONCLUSION

It was only in the decades before the British 1819–1820 expedition that the cost of security was an important factor in determining the total cost of shipping in the Persian Gulf. Ships, cargoes, indeed passengers were considered legitimate targets and booty in the almost continuous wars and skirmishes that occurred among the area's tribes and port cities. Under these circumstances, it made rational economic sense for a merchant to pay the higher cargo fees charged by British shippers than to use the "lower cost line," which may or may not have made the run safely between the Gulf and India. (Of course, it is true that British ships were not immune from attack and, indeed, in the years before the 1820 expedition, the number and intensity of attacks increased significantly.)

The terms of trade changed once the cost of security was significantly reduced by the gradually tightening British grip over the region. (The British forced the local tribes to sign a series of maritime peace treaties which were enforced by the British navy.) Purely economic costs would become the principal factor in determining competitiveness, and, on that basis, Persians and Arabs could charge lower cargo fees than their European counterparts.

36. "Charles Watkins Trade Report."

37. There was a drop in percentages in 1832–1833: English piece goods captured 19 percent of the market, while those from India, 3 percent. This is explained by the overwhelming political instability that rocked Bushire in the early 1830s; government changed hands several times and lawlessness reigned. Despite this, the British retained a significant share of the market.

Seen in longer term perspective, local shipping would only have a few decades in which it would operate in an environment relatively free of European competition. When the steamship was introduced, it quickly undercut the competitiveness of Arab and Persian ship owners. Not only were these ships faster and more reliable than native sailing vessels, but, because of their size, they could carry more cargo. This reduced marginal operating expenses, and the end result was lower cargo fees.

Persian and Arab shippers had to adapt to the challenge by purchasing the new technology or be relegated to the backwaters. There were Persian merchants and shippers who attempted to make the transition and compete using the new technology. For the most part, though, capital requirements, British administrative regulations, local government inefficiency, and the weight of tradition assured that Europeans would dominate the Gulf's carrying trade after the 1860s.

INDEX

Also from
The Middle East Institute . . .

MIDDLE EAST ORGANIZATIONS
IN WASHINGTON, DC

The indispensable guide to the 119 private organizations in Washington which are involved with the Middle East—what they do, who their officers are, what they say about themselves. You cannot tell the players without it.   **$6.00**

THE IRANIAN REVOLUTION:
THANATOS ON A NATIONAL SCALE
by Gholam R. Afkhami

An insider's examination of the Iranian Revolution and the middle class death wish that made it happen. A compelling narrative.   **$24.95**

THE MIDDLE EAST REMEMBERED
by John Badeau

The recollection of a missionary, educator, humanitarian, builder, economic developer, diplomat and raconteur, stretching over 5 decades in the Middle East—from Mosul to Cairo. A rich harvest of privileged insights and anecdotes, and dispassionate examination of the problems that have beset the United States in that area.   **$25.00**